ST PAUL'S SCHOOL
Est. 1509

WITHDRAWN
THE KAYTON LIBRARY

LANGUAGES OF CLASS

STUDIES IN ENGLISH WORKING CLASS HISTORY
1832–1982

LANGUAGES OF CLASS

STUDIES IN ENGLISH WORKING CLASS HISTORY 1832–1982

Gareth Stedman Jones

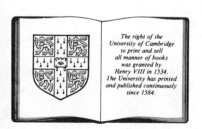

The right of the
University of Cambridge
to print and sell
all manner of books
was granted by
Henry VIII in 1534.
The University has printed
and published continuously
since 1584.

Cambridge University Press

CAMBRIDGE

LONDON   NEW YORK   NEW ROCHELLE

MELBOURNE   SYDNEY

Published by the Press Syndicate of the University of Cambridge
The Pitt Building, Trumpington Street, Cambridge CB2 1RP
32 East 57th Street, New York, NY 10022, USA
296 Beaconsfield Parade, Middle Park, Melbourne 3206, Australia

First published 1983

Printed in Great Britain by the Alden Press, Oxford

Library of Congress catalogue card number: 83-7721

British Library Cataloguing in Publication Data
Jones, Gareth Stedman
Languages of class.
1. Labor and laboring classes – Great Britain –
History
I. Title
305.5′62′0941   HD8390
ISBN 0 521 25648 8 hard covers
ISBN 0 521 27631 4 paperback

AN

To Abigail, Daniel and Sally

CONTENTS

ACKNOWLEDGEMENTS

The essay, 'Class struggle and the Industrial Revolution', originally appeared in *New Left Review*, 90 (March–April 1975); the essay, 'Class expression versus social control? A critique of recent trends in the social history of "leisure"', first appeared in *History Workshop*, 4 (Autumn 1977); the essay, 'Working-class culture and working-class politics in London, 1870–1900: Notes on the remaking of a working class', first appeared in the *Journal of Social History*, 7,4 (Summer 1974). A short version of 'Why is the Labour Party in a mess?' appeared in *New Socialist*, 3 (Jan.–Feb. 1982) as 'Why the Labour Party is in a mess'. Part of the essay, 'Rethinking Chartism', was published as 'The Language of Chartism' in J. Epstein and D. Thompson (eds.), *The Chartist Experience*, London (1982).

I would like to thank the editors of these publications for the help they gave me at the time, and for the encouragement they have given me in the republication of the essays in this book.

INTRODUCTION

Each of the studies collected together in this book concerns the relationship between society and politics in England in the nineteenth and twentieth centuries: in particular, the changing place attributed to the 'working classes' or 'working class' within the development of the polity. If this topic merits new historical attention, it is certainly not because it has previously been ignored, but rather because the ways in which it has been considered important and the reasons given for its importance have generally been taken for granted. There are of course countless studies and histories of the working class. But most of them proceed all too smoothly along tramlines welded together long ago from a rough but apparently serviceable mixture of utilitarian, evolutionist and Marxist assumptions. In the new historical epoch which we appear to have entered, in which a whole set of conventional beliefs about working-class politics have been put into doubt – both nationally and internationally – a critical scrutiny of some of the intellectual premises upon which these beliefs have been based can only be a gain. In England, what Eric Hobsbawm has recently described as 'the halting' of 'the forward march of labour' suggests the need not simply to examine 'the halting', but also to question the metaphor itself.[1] It is in this spirit that these essays have been collected together. It may not be possible for a historian to ask what sort of substantive reality 'the working class' as such might have possessed outside the particular historical idioms in which it has been ascribed meaning. But it certainly is possible to investigate how the

---

[1] Eric Hobsbawm, *The Forward March of Labour Halted?* (1981).
  (All titles published in London unless specified otherwise.)

I

historical picture changes, once certain of the assumptions informing these idioms are no longer presupposed.

Some of the most deeply entrenched of these assumptions have clustered around the notion of class. In a country like the United States, it has never been possible for historians simply to infer class as a political force from class as a structural position within productive relations. In England, on the other hand, such equations between social and political forces have been only too easy to make both because much of modern English political history has generally been thought to coincide with class alignments and because, at the level of everyday speech, one of the peculiarities of England has been the pervasiveness of the employment of diverse forms of class vocabulary. Unlike Germany, languages of class in England never faced serious rivalry from a pre-existing language of estates; unlike France and America, republican vocabulary and notions of citizenship never became more than a minor current, whether as part of everyday speech or as analytic categories; unlike the countries of southern Europe, vocabularies of class did not accompany, but long preceded, the arrival of social democratic parties and were never exclusively identified with them. In fact, in England more than in any other country, the word 'class' has acted as a congested point of intersection between many competing, overlapping or simply differing forms of discourse – political, economic, religious and cultural – right across the political spectrum. It is in this very broad sense that class, however we define it, has formed an inescapable component of any discussion of the course of English politics and society since the 1830s.

But the easy derivation of political from social forces common among English historians is not explained simply by the pervasiveness of vocabularies of class or by the apparently self-evident facts of political history. It also derives from the large theoretical superstructures built upon them. Just as eighteenth century England had proved the seedbed of theories of commercial society (in fact more Scottish than English),[2] which already contained strong notions of social

---

[2] On this, see Istvan Hont and Michael Ignatieff (eds.), *Wealth and Virtue, the Shaping of Political Economy in the Scottish Enlightenment*, Cambridge (1983). I have on the whole confined my discussion to England. In some cases, particularly when

It was not until the 1950s that this situation began to change. The apparent arrival of an 'age of affluence' posed new historical questions and rekindled interest in the character and representativeness of English social development. Internationally, Britain as a pioneer of industrialization attracted the attention of American economists and sociologists interested both in models of 'growth' or 'modernization' and in the types of social conflict which accompanied them. In Rostow's famous *Stages of Economic Growth* the English Industrial Revolution was again invoked, not this time by a dawn chorus of political economists and socialists, but by a self-appointed owl of Minerva looking back from the halcyon years of Wirtschaftswunder as if from the achieved millennium of an age of 'mass consumption'.[6] Domestically, on the other hand, from the mid-1950s, the social democratic consensus achieved by the Labour Party in the previous decade became an object of serious criticism both for Croslandite revisionists and for the New Left.[7] The stage was set for a novel and important confrontation between history and social theory.

If England from the 1950s, once again and somewhat paradoxically, became the focus of ambitious attempts to plot its development upon global economic and sociological grids, the process was further aided by the emergence of new conceptions of history on the part of historians themselves. What came to be known as *social history* derived from a variety of sources – from new ways of posing historical questions pioneered by the *Annales* and *Past and Present*, from the critique of economistic versions of Marxism which developed after 1956, and from a growing interest in the methods and preoccupations of sociology and anthropology. What came to characterize this new idea of social history at its most expansive was a totalizing ambition which would both displace the narrow concerns of traditional practitioners and make history central to the understanding of modern society and politics.

It was the historical analysis of the nineteenth and twentieth centuries which was to become the battleground upon

[6] W. W. Rostow, *The Stages of Economic Growth*, Cambridge (1960).
[7] See, for example, C. A. R. Crosland, *The Future of Socialism* (1956); E. P. Thompson (ed.), *Out of Apathy* (1960); P. Anderson, 'Sweden: Mr Crosland's Dreamland', *New Left Review* (*NLR*) 7, 9 (1961).

which so many of these new issues, both political and methodological, were to be fought out. So far as the nineteenth century was concerned there was, however, nothing new in the presumption of what it was that needed to be explained. This was the seemingly abrupt change from economic dislocation and class conflict to social peace and political stability that was thought to have occurred around 1850. As far back as the beginning of the nineteenth century, the breach in continuity between the Chartist and post-Chartist periods had been highlighted both in the work of the Webbs and in that of liberal historians for whom the 'hungry forties' represented a 'bleak age' preceding free trade.[8] Now the interpretative challenge, represented by a society which within a century had moved with such apparent rapidity from 'stable hierarchy' through bitter class antagonism to a new but class-based harmony, attracted a rich array of new efforts at theorization. Such projects could be couched in terms derived from Weber, Durkheim or Parsons, as the work of Smelser, Tholfsen or Perkin testified.[9] They could draw creatively from the insights of the Chicago school and of urban sociology in the work of Briggs and Dyos.[10] In the treatment of more recent history they could involve attempts at a synthesis of Marxian and Weberian motifs in the social analysis of Lockwood and Goldthorpe,[11] or the radicalization and resituation of cultural criticism in the work of Hoggart and Williams.[12] Finally, in the case of historians of the left, they could take the form of an ambition to revitalize a Marxist picture of social change and to overcome the gulf between theoretical expectation and actual history. The works of Eric Hobsbawm, Edward

[8] S. and B. Webb, *History of Trade Unionism* (1920 edn); J. and B. L. Hammond, *The Bleak Age* (1934).

[9] N. J. Smelser, *Social Change in the Industrial Revolution: an Application of Theory to the Lancashire Cotton Industry, 1770–1840* (1959); T. Tholfsen, 'The Transition to Democracy in Victorian England', *International Review of Social History*, VI (1961); T. Tholfsen, *Working Class Radicalism in Mid-Victorian England* (1976); H. J. Perkin, *The Origins of Modern English Society, 1780–1880* (1969).

[10] Asa Briggs, *Victorian Cities* (1963); H. J. Dyos (ed.), *The Study of Urban History* (1968).

[11] J. H. Goldthorpe, D. Lockwood, F. Bechhofer, J. Platt, *The Affluent Worker: Industrial Attitudes and Behaviour*, Cambridge (1968); id., *The Affluent Worker in the Class Structure*, Cambridge (1969).

[12] R. Hoggart, *The Uses of Literacy* (1957); R. Williams, *Culture and Society, 1780–1950* (1958).

Thompson, Royden Harrison, Perry Anderson, Tom Nairn and others could all be viewed as different attempts to marry a broadly defined Marxist conception of the working class to what Thompson called 'the peculiarities of the English'.[13]

This was the context in which the earliest written essays in this book were conceived. I began with the strong conviction both of the inadequacy of simple empiricist approaches to nineteenth and twentieth century history and of the inability of conventional Marxism or other prevalent forms of social theory satisfactorily to illuminate the actual course of events. My initial ambition was to arrive at a more fruitful juncture between history and social theory. I hoped that the combination of a non-empiricist approach to history and a sceptical relation to received social theory might become the distinguishing trait of a new type of history. As I originally conceived the problem, partial or wishful depictions of the 'social' had led to the inability to explain the political, cultural or ideological in the light of it. My scepticism did not extend to the character of social determination in itself. But as my preoccupation with this theme developed – and as the later essays in the book bear witness – I found myself obliged to redefine the problem: in short, to dissociate the ambition of a theoretically informed history from any simple prejudgement about the determining role of the 'social'. In particular, I became increasingly critical of the prevalent treatment of the 'social' as something outside of, and logically – and often, though not necessarily, chronologically – prior to its articulation through language. The title, *Languages of class*, stresses this point: firstly, that the term 'class' is a word embedded in languge and should thus be analysed in its linguistic context; and secondly, that because there are *different* languages of class, one should not proceed upon the assumption that 'class' as an elementary counter of official social description, 'class' as an effect of theoretical

[13] Eric Hobsbawm, *Primitive Rebels*, Manchester (1959); id., *Labouring Men, Studies in the History of Labour* (1964); id., *Industry and Empire* (1968); E. P. Thompson, *The Making of the English Working Class* (1963); id., 'The Peculiarities of the English', in Ralph Miliband and John Saville (eds.), *The Socialist Register*, 2 (1965); Royden Harrison, *Before the Socialists, Studies in Labour and Politics* (1965); Perry Anderson, 'Origins of the Present Crisis', *NLR*, 23 (1964); Tom Nairn, 'Anatomy of the Labour Party', *NLR*, 27, 28 (1964).

discourse about distribution or production relations, 'class' as the summary of a cluster of culturally signifying practices or 'class' as a species of political or ideological self-definition, all share a single reference point in an anterior social reality.

Because of this change in the direction of my approach, my usage of the term 'class' does not remain constant through the essays. The earliest contributions play upon a tension between Marxist definitions of 'class' and the historically observable behaviour of particular groups of workers; and attempts are made to explain the gulf between the predictions of the Marxist explanatory model and the actual assumptions which appear to have guided the activities of the groups of workers with whom I was concerned. In the later essays, 'class' is treated as a discursive rather than as an ontological reality, the central effort being to explain languages of class from the nature of politics rather than the character of politics from the nature of class. Thus, although the essays follow a rough chronological order in real historical terms, the story that the book tells is as much that of my own theoretical development as of the history of the working class itself. If this development has any claim to be of more than biographical interest, it is that of a case study suggesting how the growing explanatory ambition of social history led to an increasing awareness of its limits as a self-sufficient form of historical interpretation.

The reader should therefore be alerted to the dating of the different essays, since the order of their composition does not correspond to the order in which they are presented in this book. The essay on Chartism (Ch. 3), for example, was in fact one of the most recently written and represents my current approach. By contrast, the review essay 'Class struggle and the Industrial Revolution' (Ch. 1) represents an earlier and significantly different theorization of a similar set of themes. What follows in the rest of the Introduction is a brief résumé of the context in which each of the essays was written and some attempt to explain, at a more concrete historiographic level, the reasons that led to the shift of focus observable between the earlier and later essays in the book.

The earliest essay in the book, 'Working-class culture and working-class politics' (Ch. 4) was written in 1973–4. In one sense, it might appear to be a tailpiece to my book *Outcast London*, but its intention was to pose a question that was quite distinct from those raised in my book.[14] *Outcast London* was primarily concerned with 'the social problem' as it came to be constituted in the mid-Victorian period, not with the actual attitudes and behaviour of London workers themselves. Any investigation of the subjective character of the London working class between 1850 and 1914 entailed a direct engagement with an area of social and labour history with which I had not been previously concerned. Since at the time of writing I largely accepted the picture of working-class development in the first half of the nineteenth century presented in Edward Thompson's *Making of the English Working Class*, it seemed obvious that some explanation was required for the gulf which separated the working class depicted in his book from that existing in the twentieth century. Accordingly, the aim of the essay was to construct, in the case of London, some sort of arch which might connect the working class of the 1830s and that more familiar to the twentieth century. The text was thus pointedly subtitled 'Notes on the remaking of a working class'.

'Working-class culture and working-class politics', as the title implies, attempted to establish a systematic linkage between culture and politics at a time when historical investigation of popular culture had barely begun. It is not surprising that subsequent research and reflection has put some of these linkages in doubt. It has been questioned, for example, how far and in what sense the 'culture' described in the article was distinctively 'working class' as opposed to 'popular', 'urban' or 'metropolitan'. But so far as the analysis of London itself is concerned, such a dispute is ultimately terminological. Whether one describes the cultural milieu of the majority of London workers as a working-class culture or a mass urban culture does not bear centrally upon the argument. It was certainly never suggested that this culture was the self-conscious creation of workers or that it was confined to workers, only that, by sheer weight of numbers, the preoccupations and predilections of workers imposed a discernible

[14] G. Stedman Jones, *Outcast London: a Study in the Relationship between Classes in Victorian Society*, Oxford (1971); 2nd edn, London (1984).

imprint upon the shape taken by this culture. The example of music-hall was an attempt to illustrate this point.

More problematic was the relationship established between this culture and the politics of the period. The weakness of independent working-class political activity in late Victorian London was largely attributed to the emergence of a culture in which politics played a marginal role. That culture in turn was placed in symbiotic relation to a casualized economy and the decline of artisans as a cohesive force. While it still seems to me that these were important obstacles to political mobilization or organization, I no longer think that the character of popular politics in the period can be attributed so simply or directly to these social and cultural features. Casual labour and small workshop production remained a characteristic feature of the inter-war London economy to a far greater extent than I originally imagined, and so did many of the hallmarks of the culture which I described.[15] Yet the face of popular politics was transformed. In the aftermath of the First World War, the unemployed became a vocal political presence in working-class districts and even some of the poorest and most demoralized districts of the East End became Labour strongholds.[16] Conversely, in the period before 1850, it is by no means clear that evidence of a more widely diffused radicalism among the London working classes was in the first instance to be attributed to the condition of the trades or the culture of the metropolitan artisan.

What I did not sufficiently stress in this article, was the importance of the national political dimension. In general, the temporality of periods of heightened *political* conflict and *political* mobilization is determined, in the *first* instance, not by the conditions of the local economy nor by cultural factors,

[15] On the character of the inter-war London economy, I am indebted to the work of Jim Gillespie, see 'The Effects of Urbanisation and Urban Segregation on Working Class Stratification in Early 20th Century London', Cambridge University Ph.D., forthcoming; for an interesting examination of the political discussion about the culture I described among socialists and labour/liberal progressives in the 1890–1914 period, see Susan Pennybacker, 'The Labour Question and the London County Council 1889–1919', Cambridge University Ph.D., forthcoming.

[16] In the case of West Ham, see John Marriott, 'London over the Border: Industry and Culture in West Ham, 1840–1939', Cambridge University Ph.D., forthcoming.

but by the activity of all those institutions of government and political order, both legislative and executive, central and local, which in short we call the state. A strike is a strike. A strike in which employers are assisted by troops, or whose leaders are sentenced to transportation, inevitably acquires a political dimension. What sort of political dimension it acquires, others things being equal, depends upon the existence of a political organization or current with a capacity convincingly to portray the particular sequence of events as an instance of a coherent general position on the character of the state and a strategy for its transformation. Of course, state activity itself, when it is of an innovative or disruptive kind, may be a response to an economic or social situation which is conceived to be politically dangerous. Innovative state activity in the second quarter of the nineteenth century was primarily of this type. But it may equally be a response to a perilous situation in international relations, as it was during the First World War,[17] or a perceived threat in the international economy, as it was at least to some degree during the Edwardian period. The 'depoliticization' of late nineteenth century London was probably more pronounced than in other urban or industrial regions for the reasons I described. But, virtually everywhere in industrial England, the degree of political confrontation was higher in the 1830s and 1840s and then again in the period between 1910 and 1926 than it had been in the decades in between.

One reason for this underestimation of the political was that I did not possess a clear conception of the limits of social explanation, i.e. in what senses the political could not be inferred from the social. My ambition at the time was to show how much political history could be explained in social terms and my attitude was, 'on s'engage et puis on voit'. Secondly, however, and more specifically, I did not possess an interpretation of my own for the defeat and disappearance of Chartism. I had therefore to make the best I could from the existing historiography on the subject. It was partly from a sense of dissatisfaction with this literature, and a conviction

---

[17] In the case of the militancy of Clydeside ship-builders during the First World War, for example, see Alastair Reid, 'The Division of Labour in the British Shipbuilding Industry, 1880–1920', Cambridge University Ph.D. (1980).

that much of the interpretation of the social and political history
of the 1850–1914 period depended upon it, that I looked for an
opportunity to re-examine the character of radical and working-
class politics in the first half of the nineteenth century.

At this point, I was primarily interested, not in embarking
upon a programme of empirical research, but rather in developing a theoretical framework within which to interpret the
conflicts of the pre-1850 period. One way forward had been
pioneered by Edward Thompson. His powerful and imaginative
account of *The Making of the English Working Class* involved a
considerable revision of orthodox Marxist assumptions about
consciousness, the economy and the place of politics. Although
sympathetic to the historical fruits of these revisions and heavily
indebted at the time to his conception of 'culture', I continued
to have reservations about his conception of historical
method. My own predilection was towards a theoretical
revision in a more structuralist direction and was inspired
more by French than English currents of thinking. For me, the
relationship of the historian to theory was not an external one
– the attempted empirical validation of a pre-existing catego-
rial currency (class consciousness, class struggle, labour
aristocracy etc.) – but rather the location and construction of
an invisible structure capable both of illuminating the direction of change on the surface and suggesting the limits within
which it operated. So far as the interpretation of Marx was
concerned, I was considerably influenced by the 'reading' put
forward by Louis Althusser and his associates.[18] Particularly
important for me was their stress upon *Capital* rather than
Marx's early works, and their elaboration of the notions of
mode of production and social formation.

Especially pertinent to the problem of interpreting the
1790–1850 period was the highlighting by Etienne Balibar of
the distinction made by Marx between the 'formal' and 'real'
subordination of labour to capital.[19] I therefore re-read
Marx's *Capital*, paying particular attention to his analysis of
'manufacture' and 'modern industry', from which this distinction was drawn. During the epoch of manufacture, according

[18] Louis Althusser and Etienne Balibar, *Reading Capital* (1970).
[19] Etienne Balibar, 'Basic Concepts of Historical Materialism', in Althusser and
Balibar, *Reading Capital*.

to Marx, the control over wage labour exercised by the capitalist was only 'formal': that is to say that while the capitalist owned the means of production and was able to combine and specialize the work of wage labour in order to increase productivity, the technical basis of the division of labour remained handicraft. The means of labour, the tool, remained an extension of the human hand, the tempo of production was that of manual labour. If one followed the analysis presented by *Capital*, the Industrial Revolution could be defined in terms of the replacement of a division of labour based upon handicrafts by a division of labour based upon machines. The subordination of labour to capital now became 'real' in the sense that it rested not solely upon the structure of ownership, but also upon the character of the labour process itself. This now entailed larger units of production (factories) and a different technical relationship between labourers and means of production. If one started out from a strict application of these categories, I thought, it might be possible to develop a more adequate interpretation of the social character of the industrial conflicts of the pre-1850 period than that implied in the *Communist Manifesto* or that generally associated with Marxist approaches to nineteenth century labour history. They could be seen as battles, not about ownership but about control.

The appearance in 1974 of John Foster's *Class Struggle and the Industrial Revolution*, a forceful restatement of an orthodox Marxist–Leninist interpretation of nineteenth century working-class development, provided me with an initial opportunity to discuss these issues.[20] By focussing upon this distinction between 'formal' and 'real', I hoped not only to illuminate the social context of Chartism, but also to open up a new line of enquiry into the changed tenor of industrial relations in Lancashire in the second half of the century. For it was not the alleged emergence of a privileged section of the working class that needed explanation, but rather the changed behaviour of the working class as a whole. Of course, this was only one of the features which might help to explain such a shift; I was very conscious of the need to avoid economic determinism. But so far as the change was located at the socio-

---

[20] John Foster, *Class Struggle and the Industrial Revolution, Early Industrial Capitalism in Three English Towns* (1974).

economic level, this seemed to me a more creative use of what might remain valuable in Marx's theory than the tired and forced recourse to the notion of a 'labour aristocracy'.

In the light of what has been written since, even at the socio-economic level, my interpretation would have to be modified. While the distinction between 'formal' and 'real' remains useful for certain purposes, it must be detached from the implication that the bargaining or obstructive power of labour was necessarily much less in a situation of 'real' control. It was certainly different, but not necessarily or irreversibly worse. Undoubtedly the loss of the technical indispensability of the male mule-spinner with the adoption of the self-acting mule did change the pattern of industrial relations. Nor does it seem to mc doubtful that the threat of such a change was a potent source of the spinners' political involvement in the 1830s. But, so far as the post-1843 situation was concerned, the detailed research of William Lazonick has shown that the spinners remained well organized and retained a great deal of leverage on the organization and pace of their work.[21] In my article it was implied that employers preserved the status of the spinners primarily for social reasons. What Lazonick shows, however, is that the spinner retained his position because it made good economic sense for the employer to continue to delegate to him both the functions of supervision and of labour recruitment. In this sense the continuities were more marked and the position of the spinner was less precarious than my argument implied.

How far, at a more general level, the triumph of modern industry inaugurated a more accommodative style of popular politics in the post-1850 period remains a debated question. Interesting evidence supporting this argument is adduced by Patrick Joyce in his major study of post-Chartist Lancashire, *Work, Society and Politics*.[22] But no unambiguous connection is established. Not only were the effects of 'real' control less absolute than Ure or Marx anticipated – the growth of textile trade unionism from the 1850s was one indication of this – but

[21] William Lazonick, 'Industrial Relations and Technical Change: the Case of the Self-Acting Mule', *Cambridge Journal of Economics*, 3 (1979).

[22] Patrick Joyce, *Work, Society and Politics, the Culture of the Factory in later Victorian England*, Brighton (1980).

also the chronology of its implementation was slow and its geography uneven. Of course, no one except a strict technological determinist would expect a close correlation between advances of 'real' control in particular factory districts and concomitant changes in popular politics. Even at the economic level, many other features would play a part, most obviously the growing stability and prosperity of the cotton trade itself.[23] However, the original intention of the argument was not to establish that sort of case. It was rather to establish how structural changes in work relations consolidated and reinforced a pattern of politics which had come into existence in the first instance for other reasons. What these other reasons were was the problem left unresolved by the article.

A concern to demarcate a more adequate theoretical framework for the interpretation of social change in the nineteenth century was also uppermost in my essay, 'Class expression versus social control?' (Ch. 2), written in the autumn of 1975. The paper was the result of an invitation to comment upon a wide and representative cross-section of contributions towards a social history of leisure to be presented to a conference held at the University of Sussex. From reading these papers, it struck me that one distinctive feature of the methodology of social history, as it had emerged and crystallized, was a bland and often unconscious conflation between Marxist and functionalist categories for the explanation of social change. In the light of its origins, this was perhaps not surprising. Many of the preoccupations and some of the terminology of the new social history had begun life as an offshoot from, or reaction to, the 'modernization' theories of the late 1950s and early 1960s. In the ensuing development, the prevailing tendency among social historians had been towards the blending or incorporating of elements from opposed conceptual sets into forms of social–historical synthesis; and, if one were attempting to write a social history of social history, one might say that the result had been the growth of a new professional lingua franca serving to legitimize the autonomy of social history as a distinct discipline.

---

[23] On this, see, for example, D.A. Farnie, *The English Cotton Industry and the World Market, 1815–1896*, Oxford (1979).

Nowhere was this process more striking than in the pervasive employment of the notion of 'social control': in the case of the nineteenth century, increasingly conceived as the central mechanism through which the 'stabilization' of Victorian society had been successfully accomplished. Whether conceived as 'the triumph of the entrepreneurial ideal', the divisive aspirations of a 'labour aristocracy', 'liberalization' or 'hegemony', the common point of emphasis in all these approaches appeared to be the diversion of subversive or disruptive aims by ideological-cum-economistic means. My concern in the essay was partly to highlight the incompatibility between Marxist and functionalist approaches, partly to dramatize how little 'social control' explained. The vision of a working class thwarted in revolt by the machinations of 'social control' seemed to me inherently implausible both because it overlooked the more mundane material exigencies which framed the concerns of workers – pre-eminently, as I stressed, work itself – but also because it overdid the putative triumph of 'control'. As I had already attempted to demonstrate in the 'working-class culture' essay, Benthamites and evangelicals were no more successful than radicals and Chartists in moulding a working class in their own image.

I would now have reservations about the elements of a Marxist alternative that I offered in place of the tautologies of social control. The determinant place of relations of production was invoked far too unproblematically. Nevertheless, it still seems to me that most of the negative criticism offered by the essay remains valid, and that the registering of an elementary discordance between administrative or ideological fantasy and historically observable behaviour may be of continuing relevance as a corrective to some of the more extreme historical versions of Michel Foucault's equation between knowledge and power.[24]

The latest essays, 'Rethinking Chartism' (Ch. 3) (1981) and 'Why is the Labour Party in a mess?' (Ch. 5) (1982), are here presented in their full versions for the first time. They indicate

---

[24] For a subsequent and also critical survey of the literature, see F. M. L. Thompson, 'Social Control in Victorian Britain', *Economic History Review*, 2nd Series, XXXIV, 2 (1981).

a shift in my thinking not only about these particular topics but also about the social historical approach as such. Most important in this respect was the process of rethinking that lay behind my essay on Chartism.

I wanted to make a study of Chartism both because my work on a projected biography of Engels suggested the need to find a critical yardstick by which to judge his picture of the movement, and because no overview of English working class development was possible without an adequate interpretation of that crucial episode. The weakness of my critique of Foster's book had derived from the vagueness of its treatment of Chartism as a political phenomenon. The decline of Chartism had there been described only from a most strato-spheric angle of vision in terms of a failure of the social Weltanschauung supposedly represented by the Chartists in the face of the advance and stabilization of the national and international economy. Similarly, in accounting for its begin-nings, although I had felt a long-standing unease at the theoretical level about Edward Thompson's picture of the formation of working-class consciousness, it was impossible to provide a more satisfactory alternative without independent engagement with the primary sources.

In my initial attempt to find a way into the problem, I mistook Thompson's strength for his weakness. By situating and tying down more precisely, as an ideology, what Thompson portrayed as working-class consciousness around 1830, I thought it might be possible to account both for the strengths and the limits of the social movements in the first half of the nineteenth century. Given this hypothesis, two questions then presented themselves. Firstly, why did this type of consciousness apparently reach a peak in Chartism and then decline? Thompson's book provided no obvious answer to that question. Secondly, whose consciousness precisely was it? Was it really that of the 'working class'? Or was it that of a historically more specific group of wage earners – journeymen and outworkers faced with the pro-letarianization of their trades, rather than a proletariat in a more familiar Marxist sense? Thompson's book largely side-stepped that question, while the attempt by Foster to identify the most revolutionary form of class consciousness with a *factory* proletariat squarely posed a question which any Marx-based approach would have to confront.

In an article not reproduced here, I attempted some form of answer to both these questions.[25] Briefly, my solution was that the movement which had come into existence by the 1830s, while not confined to artisans, was nevertheless premissed upon a particular set of assumptions espoused by artisans about work, class relations and the role of the state. Such an outlook could also be identified in the use of labour theories of property derived from natural right, in the preoccupation with the land, in the focus upon the 'capitalist' as trader rather than employer, and in the location of exploitation in politically sustained forms of unequal exchange rather than in the productive process itself. Thompson's book could end on a peak because in the radical and co-operative movements of 1829–34, these peculiarities were not apparent. In Chartism, on the other hand, a much broader movement incorporating the new factory districts as well as the workshop and outwork trades, such problems came to the fore. Thus the decline of Chartism could partly be attributed to the limitations inherent in an ideology, which was dominant within it, that was incapable of articulating the new pattern of class relations in the factory districts of the North.

Further research and reflection, however, revealed the radical inadequacy of this approach. The attempt to arrive at a new understanding of Chartism through the use of the concept of ideology proved a blind alley. As a category it turned out to be inert and unilluminatingly reductive. The term 'ideology' tends to be used to link a certain set of beliefs or preoccupations with the material situation of a precisely specified social group. Yet a comparison of Chartist argument with eighteenth century radicalism made it less and less clear what was distinctively artisanal about the Chartist platform. The basic assumptions upon which the radical case was based predated the entry of artisans and other workers into politics and were not fundamentally reshaped as a result. More

[25] G. Stedman Jones, 'The Limits of a Proletarian Theory in England before 1850', Unpublished Paper presented to a conference of social historians at Bielefeld, 1977. For an important study of the politics of artisans in this period, see Iorwerth Prothero, *Artisans and Politics in Early Nineteenth Century London*, Folkestone (1979).

generally, a preoccupation with ideology simply missed what was most urgent to explain about Chartism – its political character, the specific reasons for its rise and fall, its focus upon representation and its lack of interest in the demarcation of socio-economic status within the unrepresented. The difficulty of an explanation in terms of the limitations of an artisanal consciousness or ideology, like most social approaches to the decline of Chartism, was that it did not identify with any precision what it was that declined.

Having arrived at this point, I decided to reverse my initial assumption: given the existence of good material grounds for discontent, it was not consciousness (or ideology) that produced politics, but politics that produced consciousness. This meant opening up an unfamiliar line of enquiry into Chartism – an approach which would drop all the social presuppositions which had encrusted the literature on Chartism since the beginning and would isolate the politics of Chartism as an object of study in its own right. To do this, however, was more difficult than at first appeared. For it involved not only an empirical programme of research – finding out the reasons for discontent stated by the Chartists, and the political solutions they envisaged. It also meant knowing what weight to give to these utterances in the interpretation of Chartism as a whole and the reasons why most commentators on Chartism had implicitly or explicitly discounted their significance. This problem was theoretical. It concerned the place of language, consciousness and experience.

Early observers of Chartism like Engels, and most historians of Chartism since, have worked with two sorts of evidence: on the one hand, evidence of reasons for discontent – unemployment, machine breaking, catastrophic depressions, overwork, child labour, overcrowding, extreme poverty and so on; on the other hand, evidence of the widespread employment of a language of class antagonism in the radical political movements of the period. What has been problematic has been the way in which these two types of evidence have been connected. Part of the problem is precisely that it has not been seen as a problem. Philosophical assumption – explicit or unwitting – has supplied the missing links by interjecting terms like 'experience' or 'consciousness', tying the two poles together in a way which seems intuitively obvious. What these terms suggest is that the relationship between the two sorts of evidence is one of simple expression. The stronger term 'consciousness', in its usage by social historians, is Hegelian in origin. It assumes an objective and necessary process in which what is latent will be made manifest, and it provides criteria by which the adequacy of the manifestation may be judged. 'Experience' on the other hand is compatible with a seemingly more empiricist approach to history.[26] It puts to one side the question of the necessity or objectivity of the process and presents such a process more as a matter of fact registered through the subjectivities of those engaged within it. In practice, however, the difference between the two terms is not as great as it might appear. For tacit assumptions are made about what is to count as experience, about its meaningfulness, and about its cumulative and collective character.

What both 'experience' and 'consciousness' conceal – at least as their usage has evolved among historians – is the problematic character of language itself. Both concepts imply that language is a simple medium through which 'experience' finds expression – a romantic conception of language in which what is at the beginning inner and particular struggles to outward expression and, having done so, finds itself recognized in the answering experience of others, and hence sees itself to be part of a shared experience. It is in some such way that 'experience' can be conceived cumulatively to result in class consciousness. What this approach cannot acknowledge is all the criticism which has been levelled at it since the broader significance of Saussure's work was understood – the materiality of language itself, the impossibility of simply referring it back to some primal anterior reality, 'social being', the impossibility of abstracting experience from the language which structures its articulation. In areas other than history, such criticisms are by now well known and do not need

---

[26] This is not to imply that 'experience' cannot also be conceived in Hegelian fashion. See, for example, G. W. F. Hegel, *Phenomenology of Spirit*, trans. A. V. Miller, Oxford (1977), 55–7. Nor, of course, do I mean to imply that the philosophical problem of 'consciousness' in its broadest sense begins with Hegel. For an illuminating discussion of the philosophical construction of 'consciousness' in the seventeenth century, see Richard Rorty, *Philosophy and the Mirror of Nature*, Oxford (1980), 45–69.

elaboration. But historians – and social historians in particular – have either been unaware or, when aware, extremely resistant to the implications of this approach for their own practice, and this has been so most of all perhaps when it touches such a central topic as class.

In order, therefore, to bring to the fore the politics of Chartism, freed from the a priori assumptions of historians about its social meaning, I applied a non-referential conception of language to the study of Chartist speeches and writings. Concretely, this meant exploring the systematic relationship between terms and propositions within the language rather than setting particular propositions into direct relation to a putative experiential reality of which they were assumed to be the expression. How well I succeeded in utilizing the insights to be derived from such an approach in the resulting essay, readers may judge. But provisionally it seems to me that such an approach allows a way round the otherwise insoluble riddles raised in the age-old debates about continuity/discontinuity in nineteenth and twentieth century social history by restoring politics to its proper importance.

In general, whether steeped in the older traditions of labour history or the newer conventions of social history, historians have looked everywhere except at changes in political discourse itself to explain changes in political behaviour. Starting implicitly or explicitly from an essentialist conception of class, in which all the different languages of class are measured against Marxist or sociological conceptions of class position, they have taken as their task the demonstration of concordance with, or the explanation of deviation from, positions which socio-economic logic ascribes. The implicit assumption is of civil society as a field of conflicting social groups or classes whose opposing interests will find rational expression in the political arena. Such interests, it is assumed, pre-exist their expression. Languages of politics are evanescent forms, mere coverings of an adequate, inadequate or anachronistic kind, through which essential interests may be decoded.

In order to rewrite the political history of the 'working class' or 'working classes', we should start out from the other end of the chain. Language disrupts any simple notion of the determination of consciousness by social being because it is itself part of social being. We cannot therefore decode political language to reach a primal and material expression of interest since it is the discursive structure of political language which conceives and defines interest in the first place. What we must therefore do is to study the production of interest, identification, grievance and aspiration within political languages themselves. We need to map out these successive languages of radicalism, liberalism, socialism etc., both in relation to the political languages they replace and laterally in relation to rival political languages with which they are in conflict. Only then can we begin to assess their reasons for success or failure at specific points in time. It is clear that particular political languages do become inapposite in new situations. How and why this occurs involves the discovery of the precise point at which shifts occur as well as an investigation of the specific political circumstances in which they shift. To peer straight through these languages into the structural changes to which they may be notionally referred is no substitute for such an investigation, not because there is not a relationship of some kind, but because such connections can never be established with any satisfying degree of finality.

In the last essay, 'Why is the Labour Party in a mess?' (Ch. 5), I make a preliminary attempt to suggest how the connection between the political and the social might be rethought. Firstly, I reject the notion of the Labour Party which defines it as a unitary subject, whether this be conceived – as on the left – as the expression of a class ('the party of the working class'), or of an ideology ('labourism'), or – as on the right – as a set of institutional relationships (PLP (Parliamentary Labour Party), Conference, NEC (National Executive Committee), trade union block vote, constitution etc.).[27] In this respect, it is more fruitful to treat the Labour Party as a vacant centre – as a space traversed or tenanted by groups possessing different and sometimes incompatible political languages of widely varying provenance, a changing balance of forces and their discursive self-definitions, defined primarily from without. Secondly, I argue against any picture

[27] Some of these criticisms are developed more fully in R. Samuel and G. Stedman Jones, 'The Labour Party and Social Democracy', in R. Samuel and G. Stedman Jones (eds.), *Culture, Ideology and Politics, Essays for Eric Hobsbawm* (1983).

of the Labour Party that presents it in terms of a simple history of evolution. The history of the Labour Party – or indeed any other political party – is better understood in terms of a succession of discontinuous conjunctures which enabled it to achieve specific forms of success at rather widely separated points in time. Amongst other things, this entails an analysis of the conditions in which groups and discourses of very different points of origin enter at particular moments into relationships of stable coexistence or even mutual reinforcement. That conception of the Labour Party which characterizes it as having an essential definition or a continuous evolution – 'the labour movement' – has an importance in the history of the Labour Party, not as its definition, but rather as an animating myth producing real effects upon the practices of many of the participants within that history.

Finally, a tentative attempt is made to suggest how social change might be treated within this new interpretative framework. Of course, social and structural changes in twentieth century England are of fundamental importance and no discussion of politics, labour or otherwise, could proceed in ignorance of them. But, from the vantage point of the history of the Labour Party, it is not these changes in themselves that matter. What matters are which of these changes are articulated and how, within the successive and various discourses which have coexisted within the Labour Party, or which have impinged upon it or threatened it from the outside. The place of the social would have to be, in this context, resituated within discursive relations. Messages are sent to addressees. They are amended or recomposed, according to whom they are sent. Speakers address audiences, whom they conceive (or project) to be composed of a specific type of social being. Political discourses are addressed to particular constituencies, indeed at certain formative turning points are able to constitute or reconstitute such constituencies. There is an intimate connection between what is said and to whom. Yet it cannot be said that such a connection can be conceived in terms of a recognition of the pre-existence of the common social properties of the addressees. It should rather be thought of as the construction, successful or unsuccessful, of a possible representation of what such common properties might be. Of course, the almost definitional claim of political discourse is to be a response to a pre-existing need or demand. But in fact the primary motivation is to create and then orchestrate such a demand, to change the self-identification and behaviour of those addressed. The attempted relationship is prefigurative, not reflective. Once again, it is only to observe that between the changing character of social life and the order of politics there is no simple, synchronous or directly transitive line of connection, either in one direction or the other. To begin at the other end of the chain does not obliterate the significance of the work of the social historian, but locates its significance in a different perspective.

It would be foolish to pretend that the harnessing of elementary insights derived from theories of language to problems of substantive historical interpretation is in anything other than an extremely primitive state. It could also easily be objected that what has been said about it in this introduction barely gets beyond the Bourgeois Gentilhomme's perplexed discovery that he had been speaking prose all his life. So be it. The suggestions presented here should not be read as a triumphant manifesto, but rather as a response to the breakdown or impasse reached by previous interpretative frameworks. After the many magniloquent death sentences passed upon history since the ascent of structuralism in France, it is scarcely surprising that most historians have reacted with scepticism or hostility to what they have regarded as a new species of charlatanry. But a justified reluctance to be pulled along on the coat-tails of intellectual fashion is not the same as a refusal to consider theories which have attempted to confront the implications of landmarks in twentieth century linguistics for the study of the social. The fact is that the effort to absorb the lessons of these developments for history has scarcely begun and it is foolish to judge the importance of such a project by the flaws of those few well publicized solutions which have pushed their consequences too far or too fast. If history is to renew itself, and in particular, in this context, social and labour history, it cannot be by the defensive reiteration of well tried and by now well worn formulae. It can only be by an engagement with the contemporary intellectual terrain – not to counter a threat, but to discover an opportunity.

CLASS STRUGGLE AND THE INDUSTRIAL REVOLUTION

John Foster's *Class Struggle and the Industrial Revolution*[1] is a remarkable contribution to English historiography. It represents both a continuation of, and a stark contrast to, the impressive tradition of social history which has grown up in Britain in the last two decades. If the best work of English social historians has largely grown within a Marxist tradition, that Marxism has been lightly worn. Mainly as a reaction against the positivism dominant within social science, English social historians have tended to disguise sharp analytical distinctions, and eschew sophisticated quantification or explicit theorization. If their guiding lines have been Marxist, they have also drawn much from a native socialist tradition, a tradition which remembered *Capital* as much for its moral passion as its theoretical achievement. Moreover, their methods of approach have by no means been inspired solely by Marxist sources. The less positivistic realms of sociology have obviously been drawn upon, and economic history of the more traditional kind has always provided a bedrock of support. But it is above all a drawing nearer to social anthropology which has most distinguished modern social history from traditional labour history. Ideas like 'moral economy', 'primitive rebellion' and general attempts to reconstruct 'history from below' have been attempts not only to relate forms of social thought and behaviour to their material roots, but also to uncover the social meaning of lost or disappearing forms of struggle, ritual or myth and to reconstitute their coherence. Compared to traditional labour history, social historians have reacted against the assumption that the

[1] John Foster, *Class Struggle and the Industrial Revolution, Early Industrial Capitalism in Three English Towns* (1974).

history of the working class or of any other oppressed group could be adequately understood through the history of its leadership or its formal organizations, and even more strongly against the short-hand which gauged the 'maturity' of a labour movement by tons of steel produced or miles of railway line laid down. It has shifted the attention from political vanguards to those whose consciousness traditional historiography would have labelled backward or unenlightened. It has thus been a reaction, not only against certain form of Marxist history writing, but also against a much older whig–liberal tradition.

NEW EMPHASIS

John Foster's book clearly registers a debt to the recent achievement of social history and builds upon it. But what is most striking is his abrupt departure from its dominant emphases. The questions the book seeks to answer are explicitly Marxist, the categories of analysis equally so. Quantitative analysis of great sophistication is used to support interpretation whenever possible; literary evidence is used only with the most stringent economy. In place of a detailed literary analysis of the transitional popular ideologies which accompanied the history of the Industrial Revolution, Foster emphasizes a Leninist dialectic between vanguard and mass. Questions of power and political organization are moved into the foreground. Little space is allotted to the byways of working-class life or struggle. If Foster has produced some path-breaking information about types of family and types of household characteristic of the early industrial working class, this information is strictly subordinated to the political questions it is designed to answer.

The central theme of the book is 'the development and decline of a revolutionary class consciousness' in the second quarter of the nineteenth century; its basic aim is 'to further our understanding of how industrial capitalism developed *as a whole*'.[2] The result is a rare conjuncture between a consistent application of Marxist categories and the most rigorous and detailed empirical research. Perhaps only another historian

---

[2] Ibid., 1.

could appreciate the sheer immensity of research that has gone into the substantiation of Foster's arguments. On the other hand, the employment of the most advanced quantitative techniques of sociology to establish Marxist and Leninist concepts – and, more important, to answer questions posed by these concepts – is unprecedented, at least in the English-speaking world. Foster's book will undoubtedly be a landmark not only in British historiography, but also in Marxist historical analysis.

Nevertheless, *Class Struggle and the Industrial Revolution* is a difficult book. The conceptual apparatus is not sufficiently explained. The arguments are often unreasonably condensed and the transitions abrupt. The arrangement of the book is also disconcerting. Foster's argument is based on Oldham, a Lancashire textile town, but the popular movement in Oldham is not set in any national context, indeed is not even compared to that of the neighbouring industrial towns of south Lancashire. Oldham workers appear to fight out their own autonomous class struggle, sending delegates to Westminster only to protect that autonomy. Familiar political landmarks of the period are either not mentioned, or appear in such heavy disguise that it is necessary to think twice before recognition dawns. Luddism, Peterloo, the 1832 Reform Bill, Owenism, the New Poor Law, the Ten Hours' movement and Chartism are present in the book, but it is by no means immediately apparent that these were also issues which punctuated the Oldham struggle. Most serious, it is not clear whether this refusal to situate Oldham in the context of a national political struggle is itself a substantive thesis, or merely an accidental result of the organization of the book. In either case, it remains a weakness that the method of approach is not explained, and that the reader is left to do so much of his own detective work. Because Foster's book is of fundamental importance, I shall provide a fairly full summary of his argument, and then venture some reflections of my own on *Class Struggle and the Industrial Revolution*'s contribution to Marxist history.

THE CASE OF OLDHAM

Oldham is an industrial centre a few miles north-west of Manchester. From 1750 to 1850, Oldham's main industry was cotton-spinning and weaving; from the mid-nineteenth century onwards, engineering and machine-building were predominant. Oldham reflected the general development of British capitalism in particularly bold relief. It experienced the full force of the economic contradictions of the first phase of the Industrial Revolution, and in the high noon of Victorian capitalism became one of the leading manufacturing bases of the 'workshop of the world'. Similarly, Oldham's working class reproduced in sharper than usual outline the historical progression of the British working class as a whole. Until the late 1820s, the majority of Oldham's workers were handloom weavers working in their own homes. By 1840, the majority worked in spinning and weaving factories. By 1860, the majority of male workers were employed by a few large-scale engineering firms. Politically, Oldham enjoyed a continuity of radical and revolutionary working-class leadership from the beginning of the century until the collapse of Chartism. Every significant initiative of the radical or working-class movement during that period, whether political or industrial, appears to have found strong local support there. In the mid-Victorian age, Oldham likewise starkly reflected the changed political character of the working class, epitomized by the clearcut division between the labour aristocrat and the unskilled: a tightly interlocking collection of liberal nonconformist self-help institutions on the one hand; Orangeism, Toryism and the pub on the other.

Between 1790 and 1850, the cotton industry experienced two periods of prolonged crisis. The first lasted from the mid-1790s to 1820. It was preceded by the first modern industrial slump which expressed itself not by a rise in the price of grain, but by wage-cutting and unemployment. It thus threw into disarray traditional methods of social control, which could contain a harvest crisis but had no solution to industrial grievances once wages ceased to be customary. The novel violence of the trade cycle was, however, less dangerous than the structural crisis which afflicted the cotton industry for the next twenty-five years. Its cause lay in the imbalance between the mechanized spinning and unmechanized weaving sectors. By the 1790s European producers were using English machine-spun yarn to oust England from her traditional markets for woven cloth. Thus, 'the failure to mechanize weaving brought the largest sector of England's industrial labour force into direct competition with more cheaply fed workers on the continent'.[3] The result was a sustained attack on living standards which continued for a generation.

The second crisis lasted from 1830 to 1847. The cause was no longer an imbalance within the cotton industry, for weaving was now mechanized. It was rather an imbalance between the technologically advanced cotton industry and the rest of the British economy. While there was a continual and dramatic decrease in the exchange value of cotton textiles, there was no corresponding fall in the price of food and machinery. Therefore, 'the value of industrial output relative to the costs of labour and the increasing mass of fixed capital fell from crisis to crisis'[4]: a classic example, as Foster suggests, of a declining rate of profit as Marx defined it. The result was again constant wage-cutting and frequent unemployment, affecting the whole of the cotton industry, but principally the spinners.

Foster's argument is that the first of these crises produced in Oldham 'a special form of trade-union consciousness'[5] – a coercive and extra-legal occupational solidarity, which in its struggle to maintain living standards succeeded in eliminating bourgeois political control from the town and resisted successfully all attempts by the state power to re-establish that control (although he does not sufficiently stress that radical control did not pose a direct threat to bourgeois property or to the running of the cotton industry). In the second crisis, Foster maintains, Oldham's workers consolidated the political gains of the first but went on to develop a mass revolutionary class consciousness. The Short Time movement kept the cotton workers in a permanent state of political mobilization. The resulting critique of overproduction and competition and its connection to wage-cutting and unemployment within the cotton industry was an anti-capitalist one. During the earlier period, radicals had made no systematic long-term link between their economic and political campaigns: 'national bankruptcy' had been merely a step towards an 'ill-defined

[3] Ibid., 21.
[4] Ibid.
[5] Ibid., 43.

jacobin republic'. Now Oldham's radicals were able to make fundamental political change an intrinsic part of their industrial programme. Foster emphasizes two preconditions for the existence of class consciousness: the overcoming of sectional loyalties and evidence of intellectual conviction (as opposed to mere desperation). He argues that class consciousness fulfilling these conditions was present in Oldham, not merely among a vanguard but also among the mass of the working class. To support his case, he points to the mass response of all trades to a general strike in support of Fielden's Short Time proposals in 1834 (although here he admits that the evidence to support mass intellectual conviction is ambiguous) and, with greater confidence, to the month-long general strike of 1842. The pressure for this strike came from below. It was eventually decided upon, against the advice of the Chartist executive, after ten days of discussion in Oldham in which 10,000 people were said to have taken part, and it was supported by all the trades in the town.

Thus Oldham's history between the 1790s and 1840s, as Foster presents it, roughly reproduced the stages of class consciousness outlined by Marx and Engels in the *Communist Manifesto*. Similarly, the explanation Foster goes on to develop of the dissolution of that class consciousness broadly endorses the interpretation put forward by Engels in his 1892 preface to 'The Condition of the Working Class in England in 1844'. It was not impotence or ineffectiveness that produced the collapse of Chartism. On the contrary, Foster argues, it was the strength of the Chartist challenge that forced the governing classes to make fundamental concessions, and it was these concessions which in turn first disoriented and then disarmed Chartism. The reforms associated with the mid-century period of 'liberalization' – the emergence of mass parties, the extension of the franchise, the legal recognition of trade unions, etc. – were not unconnected phenomena. Quite the reverse: 'liberalization was in fact a collective *ruling-class* response to a social system in crisis and integrally related to a preceding period of working-class consciousness'.[6]

[6] Ibid., 3.

TWO TYPES OF CONSCIOUSNESS

Before looking at the reasons for the transition from 'class consciousness' to 'liberalization' in the 1840s and 1850s, we should follow the author in examining how these two stages of consciousness were formed, and what differentiated Oldham from other comparable types of industrial town. According to Foster, Oldham's first period of 'trade-unionist consciousness' developed out of the need for industrial resistance to capitalist pressure in the period in which trade unionism was outlawed. Oldham had always had its radical enclave, partly hereditary and highly localized. In the eighteenth century, opposition had been expressed in religious terms and had clustered round the Dob Street Unitarian Church. When the French Revolution came, Dob Street was the place chosen for attack in Oldham by church and king mobs in 1792. It was the experience of capitalist crisis rather than the French Revolution which freed these radicals – by now Jacobins – from their previous isolation from the rest of the community. By 1799 the weaver's purchasing power was half what it had been in 1792; at the same time the Combination Acts illegalized all forms of trade union activity. Foster writes, 'a vanguard group is only likely to gain mass leadership in conditions where its larger social orientation (and particularly its willingness to use extra-legal, anti-system tactics) has an immediate relevance'.[7] This was the situation in Oldham. So it was not surprising that radicals should assume leadership of a movement to defend traditional living standards, for the struggle demanded not merely resistance to employers, but direct confrontations with 'state power'. By 1811–12, 12,000 regular troops were tied down for the best part of a year by a 'guerrilla campaign' (Luddism) in the Midlands and the North. In these conditions, traditional methods of social control broke down. The magistracy lost its hegemony over the district. The local yeomanry – employers on horseback – proved ineffective, and working-class leaders were able to gain control over the local administration. But, as Foster stresses, the strength of the radical leadership was

[7] Ibid., 100.

precariously dependent upon the economic misery of the weaver and, once economic conditions improved in 1819, political support for the radicals declined. Furthermore, despite the insurrectionary mood of 1811 or 1817, the views of the radical leadership were those of Paine and Cobbett; they were based essentially on an appeal to the independence of the small producer.

Oldham's radicals were able to weather out the waning of the radical movement in the 1820s without relinquishing their hold on the town administration, or succumbing to the liberalizing schemes of Brougham, Hume and Place. Foster's explanation is that Oldham's workers now had an economic incentive to resist the reimposition of bourgeois political control. Surviving statistics record no prosecutions in Oldham under the Combination Acts, and a local rate of wages that was higher than in neighbouring Manchester. These were the fruits of working-class control of the administration, and in particular its control of the police. Working-class leaders captured Oldham's local government in the second decade of the century and did not lose it until 1847. The police force was staffed with hand-picked trade union militants. Home Office reports expressed concern about 'jacobinical' constables. And not without reason. In 1816, for instance, the constables permitted the holding of universal suffrage meetings and one, Ashton Clegg, described as 'extremely disaffected' and 'violent', took the chair.[8] Without co-operation from the police, persecution of the radical and unionist movement by the state power was virtually impossible. Local employers vainly petitioned for barracks or the billeting of troops, but this was turned down on grounds of expense and the dangers of fraternization. Even the spy system broke down when Oldham's local informer, the sub-postmaster, was unmasked as a double agent.

Freed from the normal channels of state repression, Oldham's radicals consolidated their hold on the town. Poor Law administration remained under their control, and the 1834 Poor Law could not be imposed on Oldham, until the end of the 1840s. The Select Vestry, whose chairmanship appears

[8] Ibid., 57.

always to have been reserved for ex-political prisoners, acted similarly. Lastly, despite the restricted franchise, the working class controlled the Parliamentary representation of the town during the second period of capitalist crisis. Oldham's MPs were William Cobbett and John Fielden, an old Jacobin and a leader of the Short Time movement. According to Foster, their main task at Westminster was to foil government attempts to regain control over the police, the Poor Law and local administration. Their return to Parliament was secured because of working-class control over the local petty bourgeoisie. Through a policy of 'exclusive dealing', the town's shopkeepers were encouraged to vote for working-class candidates. As Foster remarks of this, trade union methods had been put in the hands of revolutionary leaders, for 'the techniques used were carried over from the traditional methods of labour bargaining – boycott, picketing and reliance on mass discipline and allegiance'.[9]

DETERMINANTS OF CLASS CONSCIOUSNESS

What, apart from dramatic but imperfect accounts of mass struggles, can establish that there *was* a revolutionary mass 'class consciousness' in Oldham between 1830 and 1847, and not just a continuation of trade union consciousness, or a momentary revolt against intolerable conditions? And if this consciousness did exist, why did it not exist in other single-industry towns where conditions were comparably bad? In order to differentiate Oldham from other industrial towns, Foster compares it with Northampton (dominated by shoe-making) and South Shields (dominated by coastal shipping and ship-building). In an intricate comparative statistical survey – employing sampling techniques to which it is impossible to do justice here – Foster demonstrates that wages and living standards were in fact better in Oldham than in Northampton or South Shields, while working conditions could only be described as equally terrible. ('Better' in this context meant that whereas in Oldham only 20 per cent of families lived beneath the line of subsistence, the proportion

[9] Ibid., 56.

was 25 per cent in South Shields and over 30 per cent in Northampton!) From these results, Foster deduces that intolerable conditions in themselves had little to do with the formation of class consciousness. Northampton, probably the most miserable of the three towns, possessed no effective organized working-class presence. South Shields, on the other hand, possessed a strongly organized working class, but no working-class political movement.

Having established no immediate correlation between class consciousness and conditions of life in the three towns, Foster goes on to compare patterns of intermarriage and neighbourhood. How far did families of different occupations, particularly craftsmen and labourers, intermarry and live next door to one another? Several objections could be advanced against the statistical significance of this comparison, and unfortunately the data refer to the decade after Oldham's period of 'class consciousness' had already come to an end. Nevertheless, the differences revealed are extremely interesting and, on the face of it, Foster's interpretation of the results is plausible. In a town where the workers are strongly organized and a high degree of sectional occupational solidarity is built up, a high degree of marriage *within* occupations is to be expected, but little between craftsmen and labourers. On the other hand, in a town where occupational loyalties are overshadowed by a strong working-class political movement, some intermarriage between labourer and craftsman families might be expected. Foster's comparison does in fact reveal this – although the differentials are not very great. In South Shields, which had the greatest income overlap between skilled and unskilled families, there was the lowest degree of intermarriage. In Oldham, which had the least income overlap, there was the highest degree of intermarriage. What of Northampton? In a town where labour has little organized presence or tradition, and where a new staple industry is continually being swollen with recruits from the countryside, different factors can be expected to affect choice of marriage. Foster's explanation of the Northampton figures, which bear more resemblance to those of Oldham than to those of South Shields, is that because Northampton was still under the cultural control of the employers, the distinction between 'respectable' and 'unrespectable' carried more weight than that between skilled and unskilled, and that different social and political allegiances were therefore to be found as much *within* as *between* occupations.

If comparisons of intermarriage (and neighbourhood) tend to suggest less social distance between sections of the working class in Oldham, what was it that created 'class consciousness' there, while blocking it in a strongly unionized and sometimes violent town like South Shields? Foster's answer is 'the logic of capitalist development expressed in particular industries'.[10] In Oldham, the development of the cotton industry, and to a lesser extent that of coal, suggested immediate 'trade unionist' solutions to the dominant problems of overproduction, competition and unemployment, which were in fact incompatible with the capitalist structure of these industries. In South Shields, on the other hand, no such logic was present. The shipping industry experienced no significant change either in its technology or in its structure of ownership. Its difficulties were caused by an overcapacity left over from the Napoleonic wars, by the gradual dismantling of the mercantile system, and by railway competition in transporting coal to London. The problem for its labour force was not an attack on its wage rates, but rising unemployment. From the late 1820s, trade unionists in South Shields increasingly collaborated with employers in a fight to retain a protected British shipping industry, on which the town's former prosperity had been based. The pattern of industrial development in South Shields did not immediately suggest any anti-capitalist solution to its problems. Thus, while the town possessed an active Chartist leadership and a working-class press, political militants always remained a minority. They were never able to converge with the wider trade union movement, as happened in Oldham.

REASONS FOR DEFEAT

Finally, how was the 'class consciousness' of Oldham transformed into the class collaborationism of the mid-

[10] Ibid., 124.

Victorian period? Foster emphasizes two processes: firstly, a liberalizing response from the local bourgeoisie which successfully broke up the proletarian-dominated radical alliance in the later 1840s; secondly, a restabilization and reorientation of the capitalist economy, of which one result was the emergence of a new form of social control, this time no longer imposed formally and externally upon the labour community by the magistrate, but operating structurally within the place of work. This occurred through the appearance of a new stratum of production workers – labour aristocrats – 'willing and able to implement technically phrased instructions from above',[11] and sharing a material interest with the employers in increasing the productivity of those beneath them.

Liberalizing initiatives at a local level were preceded by a series of legislative reforms in the late 1830s and early 1840s, designed to check the apparently suicidal course of the cotton industry, to restabilize the economy and so reduce the scale of class conflict. They included currency reform, factory legislation and the lifting of the ban on the export of machinery, and were accompanied by a modification of the earlier positions adopted by political economy – a novel stress on a stable currency, capital export and income distribution. In Oldham itself the bourgeoisie began to abandon its earlier positions in 1847. In that year, one sector of the town's capitalists came out in favour of the limitation of factory hours, while another sector came out in favour of an extension of the franchise. Two planks of the working-class programme had been appropriated by the Conservative and Liberal parties respectively. Foster then shows in microscopic detail how, in the ensuing confusion, the working-class alliance broke up. The shopkeepers moved behind the Liberal candidate, whose platform also contained the demand for the disestablishment of the Church. The small masters fell in behind the Tory demand for factory legislation. Deserted by their petty-bourgeois allies, working-class activists were also gradually absorbed into the two bourgeois parties. By the early 1850s, the Chartists had been reduced to a small rump.

This defeat of the working-class alliance through the

[11]   Ibid., 224.

modification of bourgeois positions was cemented, according to Foster, by parallel changes in the structure of Oldham's workforce. Oldham's machine-making industry had overextended itself by the end of the 1830s to meet the demand created by the mechanization of weaving. In the ensuing slump, capitalists began to cut costs by attacking the craft control of the trade. The end of the ban on the export of machinery gave further incentive to increase the scale of production and transform the labour process. There followed a battle between workers and employers which lasted for ten years ending in the complete defeat of the Engineers' Union in the national lockout of 1851. In place of the skilled artisan possessing control over access to the trade and work practice, there stepped the labour aristocrat, stripped of craft control and transformed into a 'pace-maker' of his unskilled assistants. A similar process, Foster argues, took place in the cotton industry where the spinner, spared from elimination by the automatic mule, was instead made into the 'pace-maker' of his piecers – an important reason why the Ten Hours' Movement faded away towards the end of the 1840s. The growth of this aristocratic stratum – Foster estimates that by the 1860s it constituted one-third of the adult male workforce – was accompanied by a cultural mutation and fission within the working class. The new aristocrat was surrounded by a cocoon of new institutions – adult education, temperance, the co-op, methodism, etc. – linking him to his employers and separating him from the unskilled population beneath him. Foster's conclusion is that the creation of this privileged grade within the labour force was the 'key component' in the mid-nineteenth century restabilization 'and that it was around this dimension of inequality that the social structure later crystallized'.[12]

There are many individual questions of interpretation that could be taken up in a book as rich and important as this. But such questions are better left to other historians with a specialized knowledge of Lancashire history. The scope of the present critique is confined to Foster's overall argument and the type of Marxist analysis used to support it.

[12] Ibid., 254.

CONVINCING ANALYSIS

It should at once be stressed that Foster's exciting analyses of the structure and evolution of the Oldham bourgeoisie and petty bourgeoisie mark a major advance over previous studies. They demonstrate more irrefutably than any other section of the book the immense gains that can be registered by a quantitative social history informed by Marxism, particularly when that Marxism is unhampered by some formal touchstone of orthodoxy to which the material is made to conform. The origins of all the major manufacturing families are traced back to the seventeenth century and the still widespread notion that the Industrial Revolution was led by men who rose from rags to riches is, in Oldham at least, wholly disproved. Nearly all Oldham's factory owners began their social ascent not in the 1770s but in the 1650s. Foster goes on to provide a meticulous dissection of the divisions within this ruling stratum, distinguishing the social and political outlook of those whose livelihood depended upon connection with Manchester from that of those who needed the goodwill of the neighbouring gentry. This dissection does not rest merely on literary impression or historical intuition. It is exhaustively demonstrated by systematic investigation of probate records, marriage registers and census data. Foster provides practically irrefutable proof for each of his propositions. Yet the reader is not dragged down by an academic discourse on source material and research methods. Within the framework of a Marxist analysis, he is left with a vivid impression of what these people were like, whom they married, whom they consorted with, what sort of houses they lived in, what they did after work, how they made their money and how this affected their outlook.

Particularly striking is Foster's examination of the religious divisions within the local bourgeoisie. Against Weber, he demonstrates that the relationship between capitalism and Calvinism was based on experience, not tradition.[13] In the early phase of industrial capitalism, where capitalist control of the economy was still very incomplete, it was necessary for the

---

[13] Ibid., 177.

capitalist to bind his workforce to him. He minimized the social distance between himself and his labourers, and exercised a patriarchal face-to-face supervision, legitimated by a Calvinist interpretation of Christianity – in which of course the evils of sloth were particularly emphasized. Where this form of relationship was impossible, as it was, for example, in the Oldham coal-mines, the capitalist tended to adopt the manners and theology of the neighbouring gentry; and when this relationship broke down, as it did in the centre of Oldham once the size of the labour force grew too large, the capitalist opted for a more easygoing religion and a more consumption-oriented way of life. This priority of material situation over doctrine was confirmed by the religious geography of Oldham. As Foster observes, 'the Church of England, gaudy in the town centre, became conscientious in the out-townships, merging in doctrine, as its congregation did in marriage and friendship, with dissent'.[14]

IMBALANCES

But if the analysis of the bourgeoisie and the petty bourgeoisie carries great conviction, important parts of the analysis of the working class do not. There is no decline in the quality of the research. What jars is the overall categorization and the way in which it imprints upon certain features of the story an overbold relief, while leaving others in an unjustifiable obscurity. The treatment of the origins and the eighteenth century structure of the labour community is excellently done. The trouble begins at the point where Foster starts to apply the full weight of his categories to the development of the Oldham class struggle.

It will be noticed that the exposition of the book is arranged around a limited number of guiding concepts: *alienation, trade union consciousness, class consciousness* and the *labour aristocracy*. Foster is particularly anxious to prove that the struggle of the period (1790–1820) was limited to 'a special form of trade-union consciousness', qualitatively different from the second period of 'class consciousness'. The importance of this distinction for Foster is that capitalism, through the alienation it

---

[14] Ibid., 178.

inaugurates, engenders among the proletariat a series of sectional 'false' consciousnesses, which in turn provide a socially stabilizing mechanism within capitalist development. In what circumstances can this 'false consciousness' be transformed into a 'class consciousness'? 'Only when capitalism itself reveals its full contradictions', writes Foster, 'will people begin to understand why and how it is to be overthrown.'[15] This, it is argued, is what happened in Oldham in the 1830s.

However, despite the rigour and imaginativeness of much of the analysis, the fundamental point of distinction remains somewhat intangible. A large number of comparisons are offered, but none are conclusive. They establish an empirical possibility, but not a conceptual certainty.

Firstly, Foster suggests that, in comparison with the second period, the earlier political radicalism was narrowly dependent on economic conditions and lacked the staying power which only intellectual conviction could have provided. However, on the face of it, the waning of the political radicalism of the spinners after 1842 appears not dissimilar to that of the weavers after 1819.[16] Secondly, he argues that the earlier radicalism, however egalitarian, possessed no conception of an alternative economic order for which the conquest of political power would be merely a means: that an 'ill-defined jacobin republic' was the end and 'state bankruptcy' was a step towards it.[17] In the 1830s, on the other hand, Foster argues, working-class leaders were able to make radical political change an intrinsic part of their industrial programme. Against this, a number of points can be made. The

[15] Ibid., 124.

[16] At another point Foster states: 'the various fiascos of 1839 are well known (and the north-west was probably wise to keep clear of them)' (p. 143). In fact there were Chartist attempts from June to August in the Manchester area to organize a 'National Holiday', and the thinking behind this does not seem to have been very different from that in the 1842 general strike. It met with no response in Oldham, where trade had temporarily improved. A meeting there declared that the National Holiday was unnecessary and that the Charter should only be worked for by peaceable means. It may well be that the Oldham workers rejected this on sound political grounds. But the other possibility should also have been discussed; i.e. the apparently close relationship between support for a general strike and the presence or absence of distress. For details, see Asa Briggs (ed.), *Chartist Studies* (1962 edn), 47–9.

[17] Foster, *Class Struggle*, 147.

Jacobin republic *did* imply a specific form of economy – that of small, equal, independent commodity producers – which was certainly 'an alternative economic order', even if a backward-looking one. Moreover, it is unlikely that this small-producer ideology disappeared as abruptly from Oldham's radicalism as Foster implies, given what we know of its continuing strength nationally during the Chartist period (we should not forget that the majority of Oldham's workers remained handloom weavers until the end of the 1820s). Lastly, even if the aims of the Oldham workers could be wholly summed up in the demands of the Short Time movement in the 1830s, this was a *de facto* anti-capitalist, not a consciously socialist programme. Foster further supports his argument by pointing to the richness and depth of a revolutionary culture in Oldham during the period of 'class consciousness'. But working-class political control of the town was continuous from the 1810s to the 1840s. No sharp breaks appear. In itself, this argument is as compatible with a thesis of quantitative growth as it is with that of a qualitative leap. Similarly, the evidence from social structure that Foster draws upon – intermarriage, neighbourliness, etc. – while in itself a major step forward in the precision of English social history, nevertheless remains in principle open to alternative types of explanation. It supports his argument, but it cannot establish it. Finally, to set against the evidence of a break, Foster reveals that there was a high degree of continuity in political leadership between the two periods, and that both periods of struggle were peculiarly industrial in form and inspiration.

CONCEPTUAL PROBLEMS

The difficulty of his argument lies not in a lack of information, nor in any lack of proficiency in the way concepts are employed, but in an arbitrariness and lack of precision in the concepts themselves. The historical distinction Foster attempts to establish is based upon two distinct theoretical couplets – alienation/class consciousness and trade union consciousness/class consciousness. Each of these couplets presents considerable difficulty. When combined, a further problem is introduced.

The couplet of alienation/class consciousness derives from the early Marx. Consciousness, in this sense, implies the recuperation of an alienated essence. The subject alienates his essence in an inhuman object (God, the state, private property, etc.). At a determinate moment, he is enabled to reappropriate this object and become identical subject/object. As is well known, Marx derived this schema from an application and extension of the Feuerbachian critique of Hegel. The moment of 'consciousness' here is not historical, but ontological. It appeals to a moment of absolute truth, to which no concrete historical process could ever aspire. Indeed, this is its most obvious defect for – quite apart from other epistemological objections which could be raised against it – it bears only the most notional and abstract relation to material history. It makes no reference to the specific historical development of the capitalist mode of production; only to a world in which Man has lost himself through the institution of private property. The subject of the process is not the working class, but Man as he developed in the thought of classical German philosophy.

I am not suggesting that Foster's argument in any sense depends on this idealist logic, or even that he makes any use of it. Foster attempts to provide an empirically workable definition of alienation at the beginning of the book, and thereafter it plays a very subordinate role in his general interpretation of the Oldham struggle. Nevertheless, it is difficult to apply this schema in any form without falling victim to some of its implications. In Foster's case it leads to an excessively formalistic conception of 'class consciousness'. For if alienation is identified with 'sectional' or 'false' consciousness, then 'class consciousness' becomes its opposite, the transcendence of sectionalism, the consciousness of class identity and therefore, by implication, true consciousness.

The couplet of trade union consciousness/class consciousness has a quite different genealogy. It derives from a distinction made by Lenin in 'What is to be done?' and has no affiliation to the early Marxist couplet. Lenin's argument, which is proveable or disproveable in historical terms, was directed against 'the economists' – those who glorified the spontaneous trade union struggle as *the* proletarian class struggle and objected to the emphasis of the social democrats upon the revolutionary political struggle against the Tsarist autocracy. Trade union consciousness, Lenin argued, emerges spontaneously through the day-to-day struggle between workers and employers; in itself it remains 'the bourgeois politics of the working class'.[18] Socialist class consciousness, on the other hand, is always brought to the working class 'from the outside'; i.e. in the first place it is brought to the working class by individual bourgeois intellectuals, through the medium of a revolutionary socialist party. It is not intended here to discuss the general validity of the Leninist distinction, but it is quite clear that formidable difficulties are encountered when an attempt is made to apply it to Oldham, along the lines of the argument of 'What is to be done?'. In the first place, we are talking about a period before either a revolutionary socialist theory or a revolutionary socialist party existed. It was, indeed, only as a result of this formative period of class struggle that either could come into existence. We could, of course, attempt to find analogies – certain strands of Chartist organization, for instance – but when set beside Leninist definitions of the 'Party', its aim and its unifying political task, such analogies would be very forced. This is especially so if we set it in relationship to the other pole of the Leninist distinction – trade union consciousness. 'The history of all countries', wrote Lenin, 'shows that the working class, solely by its own forces, is able to work out merely trade-union consciousness, i.e. the conviction of the need for combining in unions, for fighting against the employers, and for trying to prevail upon the government to pass laws necessary for the workers, etc.'[19] 'Solely by its own forces' raises difficult problems of definition. But it is clear enough that, if there was a transition from 'trade-union consciousness' to 'class consciousness' in Oldham in the 1830s, what primarily generated it was not an infusion from outside but, as Foster says, the logic of capitalist development in Oldham itself. 'Class political consciousness', wrote Lenin, 'can be brought to the worker *only from without*, that is from outside the economic struggle, outside the sphere of the relations between the workers and the employers.'[20] Yet

---

[18] Lenin, 'What is to be done?', *Selected Works*, 3 vols., Moscow (1970), 186.
[19] Ibid., 143.
[20] Ibid., 182.

the peculiarity of Oldham, in Foster's account, is precisely the extent to which 'class political consciousness' did develop within the economic sphere. Faced with the awkwardness of fitting Oldham into the Leninist distinction, Foster appears to shift back to the early Marxist conception of class consciousness: capitalism itself reveals its full contradictions and then people realize the necessity of overthrowing it; the proletariat is the self-consciousness of the contradiction of capitalist society.

Other historians have shown that workers began to consider themselves as members of a separate and antagonistic class from the 1830s, and that the language of populist radicalism in many areas gave way to one of class polarization. It would not, therefore, be surprising to find that Oldham workers in the 1830s were class conscious in this sense, as they had not been in the first two decades of the nineteenth century. But Foster's claim involves more than this. 'Class consciousness', as he employs the term, is virtually synonymous with 'revolutionary class consciousness'. This is much more debatable. Absence of sectionalism and 'intellectual conviction' by no means of themselves entail a revolutionary standpoint. Indeed, in principle, they are quite compatible with Lenin's conception of trade union consciousness.[21] Only an examination of what the content of that conviction was, and the way in which it informed the struggles of the period, could establish whether it was revolutionary – and, if so, what sort of revolution it was aiming at. Here Foster's analysis is at its weakest. The skill and ingenuity of his attempt to establish the fact of class consciousness is offset by a disappointingly cursory and somewhat evasive analysis of its content.[22] What was the content of the industrial and political struggles of the 1830s and 1840s and what was the connection

---

[21] Lenin's conception of trade union politics included *political* struggles of the working class *as a whole* at the level of the state. He defined these struggles as 'the common striving of all workers to secure from the government measures for the alleviation of the distress characteristic of their position, but which do not abolish that position, i.e. which do not remove the subjection of labour to capital'. Ibid., 153.

[22] See, for example, p. 73 where Foster leaves aside 'the initial difficulty of defining something (i.e. class consciousness) whose ideological content is always historically relative and specific'. See also p. 148.

between them? It is impossible to characterize the 'class consciousness' of Oldham workers during this period without some sort of answer to these questions. We shall, therefore, examine the industrial and political struggles in turn.

THE INDUSTRIAL STRUGGLE

Firstly, Oldham's industrial struggle. If we wish to find Marxist concepts which will help us to interpret it, they are to be found in *Capital* rather than the 1844 'Manuscripts' or 'What is to be done?' Like any other mode of production, the capitalist mode, as Marx defines it, is characterized by two distinct forms of appropriation. It is a specific mode of appropriation of the product and a specific mode of appropriation of nature. In other words, it embodies a double relation, a specific form of ownership of the means of production and a specific form of control over the labour process. These two types of appropriation are relatively autonomous. They cannot simply be reduced to one another, since – most obviously – their temporalities are different.

If we follow the analysis of the Industrial Revolution presented in *Capital*, we see that it involved not so much a change in ownership of the means of production as a change in the form of the labour process. As a specific form of ownership of the means of production, capitalism began around the sixteenth century when labour power became a commodity. As a specific form of control over the labour process, however, capitalism began with the Industrial Revolution. The intervening period was what Marx called the period of manufacture. During this period, the control exercised by the capitalist over wage labour was 'formal' not 'real'.[23] Through his ownership of the means of production the capitalist was able to combine and specialize the work of labourers in such a way as to increase the productivity of labour, and thus the rate of surplus value. The main distinguishing feature of manufac-

---

[23] See *Capital*, vol. 1, Moscow (1961), 510. For a discussion of this distinction as one crucial division between Marxist and Neo-Ricardian economic theory, see Bob Rowthorn, 'Neo-Classicism, Neo-Ricardianism and Marxism', *NLR*, 86 (July/August 1974), 63–88.

ture, as Adam Smith defined it, was the sophistication of its division of labour. But however sophisticated this division, the technical basis of manufacture remained handicraft. The means of labour, the tool, remained an extension of the human hand; its tempo of production was, therefore, necessarily that of manual labour. Through the dissolution of the production process of a particular commodity into its component parts, manufacture created a distinction between skilled and un-skilled labour, a distinction, as Marx observes, strictly excluded from the preceding handicraft era. But the power of the skilled 'detail labourer', the artisan, remained a formid-able obstacle to capitalist development. Through the pos-session of a scarce craft skill, the journeyman could control access to his trade (through apprenticeship) and retained considerable control over the content and pace of the labour process. 'St Monday' was symbolic of the residual power he possessed.

Conventional economic history tends to date the Industrial Revolution from the discovery of new sources of power (Watt's steam engine). But the point stressed by Marx is not the application of a new source of energy, but the elimination of the handicraft basis to production and the division of labour based upon it. 'The steam-engine itself ... did not give rise to any industrial revolution. It was, on the contrary, the invention of machines that made a revolution in the form of steam-engines necessary. As soon as man, instead of working with an implement on the subject of his labour, becomes merely the motive power of an implement machine, it is mere accident that motive power takes the disguise of human muscle.'[24] This use of the machine tool in place of the manual tool was, for Marx, the specific mode of production of the capitalist mode of production and, like any other form of the mode of appropriation of nature, it defined a specific social relationship. It was this revolutionary change in the labour process which replaced the 'formal' subordination of wage labour to capital by its 'real' subordination; it was also capitalism's most portentous achievement, since it made the socialization of labour a technical necessity.

[24] *Capital*, vol. I, 375.

Of course, we must be careful to distinguish the general transformation of a mode of production (a purely theoretical concept) from the particular form of its transformation in a particular place at a particular time. Historians date the Industrial Revolution in the cotton textile industry to the second half of the eighteenth century. But if we wish to find evidence of its *direct* social impact upon the labour force, we must look much later. The transition from 'formal' to 'real' capitalist control over production was a long and bitter process – and even in the leading sectors of the economy was only partially achieved by the end of the Chartist period.

IMPACT OF THE INDUSTRIAL REVOLUTION

What were the initial effects of the Industrial Revolution in the cotton industry upon the *adult male worker*? Apart from inaugurating the modern industrial trade cycle and thereby, as Foster notes, undermining customary forms of wage regulation, its effect was ostensibly to increase the proportion of unskilled to skilled within the shell of manufacture, and in the case of the handloom weaver to increase the tyranny of the merchant capitalist. The first modern industrial proletariat in cotton spinning was composed of women and children (piecers, machine-minders, etc.). These were two sectors of the labour force which had always been excluded from the skilled sector of manufacture, which was precisely why they were the most obvious initial source of the type of labour power required by modern industry. With the rise of mule-spinning, they were followed into the factory by a skilled minority of adult male cotton spinners. The latter were not, of course, traditional handicraft workers; before its mechanization, spinning had been performed by women with the help of children. Nevertheless, their work required a manual skill and mechanical ability. Almost from the start, the cotton spinners described their occupation as a 'trade', were strongly organized, successfully imposed a wage level comparable to that of the artisan, and achieved limitation of entry into the trade and a degree of control over hours of work – in other words, a form of craft control comparable to that within manufacture.[25] Their technical position was not effectively challenged until the invention of the automatic mule in the 1820s and, if we wish to understand their early struggles, they should be interpreted not so much as the first struggles of the epoch of modern industry, but as an extension of the form of industrial struggle characteristic of manufacture. The same *a fortiori* must be said of the early struggles of the handloom weaver. The enemy of the handloom weaver up to the 1820s was, as Foster emphasizes, not the power loom but foreign competition. It was not, therefore, really until well into the 1820s that the position of the adult male handicraft worker within the labour process was directly threatened by modern industry in the cotton industry.

'It would be possible to write quite a history of the inventions made since 1830, for the sole purpose of supplying capital with weapons against the revolts of the working class', wrote Marx. 'At the head of these in importance, stands the self-acting mule, because it opened up a new epoch in the automatic system.'[26] The threatened effect of the self-acting mule was to transform the operative from a specialized worker into a machine-minder and to allow the replacement of the male artisan by female or juvenile labour. This had been the actual effect of the replacement of the handloom by the power loom, except that it had also involved two additional features: the transference of the work from the home to the factory and a change in ownership of the means of production (to the extent that handlooms were still owned by individual weavers). This technical transformation of the cotton industry was followed by an analogous change in production methods in engineering and machine-making. Here, the battle against craft control, with the help of inventions like Maudsley's slide rest, was also intended to break the hold exercised by the artisan over the method and pace of production.

In Oldham, these three struggles took place at different

[25] Foster, *Class Struggle*, 231; see also S. D. Chapman, *The Cotton Industry in the Industrial Revolution* (1972), 58; Eric Hobsbawm, *Industry and Empire*, (1968), 65.
[26] *Capital*, vol. 1, 436. It should be noted, however, that modern economic historians have stressed the relative slowness with which such inventions were applied in nineteenth century Britain. For a stimulating discussion of the problem, see H. J. Habakkuk, *American and British Technology in the Nineteenth Century*, Cambridge (1967).

times. The handloom weavers had been defeated by the end of
the 1820s; the spinners' struggle dominated the period from
1830 to 1842; that of the machine-makers lasted from the early
1840s until the defeat of 1851. It is perhaps surprising to find,
from Foster's account, that the weavers played so small a part
in the struggles of the 1830s and 1840s. But it does at least
seem to be confirmed by a change in the dominant form of
struggle. Strike movements among domestic workers were
exceptionally difficult to organize. Therefore, at moments
when discontent among handloom weavers was at its height,
thoughts were more likely to turn to machine-breaking or
insurrection. The insurrectionary mood of 1817 and 1819 and
the attack on the factories in 1826–7 reflected the desperation
of the weavers. In the 1830s and 1840s, insurrectionism
receded. It did not disappear, but it was displaced by the
strike as the dominant weapon. Concentration upon the
possibilities of the strike as a political or industrial weapon
was closely associated with the history of the spinners. This
becomes much clearer once the exceptional position of the
spinner is understood. Unlike the weaver, the spinner had
little 'independence' to lose; nor was his struggle to retain
control over the productive process linked to maintenance of
individual ownership of the means of production. On the
other hand, unlike the machine-maker, he was not the
embattled guardian of the craft secrets of an established
manufacture. He was the product of modern industry, inseparable from the factory, yet carrying into it the aspiration
to a form of control over the productive process similar to that
exercised by the artisan in the manufacturing workshop. To
the extent that this control was successfully achieved, it
demanded from the spinners a form of trade unionism far
more comprehensive in ambition and far more coercive in
practice than that required in a craft workshop. It was the
Spinners' Union which had pioneered the first attempt at
general unionism, the *Philanthropic Hercules* of 1818, and the
coerciveness of their trade union practice is amply illustrated
by Foster's book.[27]

---

[27] See, for example, Foster, *Class Struggle*, 101.

THE SPINNERS' FIGHT

If there was a revolutionary class struggle in Oldham in the 1830s and 1840s its industrial basis was the spinners' battle to defend their social and industrial position. Compared with the spinners' struggles, the battle of the machine-makers in the 40s appears to have made little impact on the community as a whole. (Only one machine-maker is recorded in Foster's list of Oldham political militants between 1830 and 1850.) Three factors appear to have bestowed upon the spinners' struggle its exceptional importance. Firstly, the strategic position of cotton in the national economy: until railway building began to provide a stabilizing element in the 1840s, the fortunes and even the survival of the industrial economy appeared to be precariously dependent upon the fate of the cotton industry; from 1815 to 1850, cotton accounted for approximately 40 per cent of the total income from exports, despite a continuous decline in prices. Secondly, the nature of the crisis in the cotton industry: the first phase of industrialization of Oldham's engineering industry in the 1840s was a response to the huge expansion of the export market for machinery. The aim was not so much to cut labour costs as to streamline and speed up production. Mechanization took place against the background of full employment. This left elbow-room for compromise. In the cotton industry in the 1830s and early 1840s, on the other hand, mill owners pressed forward with mechanization in an attempt to halt the catastrophic decline in their rate of profit by reducing labour costs. Compromises with the workforce only became possible once the extreme imbalance in the national economy had been reduced and mill owners began to switch to capital-saving economies. This process began after the depression of 1842. Thirdly, a point not sufficiently emphasized by Foster, the persistence of family economy within the cotton factory: in 1838, nationally, only 23 per cent of textile factory workers were adult men. The workers in the unskilled departments of spinning and weaving factories and the assistants of the spinner himself were to a considerable extent the latter's wives, children and relatives. This meant that the industrial struggles of the spinners were far more communal in form and widespread in effect than those in industries like engineering where the majority of workers were adult men.[28]

The spinners' battle could not be restricted to wage demands. In the precarious situation of the 1830s and early 1840s, it became inseparable from a battle for control over production in the industry. The high points of class confrontation in Oldham, according to Foster's account, occurred in 1834 and 1842. Both were sparked off by struggles in the cotton industry. The background to the 1834 general strike was to be found in the plans of the 'Regenerators' and the leaders of the Short Time committee: these involved the democratic control of investment in the cotton industry and the introduction of the eight hour day as a solution to wage-cutting and unemployment. How far the Regenerators' aims enjoyed mass support is not clear. But other trades were at least prepared to support a general strike (and struggle on the streets) to prevent a Tolpuddle-style victimization of militants in the Spinners' Union. The general strike of 1842 was political, although not unequivocally so. The Chartist Petition had been thrown out of the House of Commons. Short time, unemployment and distress were at their height in the cotton industry. The general message of radical speakers in the months leading up to the strike was to attribute, 'the present distress to the misapplication of machinery by which means a vast extent of human labour has been superseded and wages greatly reduced'.[29] The strike movement appears to have been set off by a further threatened wage reduction. Workers in Ashton struck on 5 August. A mass meeting on Mottram Moor on 7 August called for the Charter and 'a fair day's wage for a fair day's work'.[30] On 8 August, Ashton workers marched into Oldham, appealing for all to join in a general strike until the Charter was won. Thereafter, the strike spread throughout the cotton districts. The non-textile trades also

---

[28] It should also be stressed that united action between skilled and unskilled in the spinning industry in the 1830s had a solid material basis, since both were affected by successive speed-ups of production. 'In mule spinning the number of motions that had to be completed in a minute more than trebled between 1814 and 1841, and the daily distance walked by the piecer went up from 12 miles to nearly 30.' Ibid., 91.

[29] Ibid., 115.

[30] Briggs (ed.), *Chartist Studies*, 53.

joined in. Chartists supported the strike movement, but they did not inaugurate it.

It is exceptionally difficult to produce neat dividing lines between the political and industrial struggles of the 1830–50 period. There is still not overall agreement among historians about how the 1842 strike is to be interpreted. Foster's statement that the class struggle in Oldham was peculiarly industrial in form is another example of this difficulty. Nationally, the form of struggle tended to change with the state of trade, but the desire for a different social and political order which lay behind these different struggles remained fairly constant. Clearly, economic and political discontent were closely connected. But it is no explanation to describe this phenomenon as 'the politics of hunger': hunger in Northampton had a quite different political meaning from hunger in Oldham, as Foster clearly shows. Hunger lent urgency to a discontent whose sources lay elsewhere. The guiding thread of class struggle in this period was a different estimation of the social worth and position of the worker from that accorded to him or her in the newly developing production relations of industrial capitalism.

The peculiarly radical course of the spinners' industrial struggle becomes clearer once it is understood that they were fighting not merely against immiseration, but also to retain the traditional place accorded to the artisan within the labour process. Although Foster incorporates this battle over production within his interpretation of the 'logic of capitalist development', he assigns no particular prominence to it. It appears as only one manifestation among others (overproduction, wage-cutting, cyclical unemployment) of a capitalist crisis resulting from a declining rate of profit. It is, however, not so much the fact of capitalist crisis as the form it takes which will determine what type of resistance it will generate. The spinners had the example of the handloom weavers before their eyes. The threat of the self-acting mule, the attempt by employers to complete their 'real' control over production, endangered not merely living standards, but all means of control over recruitment, hours and conditions of work until then enforced by the spinners. Beyond this, it put into question the basic sexual division of labour within the factory. Overwork, wage-cutting and unemployment (not in themselves new phenomena) acquired a more radical significance in the light of this fundamental threat.[31]

It is also worth stressing that the industrial battles of the 1830s and 1840s did not concern the capitalist *ownership* of the means of production, but capitalist *control* of the production process. Oldham's militants do not seem to have questioned in any direct way capitalist ownership of the means of production. Even the radical proposals of the Regenerationists in 1834, although effectively transferring control over the cotton industry from the capitalists to the workforce, did not formally challenge capitalist ownership of the industry. Only Owenites believed in social ownership and they did not generally connect this belief with the necessity of class struggle. The conflict over hours and machinery similarly raised issues of control rather than ownership.

This is why it is difficult to analyse Oldham's industrial militancy in the terms laid down by Lenin. Lenin's distinction between class consciousness and trade union consciousness effectively equated industrial struggle with wage struggle, and equated both with reformism, 'the bourgeois politics of the working class'. But it is clear from Marx's analysis in *Capital* that two distinct forms of industrial struggle are possible: struggles over the appropriation of the product and struggles over the appropriation of nature. However much in practice these two forms of struggle overlap, and however non-existent either may be in a pure form, they cannot simply be reduced

---

[31] In 1841 Doherty claimed that the number of spinners in Manchester had fallen between 1829 and 1841 from 2,000 to 500. According to a report instigated by the military commander, General Arbuthnot, in 1844: 'At certain places the adult male population has been thrown out of work to a much greater extent than had been supposed by the improvement of machinery ... and the employment of women' (Foster *Class Struggle*, 296–7). Elsewhere Foster states: 'more dangerous in the long run (because they represented losses which could not be regained) were attempts to dilute the labour force, cut down the number of well-paid jobs and substitute women and children for men. This was the real threat to the spinners' position.' (p. 83). But he does not draw out the full consequences of this statement, i.e. to analyse what sort of industrial struggle it was and what the links between industrial and political struggle would therefore be.

to one another. The struggle over the appropriation of the product takes place in the sphere of circulation. Short-term wage demands may coexist with long-term political goals, but there is no necessary relationship between them and over long periods of time they can remain in a state of separation. In certain circumstances, such struggles may directly contest the capitalist ownership of an industry and be accompanied by demands for nationalization. But unless an explicit socialist content is injected into it, the struggle for the appropriation of the product is simply a struggle for the betterment of the situation of the worker on the basis of the wage contract. It is, in other words, the wage struggle, the dominant feature of trade union consciousness as Lenin defined it. The struggle over the appropriation of nature, on the other hand, takes place within the labour process, within production. Such struggles are less frequent than wage struggles, but tend to predominate when an industry is revolutionized by new methods of production. They tend to form the core of industrial conflicts in periods of exceptional militancy among skilled workers. In themselves, such struggles are neither more nor less significant than struggles over the appropriation of the product. But their dynamics are undoubtedly different. In particular, the very nature of such struggles renders problematic the coexistence between the short term and the long term. Industrial discontent and the political expression of that discontent tend to converge.

Struggles of this kind necessarily begin with the defence of a relatively privileged position in production, and they may retain a conservative or even reactionary form. Whether or not they do so will depend partly upon the nature of the occupation and partly upon the political situation in which they take place. The craftsmen responsible for the 'Sheffield outrages' in 1867 had no political perspectives beyond Gladstonian liberalism. The silk weavers of Spitalfields became protectionist and conservative. On the other hand, at the beginning of the twentieth century, when the semi-handicraft basis of the metal trades was radically undermined, according to Eric Hobsbawm:

metal workers, hitherto rather conservative, became in most countries of the world the characteristic leaders of militant labour movements. The history of such movements since the British lock-out of 1897 can be largely written in terms of the metal workers, so much so that – for instance – the anti-war movements of 1916–18 followed a pace set almost exclusively by them. (We need merely think of Merrheim's union in France, the Berlin shop stewards, the British shop stewards, the Putilov works in Petrograd, the Manfred Weiss works in Budapest, the Turin and Milan metal-workers.)[32]

BETWEEN REFORM AND REVOLUTION

If the Oldham industrial struggle is interpreted as a struggle of this kind, two things become clear. Firstly, the struggle over control does not comfortably fit the Leninist equation between trade union consciousness and reformism, although, on the other hand, it certainly fell short of what he would have accepted as 'revolutionary class consciousness'. Fielden's plans for the reorganization of the cotton industry were certainly incompatible with capitalist ownership of that industry. But, on the other hand, they also fall short of a consciously planned revolutionary overthrow of capitalism. Secondly, after 1830 the dividing line between industrial and political militancy became blurred in a way which eludes Lenin's distinction between industrial and political struggle. The apparently unproblematic shifting between industrial and political struggle and the ambivalent character of the 1842 strike bear this out.

Foster tends to treat the ease of interchange between industrial and political demands as a sign of the presence of a mass revolutionary class consciousness. The events of 1834, according to Foster, 'reveal the ease with which the radical leaders could move from industrial to political struggle without losing their mass support',[33] while the enthusiastic mass response to the call of the Ashton workers for a general strike in August 1842 is seen as 'perhaps the clearest case of how far Oldham's workers had passed beyond a purely trade-union consciousness'.[34] But, as we have already argued, the fact that the industrial struggle in Oldham does not fit Lenin's conception of trade union consciousness does not necessarily establish it as a form of revolutionary class consciousness.

[32] Eric Hobsbawm, *Labouring Men, Studies in the History of Labour* (1964), 360.
[33] Foster, *Class Struggles*, 114.
[34] Ibid., 116.

That could only be established by an analysis of the political
and social aims of the Oldham workers.

Foster's concentration upon the form rather than the
content of class consciousness makes such a task difficult.[35]
Oldham politics are never adequately set in a national
political context, and the comparison with Northampton and
South Shields, however illuminating, cannot remedy this
defect. Revolutionary class consciousness, in the socialist
sense, must at least imply a commitment to the revolutionary
overthrow of the state accompanied by the expropriation of
the expropriators. There were theorists in the 1830s who
argued this case. Bronterre O'Brien envisaged such a revolution in the immediate aftermath of universal suffrage. 'From
the laws of the few have the existing inequalities sprung; by
the laws of the many shall they be destroyed ... Property –
property, this is the thing we must be at.'[36] But this theme of
expropriation does not appear to have found any audible echo
in Oldham. Foster's account of working-class political control
of the town and the alliance between working class and petty
bourgeoisie would scarcely be credible if it had; nor would his
discussion of the relationship between the town bourgeoisie
and the state. Oldham's capitalists may have petitioned for
troops and railed against their inability to control local
administration, but it did not stop the running of their
factories and even without military protection in the late
1830s and early 1840s they did not leave the town. Nevertheless, it would be wrong to deduce from this that Oldham's
militants were still simple Jacobins. Clearly, Foster is right to
argue that political and industrial demands after 1830 embodied a different social content. The social vision of a Paine
or a Cobbett could no longer have an immediate relevance to
a population of factory workers.

[35] Foster's habit of renaming the struggles and movements of the period goes
together with this formalistic tendency. Thus, for example, the Chartist National
Convention of 1839 is renamed 'the workers' parliament'. What is thereby
obliterated is the specific politics and ideology of Chartism. The choice of the word
'Convention', with its memories of Jacobinism and the French Revolution, was not
accidental and, of course, tells us a great deal about what the Chartists thought
they were doing.
[36] Edward Thompson, *The Making of the English Working Class* (1963), 822. Also, for
the character of working-class consciousness in this period, see pp. 711–833 *passim*.

FROM REFORM BILL TO CHARTER

What nationally distinguished the years before and after 1830 were the 1832 Reform Bill and the effects of Owenism and an anti-capitalist political economy. These developments are perceptible in Oldham and are surely as important as the politics of the cotton industry in explaining the changing form of political language to which Foster refers. The Reform Bill was regarded as the great betrayal of what had been thought of as a common struggle. The measures of the Whig government which followed it – the Irish Coercion Bill, the rejection of the Ten Hours' Bill, the attack on Trade Unions, the Municipalities Act and the New Poor Law – were seen as confirmation of the treachery of the middle class. The practical consequence to be drawn was that the working class must fight for its own emancipation. Thus the proletarian consciousness which developed in the 1830s and 1840s was as much the result of this political breach as of the growth of industrial capitalism, and in this sense it developed just as distinctly in London as in Oldham.[37] The other main catalyst, Owenism, tended to be interpreted by different types of worker according to their different industrial situation. But three of its most general legacies in the following two decades were the beliefs that labour was the source of all value, that the aim of production should be use not profit and that society should be based on co-operation, not competition. None of these ideas was peculiar to Owen, but it was in the Owenist period (1830–4) that they received their maximum diffusion. The ferment in Oldham in 1834 is incomprehensible unless it is situated in the nation-wide enthusiasm for co-operative schemes which seized working-class communities at this time.

Although these ideas were anti-capitalist, their logic did not lead to demands for expropriation. The labour theory of value, as it was developed by Thompson and Hodgkin in the 1820s, looked back to Locke as much as it looked forward to Marx. Its basis was not a theory of exploitation within production, but a theory of unequal exchange. Capitalists

---

[37] See Thompson, *Making*, and Iorwerth Prothero, 'Chartism in London', *Past and Present*, 44 (1969).

were still primarily seen as middlemen or monopolists. The capitalist merely owned the means of production which were put at the disposal of the producers. Profit was thus a deduction from the product of labour, enforced through ownership of the means of production. Property was justified so far as it was the product of labour. What was unjustified was wealth acquired through unequal exchange. Through their monopoly position in exchange which had enabled them to acquire ownership of the means of production, and through the increasing competition of labourers deprived of their independence, capitalists were able to exchange subsistence wages against an increasing proportion of unpaid labour.

The situation described by these writers corresponded most closely to that of the depressed artisan or outworker. When, however, this kind of analysis was applied to the situation of the factory worker, its main effect was to reinforce the demands of the Short Time movement. By forcing labourers to work overlong hours or speeding up their work through machinery, manufacturers were depriving them of a portion of their proper reward. All the gains of increasing productivity were monopolized by the capitalist. Overwork created unemployment and increasing competition among labourers, which in turn reinforced their unequal position in exchange. The answer was to replace competition by co-operation among workers, to form one large union which would breach the monopoly position of the capitalists and reduce working hours, thereby abolishing unemployment and overproduction. Thus the plans of Fielden and the Regenerationists in 1834 were far from a mere attempt to ameliorate the factory worker's condition. They could logically be seen as the beginning of 'the Great Change'.[38]

It is difficult to separate political and industrial demands in the 1830s and 1840s because working-class leaders themselves rarely did so. Universal suffrage, according to Doherty, the leader of the spinners, 'means nothing more than a power given to every man to protect his own labour from being devoured by others'.[39] After the government persecution of the trade unions in 1834–5, the emphasis shifted once more to

---

[38] 'Cobbett to Fielden', Foster, *Class Struggle*, 114.
[39] Thompson, *Making*, 820.

the suffrage. But the Charter did not mean liberal democracy. It meant working-class power to determine its own destiny. How it would do so was not always clear. For the politically articulate sectors of the working class, however, it seems that the new society which was to follow the Charter would be composed of large and small units of co-operative production exchanging their products on the basis of labour time expended. Machines would be used to lessen the extent of necessary labour time. This at least was the vision of the two most impressive theorists of the early Chartist period – Bronterre O'Brien and J. F. Bray. Foster's quotations from the Oldham leader, John Knight, convey a similar impression.

CENTRAL PROBLEM

The very last sentence of Foster's book states that 'the class consciousness we have been examining does bear the marks of being *first*'[40] (i.e. historically, within the international labour movement). But this is the problem he should really have posed at the beginning. For this is the core of the problem of trying to define the character of the proletarian consciousness of the 1830s and 1840s. Almost a century and a half later, it would be easy enough to reduce the early proletarian movement to a catalogue of mutualist, syndicalist, labourist, rationalist, utopian and democratic illusions. But there was no 'correct' historical path from which it could deviate. It had only its own experience to rely upon. The elements of working-class politics had to be forged together from the mixed inheritance of the Enlightenment, Jacobinism, Dissent and traditional notions of moral economy, in a situation which had no precedent.[41] It was this mark of 'being first' which coloured the whole character of the movement. Most important of all, there was no belief in the inevitability of industrial capitalism in the 1830s and early 1840s. Manufacturers and political economists themselves believed that they might be heading towards a stationary state, and given

---

[40] Foster, *Class Struggle*, 254.
[41] For the importance of the last of these, see Thompson, *Making*, 401–51; also the same author's 'The Moral Economy of the English Crowd', *Past and Present*, 50 (February 1971).

the dramatic decline of the profit-rate in the cotton industry, this pessimism was understandable. Conversely, for workers, the precariousness of the new system, however terrible its effects, offered sources of hope. New productive possibilities were acknowledged but capitalism was an aberration, an unnatural state of affairs. Perhaps it did not need to be overthrown, it could be by-passed, isolated and left to wither away. If workers could unite, overwork, unemployment and poverty could be ended and labour would receive its just reward. After the failures of 1834, this vision had to be modified. Social transformation would not be possible until workers had secured political power. 'Peaceably if we may, forcibly if we must.' But the general tendency to equate the Charter with the end of hunger and exploitation, shows how close these two aims remained.

Was, then, the class consciousness of Oldham workers revolutionary? If it was, it was in a democratic not a socialist sense. The distance which separated Owenism and Chartism from a fully developed socialist platform was also the distance which separated a primitive and unforeseeable process of industrialization from a developed industrial capitalism in which the limits of industrial action and political democracy could be seen more clearly. Of course, Oldham after 1830 had moved a long way from the world of Paine and Thelwall. Both the means and the ends of struggle had changed. As outwork gave way to the factory, so insurrection and conspiracy receded before quasi-syndicalist schemes of industrial transformation, nourished by a working-class political economy. Similarly, the aim was no longer simply a Jacobin republic of free and independent producers, but a co-operative commonwealth of associated producers.

But the transformation should not be exaggerated. Varieties of Owenite socialism still reflected more accurately the situation of the artisan than that of the factory proletariat, and the mental world of the cotton spinner was still much closer to that of the radical artisan than the modern factory proletarian. Moreover, this mental world could still to some extent be shared by the small master, the smallholder, the small shopkeeper and the self-employed journeyman. Foster shows clearly enough the divergences of outlook between working class and petty bourgeois, especially as they emerged into the daylight in 1847. But he perhaps exaggerates the extent to which the alliance was forced in the 1830s and early 1840s. Political hopes were still above all fixed upon the vote and the six points, as they had been for the previous forty years. Arguments about moral and physical force were centred upon the attainment of manhood suffrage, not upon social revolution and the expropriation of property. Had Oldham's revolutionary class consciousness been of a more socialist kind, it is hard to see how it could have succumbed so completely to bourgeois blandishments in 1847. The end of Chartism as a mass political force was not merely a failure to adapt tactics to a changing situation. It was the end of an epoch – an epoch above all in which the existence of industrial capitalism itself had hung in the balance. Undoubtedly, in the last years of Chartism, something like the beginning of modern socialism could be detected. 'Chartism in 1850', wrote 'Howard Morton' in the first issue of Harney's *Red Republican*, 'is a different thing from Chartism in 1840. The leaders of the English proletarians ... have progressed from the idea of simple *political reform* to the idea of *social revolution*.'[42] But by the time the *Red Republican* appeared, the huge hopes and heroic struggles of the Oldham workers were a thing of the past. The *Red Republican* was the beginning of a different history.

I have argued that Foster's use of a distinction between trade union consciousness and class consciousness is not appropriate to the class struggle in Oldham. Firstly, because Oldham's class consciousness was not socialist in the normal sense of the term, and this means that the distinction between the period before and after 1830 can only be one of degree, not of kind. Secondly, because a whole range of industrial struggles elude this distinction, so far as it is based on Lenin. These struggles, struggles over the appropriation of nature, have been particularly prominent during periods of industrial transformation. What is especially characteristic of them is the closer intertwining of industrial and political demands. But the way in which they are intertwined will depend upon

---

[42] Quoted in Briggs (ed.), *Chartist Studies*, 290.

the general political situation and the forms of thought and tradition prevalent within a particular working class. After 1830, the industrial battle of the spinners was of this type (although not, of course, only so) and the general situation in which it took place was one in which the political polarization created by the 1832 Reform Bill was accentuated by the diffusion of a proletarian political economy and a deepening capitalist crisis. This situation did indeed create a class consciousness which had not existed before. The commitment to transcend sectional division was an essential component of this new consciousness. It was in different ways a guiding thread both to Owenism and Chartism. But we cannot stop there. This idea of the unity of the working class, of co-operation between its different elements, occupied a particular place in working-class thought in the 1830s and 1840s. It was intimately linked to the social and political diagnosis of its thinkers, visionaries and political activists. The form cannot be divorced from the content. It is here that the shortcomings of Foster's formalism show up most clearly. Firstly, the particular form of class consciousness characteristic of Owen-ism and Chartism is taken out of its specific historical context and erected into the defining feature of revolutionary class consciousness in general. Secondly, applying this criterion of revolutionary class consciousness, Foster is able to find evidence of its presence in Oldham in the 1830s and 1840s. The argument is circular.

LABOUR ARISTOCRACY

If this was the historical context of Oldham's 'class consciousness', how does it affect the use of Foster's final explanatory concept: the labour aristocracy? In most Marxist writing, the use of this idea has been ambiguous and unsatisfactory. Its status is uncertain and it has been em-ployed at will, descriptively, polemically or theoretically, without ever finding a firm anchorage. Engels did not construct a theory of labour aristocracy, he took the term over from the everyday parlance of nineteenth century English trade union debate. Since then, the term has often been used as if it provided an explanation. But it would be more accurate to say that it pointed towards a vacant area where an explanation should be. Indicative of its lack of precision is the elasticity of the stratum of the working class referred to. For Engels, it meant the organized trade union movement of the mid-Victorian period, by which he intended primarily those whose craft skill was not threatened by the machine. By Lenin, it was variously applied to trade union and social democratic leadership, the upper strata of the working class and even, at some points during the First World War, the whole of the working class in imperialist countries. Since the Russian Revolution, in addition to its more traditional definitions, the term has also been used in conjunction with critiques of bureaucracy within the labour movement, or as a description of the relationship between an indigenous metropolitan working class and an immigrant, female or neo-colonial proletariat.

The methods by which the labour aristocratic strata are said to have been bought off have been almost as various as the personnel included within it. These have ranged from the bribery of labour leaders, sub-contracting at the place of work, high wages derived from imperialist super-profits through tariff and welfare measures to unequal exchange. Clearly there is, as yet, no definitive material theory of the labour aristocracy, and it is questionable whether there could ever be one. For it is not evident what sort of question such a theory would answer. If it is designed to explain the non-occurrence of revolution, it is simplistic and misconceived; for the working class at no time and in no place has been an undifferentiated mass of wage slaves. Nor has there ever been any simple correlation between degree of 'privilege' and political or industrial behaviour. What matters is not the fact of differentials but what type of differentials and, above all, in what political and social context they operate.

At one level, Foster's use of a labour aristocracy thesis is both rigorous and complex. It avoids the cruder variants where emphasis is placed unilaterally on bribery and betrayal, and attempts to provide a more structural explanation. Foster's labour aristocracy is firmly identified with the use of sub-contracting and pace-making, following the elimination of craft control, and is seen as a fundamental new form of capitalist social control, now operating in the place of work itself rather than externally upon the labour community as a whole. Foster's use of the concept thus implicitly rejects Engels' identification of the labour aristocracy with that part of the trade union movement which *retained* craft control. Moreover, a clear distinction is maintained between the immediate factors which precipitated working-class defeat ('liberalization') and those which then solidified the newly stabilized social structure (the emergence of the labour aristocracy and the panoply of cultural institutions which supported it). These are very substantial advances in the argument. Nevertheless, it is precisely the precision and scrupulousness with which Foster deploys his argument that reveals its inherent limitations. For, in the last instance, it is still pace-making which has to bear the whole weight of the subtle and complex analysis which is built upon it. These limitations show up both at a national and at a local level.

LIMITATIONS OF THE ANALYSIS

Firstly, at a national level, no direct or general correlation can be made between the restabilization of the post-1850 period and the emergence of a labour aristocracy based on sub-contracting and pace-making. Sub-contracting was certainly not a creation of the 1840s (and, surely, all forms of sub-contracting involve some form of pace-making?). According to Edward Thompson, writing of the period 1790– 1830, 'sub-contracting was predominant in the mining, iron and pottery industries, and fairly widespread in building whereby the "butty" or "ganger" would himself employ less skilled labourers; while children – pieceners in the mills or hurryers in the pits – were customarily employed by the spinner or the collier'.[43] Nor was a social hierarchy of labour, with an 'aristocracy' at its summit, a new phenomenon. Such a hierarchy had existed throughout the period of manufacture and had encompassed both a strong distinction between those with a 'trade' and those without, and a relative scale of prestige between the various trades themselves. Foster's

[43] Thompson, *Making*, 243.

achievement is to have provided, on the one hand, an extraordinarily skilful dissection of the political dissolution of working-class power in Oldham and, on the other hand, a subtle analysis of the cultural institutions, political affiliations and work attitudes which stratified the mid-Victorian working class of Oldham. But the causal connections which he seeks to establish between these two phenomena via pace-making, the labour aristocracy and a general change in English capitalism of which the labour aristocracy was an expression do not hold together.

The weaknesses of Foster's argument become even clearer when the local industries are examined individually. He has no difficulty in demonstrating the establishment of a labour aristocracy based on pace-making in Oldham's engineering industry. But the engineering industry has always been the *locus classicus* of the labour aristocracy thesis. Far more difficult is to demonstrate its presence in cotton-spinning and coal-mining. In the spinning industry, the relation between the pace-making stratum and its unskilled assistants was predominantly, and remained, a relationship *within* the family. Surely any attempt to divide the post-1850 labour community into two almost hermetic castes on the basis of this criterion must be mistaken? Again, it is clear that the threat to, and the restabilization of, the sexual division of labour within the cotton industry played a crucial part in determining the changing character and intensity of the industrial struggle in Oldham; the failure to analyse this relationship is one of the major weaknesses of the book. Finally, in mining no local labour aristocracy in the material sense is demonstrable at all. Even if Foster is right to suggest that the establishment of the checkweighman marked a turning point in the militancy of the miners' struggle, it cannot be assimilated in any sense at all to the new pace-making stratum in the engineering industry.[44] It was, after all, a victory for the miners not for the employers; and it was a strengthening of democratic control from below not despotic control from above. To sum up, in mining there emerged the *ideological* presence of a labour aristocracy, but no tangible pace-making stratum in the labour force. In spin-

[44] Foster, *Class Struggle*, 235.

ning, there existed a sub-contracting stratum of the labour force before, during and after the heroic period of Oldham's class struggle. Only in the case of engineering do sub-contracting and reformism convincingly coincide (but there, conversely, evidence of previous political militancy on the part of the engineers is not very ample).

RESTABILIZATION

Clearly there was no *necessary* relationship between pace-making or sub-contracting and the syndrome of behaviour associated with the mid-Victorian labour aristocrat. If such a relationship did come into being, its causes lay elsewhere. The real cause of the changed industrial attitudes of the spinner and the engineer is stated by Foster himself, but not given sufficient emphasis, since the whole weight of explanation is transferred from cause to effect. The real cause was an effective breach in craft control and the restabilization of the labour process on a new basis: a decisive stage in the elimination 'of the handicraftsman's work as the regulating principle of social production'.[45] Or, to follow Foster, the significant point in the transition in Oldham was the replacement of 'the restrictionist psychology of the craftsman' by that of a labour force 'willing and able to implement technically phrased instructions from above';[46] It was not the establishment of a pace-making form of sub-contracting, which was only one among other possible forms of organization of a socialized labour force – and a rather primitive one at that.

Industrially, what Foster imputes to the emergence of a labour aristocracy was in fact nothing but the effect of a restabilization of the labour process on the basis of modern industry. In cotton, despite the self-acting mule, the cotton-spinner was not displaced by a poorly paid female operative, as he was in virtually every other European textile industry.[47] The former division of labour and the relative degrees of status associated with it were preserved, and this certainly

---

[45] *Capital*, vol. I, 368.
[46] Foster, *Class Struggle*, 224.
[47] See G. Schulze-Gaevernitz, *The Cotton Trade in England and on the Continent* (1895).

had something to do with the marked conservatism of cotton spinners in the second half of the nineteenth century. A comparable development was to be observed in engineering. According to Marx:

Modern Industry was crippled in its complete development, so long as its characteristic instrument of production, the machine, owed its existence to personal strength and personal skill, and depended on the muscular development, the keenness of sight and the cunning of hand, with which the detail workmen in manufactures, and the manual labourers in handicrafts, wielded their dwarfish instruments ... At a certain stage of its development, Modern Industry became technologically incompatible with the basis furnished for it by handicraft and manufacture.[48]

A decisive step along this road was accomplished with the complete defeat of the engineers' strike in 1851. Its immediate effects should perhaps not be overestimated. The engineering industry was expanding and skilled men were not faced with the prospect of a complete undermining of their former position, as the spinners had been. They did lose their previous control over production and this was extremely important in determining their subsequent industrial behaviour. But their position remained a favoured one both before and after this industrial transformation. It was not until the twentieth century that the status of the engineer was irreversibly undermined.

NEW RULES

Industrially, therefore, the significant developments were first the breach in craft control and then a restabilization of the labour process which left formal distinctions of status untouched. The breach of craft control and its replacement by a division of labour based upon the interaction of machines, rather than the co-operation of specific groups of 'detail' labourers, changed of itself the pattern of conflict within the factory and affected that in the social structure built around it. The triumph of modern industry did not merely set former partners against each other, as Foster implies; it fundamentally altered what Hobsbawm has called 'the rules of the game'.[49]

[48] *Capital*, vol. 1, 382–3.
[49] Hobsbawm, *Labouring Men*, 344–71.

These new rules could only be learnt slowly and painfully. The methods inherited from craft unions could not simply be adapted to a new situation, even by skilled men, and certainly not by the unskilled. It was to be a further forty years before a viable form of unskilled unionism squarely based on the structure of modern industry came into being. But even the skilled sectors of modern industry bore only a superficial resemblance to those of handicraft. Such skills were precarious and transformable at the will of the capitalist in a way which those of handicraft had not been. In the cotton industry, the artificial position of the cotton spinner has already been noted. In engineering, apart from a residuum of semi-handicraft skills, the new forms of skill were based upon a quantum of literacy and technical instruction, and often included quasi-supervisory functions. They did not possess the direct purchase over the production process enjoyed by handicrafts, and were unusable except in the factories for which they had been acquired. This is part of what is meant by the 'real' subordination of wage labour to capital. Thus the explanation for the changed industrial behaviour of certain groups of workers (notably the spinners and to a lesser extent the engineers) is not to be attributed to the emergence of a labour aristocracy based on pace-making. Pace-making was at most a secondary phenomenon. What was decisive was the effect of modern industry upon their technical role in the labour process. It was not so much their privileged position as the vulnerability of that position that changed their industrial outlook.

Equally important was the *restabilization* of the labour process on this basis, not so much because of its psychological effect, but simply because it excluded certain forms of industrial struggle: notably those characteristic of the 1830s and 1840s. The most visible point of contradiction was displaced away from the place of work, and eventually into the political arena. For, once control and the division of labour were no longer live issues, industrial struggle increasingly assumed the form of wage struggle, by definition sectional and accepting the wage contract as its starting point. Similarly, when the aspiration towards collective control over the means of production re-emerged, it now predominantly took the form of a programme demanding collective *ownership* of the means of production. But a struggle to change the ownership of the means of production could not be the direct product of wage struggle. It demanded the acceptance of a theory of society which did not of itself emanate from the struggle in the factory – i.e. socialism – and the creation of a directly political form of organization to achieve it. We can now see yet another reason why the Leninist distinction between 'trade-union consciousness' and 'class consciousness' applied specifically to the conditions of modern industry, and even then only to those where the labour process itself was not seriously at issue.

ROOTS OF REFORMISM

As a *social* and *ideological* phenomenon, the labour aristocracy undoubtedly existed in mid-Victorian England; but it is impossible to explain its existence in abstraction from the general political and ideological conjuncture. Labour-aristocratic attitudes do not coincide in any simple way with particular strata of the labour force, and our intention is certainly not to substitute the technical effects of modern industry for pace-making as an adequate explanation of mid-Victorian reformism. For, to cite coal-mining once more, not only did no pace-making stratum exist, but the effects of modern industry on the labour process also remained minimal.

Foster is quite right to insist upon the connection of reformism with a wider overall change in the nature of English capitalism. But the actual connection he makes is not convincing. He attempts to link the emergence of working-class reformism with arguments produced by Lenin in *Imperialism*. Thus the general switch to capital export, which Lenin (following Hobson) argued took place around 1870, is pushed back to the 1840s. Even when this argument is applied to England in the 1870s the evidence is inconclusive, but applied to the 1840s the argument is untenable and Foster is forced to admit that 'what cannot be demonstrated as easily is that this *local* restabilization was indeed part of an overall change in the nature of English capitalism, part of the switch to a new capital export imperialism'.[50] Foster produces no direct evidence for his claim. It is incontestable that the lifting of the ban on export of machinery provided a huge stimulus to the development of British engineering. But it is a play on words to equate export of capital goods with export of capital (Lenin was very emphatic that what was involved was the export of capital not goods), and it is fanciful to imply that the Bank Charter Act had much to do with finance capital in a Leninist sense. Moreover, if the Leninist argument is to be applied consistently, colonialist superprofits and monopoly would also have to be brought forward. But the argument would then become patently absurd. If reformist attitudes were prevalent in Britain before 1870, this points not to the necessary presence of capital export, but to a deficiency in the connection made by Lenin between reformism and capital export. This deficiency cannot be rectified by shifting the connection thirty years backwards, and the attempt to find such a connection can only be described as misguided piety.

There was undoubtedly a connection between a change in British capitalism and the decline in working-class struggle, and Foster's analysis points to the connection. If the crisis in the cotton industry was the result of an extreme imbalance between the industrialized sector and the rest of the economy, then the end of the crisis was primarily the result of a new stage of industrialization which removed, or at least lessened, this imbalance. If one wants to identify the most obvious feature of this new stage of industrial capitalism, it was not capital export, but railway-building. Although it may not have played a primary role in Oldham, railway-building is what, more than anything else, resolved the capitalist crisis of the 1830s and early 1840s. It lessened the impact of cyclical crisis, stimulated coal, iron, steel and machine production, and resolved the crisis of profitability. More than any other single factor, it assured the successful transition to a modern industrial economy.

But the true factors that resolved the crisis must be distinguished from the way in which people experienced that resolution. The middle class attributed it to the statesmanship

---

[50] Foster, *Class Struggle*, 250.

of Peel and the repeal of the Corn Laws (although in material terms this made very little immediate difference). For the working class, the failures of the strike of 1842 and the Kennington Common demonstration in 1848 were demoralizing defeats (even if Chartism did not come to an end in 1848, as the middle-class myth would have it). The general failure of the 1848 Revolutions could only add to this disillusion. Above all, the permanence of industrial capitalism now seemed assured, and all except the most despairing of the outworkers were forced to adapt to this fact. A continued struggle against capitalism needed something more than the variants of Owenism and Chartism could provide. It meant the acknowledgement that there was no way round the new industrial system, and that the only way to end it was to overthrow it. It meant also a recognition that the victory of the Charter would not in itself achieve this aim. It meant, in other words, the acceptance of some form of socialism.

But in the restabilized conditions after 1848 (and in Lancashire, perhaps, some years before) few were prepared to make this step. More had listened to O'Connor than to Harney or Ernest Jones, and in Oldham the failure of 1842 seems to have paralysed further political development. Foster shows with great perception how workers in Oldham adapted to this new situation and how, as a result, the unitary vision which had held the working class together was dissolved, particularly once the industrial basis of common action had been removed. Not only does he systematically study the interrelationship between the temperance movement, the Co-op, the Sunday school, methodism and adult education as breeding grounds of the labour aristocracy; he also examines the underside of Oldham working-class life – the pub, the Orange lodge, dialect speech and 'thriftless' behaviour – as refuges of the simple factory operative. He further reveals how this new structure of Oldham's workforce bestowed new meanings and functions on older working-class institutions and upon traditional mechanisms of social control. The way in which he shows how completely a new cocoon of protective institutions spared the 'aristocrat' from contact with the non-aristocratic workforce outside the place of work is particularly impressive. Finally, he exposes very strikingly the vital role played by nationalism as an ideology capable of uniting the stratified workforce on capitalist terms, and demonstrates how it was used to 'block out' a class analysis just because the latter 'posed such a devastating challenge to the protective assumptions so carefully built up over the previous years'.[51]

This discussion of the new pattern of working-class politics and ideology in Oldham is extremely impressive. Free from the formalism which mars Foster's treatment of the 1790–1820 and 1830–47 periods, in many places it breaks entirely new ground. In particular, the dissection of the 'protective assumptions' of the new types of working-class ideology gets much closer to the heart of mid-Victorian reformism than do the hunt for pace-makers and the divination of capital-export imperialism. For what these 'protective assumptions' concealed was how the struggles of the 1830s and 1840s were reinterpreted on the basis of the compromise with which the battle had ended. This compromise was not simply the result of the political overtures of the town bourgeoisie in 1847. It evidently involved a larger social compromise. We can agree with Foster's emphasis upon the effectiveness of the Chartist movement, rather than its impotence; also with his general suggestion that important working-class struggles have a 'ratchet effect', i.e. that certain advances, once gained, cannot again be put into question without politically explosive consequences.[52] But we should not underestimate the gains made by the bourgeoisie in return.

THE BALANCE SHEET

One undoubted working-class victory in this battle had been the creation of the principle of the normal working day. Not only did it place exploitation within prescribed limits, it was also the first major victory of the political economy of the working class and pointed towards the new political relationship that would have to be fought out between worker and state in the conditions of modern industry. But, beyond this, it is difficult to speak unambiguously of working-class victories in the Chartist period. Cer-

[51] Ibid., 242.
[52] Ibid., 6.

tainly the Chartists indirectly forced a realignment of British capitalism. The measures of the Peel government are the best indication of this (although it is difficult there to separate the effect of Chartist activity from the direct pressure of manufacturers). On the other hand, it must be conceded that the general battle over control of production was fought through to a successful conclusion by Oldham's capitalists. Such compromises as they made in this area came only after the point of the battle had been won. And it is tempting – though speculative – to suggest that the political concessions of liberalization could only be made once the conditions for the unhampered development of modern industry had been assured. This is not to deny the effectiveness of Chartism. But what held Chartism together was not simply a set of political demands, but the vision of a different society and economy. Once the visionary hopes behind the Charter had been destroyed or abandoned, it was scarcely surprising that the movement faltered. This would seem to explain the loss of political initiative by Oldham's political militants after 1842, although their formal political control was not overthrown until 1847. By 1847, when Oldham's capitalists began making concessions, the handloom weavers had disappeared, the spinners' struggle was virtually resolved and the engineers were losing ground. Nor should the concessions associated with liberalization be exaggerated. They were only carried through at a national level in the late 1860s, by which time Lenin's distinction between economic and political struggle had become a general reality – at least in Britain's leading industrial sectors.

What in effect had happened was that, in return for their recognition of certain points in the proletarian programme, Oldham's bourgeoisie had gained a *de facto* acceptance of the new productive relations of industrial capitalism.[53] This change, of course, could scarcely have occurred without a resolution of the crisis in the cotton industry, the expansion of engineering and the restabilization of the labour process. But it also could not have occurred without the national political defeat of Chartism. Many of the elements which Foster

---

[53] For some effects of this development in London, see Ch. 4 in this volume.

identifies with the labour aristocracy – self-education, temperance, co-operation, for example – had been present within the Chartist movement, but they had been harnessed to different ends. Deprived of a general political horizon, they could easily become compatible with reformism, or merely a badge of superior status. The same was true of economic struggles. The Oldham miners continued a militant industrial battle into the 1850s, but it no longer possessed any political focus.

Conversely, the renewed stability of engineering and cotton, especially the latter, reinforced the conservatism of the 'protective assumptions' discussed by Foster. Cotton, the sector which had spearheaded the breakthrough of modern industry in the first half of the nineteenth century, exhibited increasing signs of technical conservatism, as the survival of the spinner testified (how far this was connected with the previous period of class struggle is not clear). The sexual division of labour resumed its former constancy and the working-class family regained an apparent fixity. Against a general background of apparent invulnerability conferred on Britain as workshop of the world, the pace of industrial transformation slackened. Moreover, although Marx was right in a general sense to state that the progress of modern industry tended to eliminate sectional divisions within the labour force, in fact (even in the advanced engineering industry) new differentials and demarcations were established and consolidated, which involved distinctions not merely between aristocrat and non-aristocrat, but between English and Irish, men and women. The class combativity of the previous period was not forgotten, but was channelled into a narrower form of labourism which embodied a distinctly conservative and nationalistic moment within it. In this sense, we should attempt to understand the ebbing of class struggle after the Chartist period not merely in terms of the detachment of a labour-aristocratic leadership, but in terms of the consolidation of a new structure involving the whole of the labour force, against a background of the apparent inevitability of capitalism. It is only in such terms that we can understand the relative political stability of Britain's industrial heartlands in many places up to the years before the First World War.

Foster states that his book is 'experimental'. It must be stressed that the tentative suggestions put forward here are much more so. What is really important is that Foster has not merely re-opened a large number of important historical debates, but he has also redefined the terms in which many of those debates will henceforth have to be conducted. His book marks a major step forward in the interpretation of British history and in Marxist methods of historical analysis. For the magnitude and scrupulousness of his 'experiment', we shall all remain deeply in his debt.

2

CLASS EXPRESSION VERSUS SOCIAL CONTROL? A CRITIQUE OF RECENT TRENDS IN THE SOCIAL HISTORY OF 'LEISURE'

For social historians, systematic interest in popular recreation and debate over the use of leisure is relatively recent. Pioneering research on the subject scarcely goes back beyond the end of the 1950s; and, undoubtedly, the growing attention which historians have paid to it has owed a lot to the increasing recourse to sociology and anthropology in the definition of problems worthy of historical research. The amount of work going on in this area is now on a sufficient scale to make it possible to step back and make at least some interim judgements on the ways in which the problem seems to have been conceived and to examine how far the conceptual instruments employed have been adequate either to posing the right questions or to resolving them.[1]

But, before examining the concepts employed, it is first necessary to stress that knowledge of this area still remains very uneven. Certain well defined themes have emerged and this has encouraged research along a few oft trodden routes, while leaving large parts of the landscape almost unmapped.

[1] This article was a contribution to the conference, 'The Working Class and Leisure', organized by the Society for the Study of Labour History at the University of Sussex in the autumn of 1975. Apart from minor stylistic changes to make the theme comprehensible to the general reader, the text remains unchanged. This text has been reproduced here because it was thought that discussion of the notion of 'social control' possessed wider historical relevance. (Needless to say, these remarks also apply to my own *Outcast London*, 2nd edn, London (1984).) But in so far as the text deals with trends in research on popular recreation, no attempt has been made to bring it up to date.

The researches referred to in the text were contributions to the conference at Sussex. A full collection of the conference papers is available from the University of Sussex through inter-library loan. In addition to these, two other works particularly relevant to this theme are: R. W. Malcolmson, *Popular Recreations in English Society 1700–1850*, Cambridge (1973); and Brian Harrison, 'Religion and Recreation in Nineteenth-Century England', *Past and Present*, 38 (1967).

Research has tended to concentrate upon the advance of a methodical capitalist rationality and the disappearance or decline of traditional forms of popular recreation in its wake. Problems which cannot be so comfortably contained within the terms of this juxtaposition have tended to be neglected. There is no substantial study, for example, of how far changes in the sexual division of labour before, during and after industrialization produced changing sexually segregated patterns of leisure, or indeed of the pattern of segregation itself. We have a few tantalizing glimpses – if men spent St Monday drinking, women spent it washing – but it is a fair generalization to say that the relation between one half of the working class and 'leisure' remains to be explored.

There are other areas too which, if not unknown, are certainly underplayed in the prevalent approach to the subject. Far more attention has been paid to the ways in which entrepreneurs or the propertied classes attempted to change popular uses of leisure time than to the ways in which craftsmen, artisans or working-class activists attempted to organize their non-work time or sought to reorientate the use of non-work time by others. Of course, something is known about the attitudes of Levellers, Jacobins, Owenites, Chartists, village radicals, nonconformist trade unionists and socialists towards popular culture. In some cases, extremely good work has been done. But it has not generally been integrated into the dominant approaches to popular and working-class recreation.

As a result of this unevenness of knowledge or emphasis, the cumulative picture conveyed by research into popular recreation and leisure is out of perspective. The sharply delineated foreground is occupied by puritan, methodist and evangelical moral reformers, gentry deciding where to place their patronage, prescient magistrates, calculating employers, prurient municipal elites, entrepreneurial publicans and rationalizing merchants of leisure. Behind this obtrusive phalanx, we can just make out the blurred and rather undifferentiated features of the rural and urban masses. Once or twice, their generally dim profiles are illuminated by 'a flashpoint of class conflict'. Forms of resistance may momentarily be discerned. But since, at this distance of time, evidence of their resistance can only be found generally in non-verbal activity – a burnt hayrick for example, or a pitched street battle – it is then difficult to situate these 'flashpoints' in their surrounding terrain. It is as if the only records of the bourgeoisie came from the bankruptcy courts, the only evidence of marriage from divorce petitions. It is a major step forward to have opened up this vast area of social history – one, potentially, that will enable us to re-examine a lot of labour history in the light of a much broader knowledge of the ideologies of poor villagers, rural craftsmen, manufacturing artisans, factory and casual labourers – but it would be very dangerous to assume that our knowledge of these ideologies and the material situations which they articulated is still in anything but an extremely primitive state.

Some of the best studies have acknowledged this ignorance and conceded that if the problem is to be posed adequately, then the case of the accused cannot satisfactorily be deduced from even the most discerning reading of testimonies bequeathed us by the case for the prosecution. But not all work has escaped the temptation to translate archival silence into historical passivity. Combined with the relative absence of studies examining active working-class attempts to determine the use of their non-work time, the composite picture presented of capitalist development, class relations and 'leisure' appears unduly slanted in one direction. It is as if class conflict in England has been a largely one-sided affair conducted by capitalism and its representatives; as if the rural and urban masses, like the newborn child in Locke's psychology, were simply a blank page upon which each successive stage of capitalism has successfully imposed its imprint. We have a picture in some ways uncannily similar to the grey, secularized, bureaucratized, rationalized landscape painted by Max Weber – a dismal progression from the poor commonwealth villager deprived of his village customs, through the Padstow miner forced to exchange his hobby-horse for a methodist hymnal, the poor Londoner constrained to abandon the spontaneity of the free-and-easy for the 'controlled' decorum of a Palace of Variety, the tea-drinking Whitsun rustic obediently enjoying his new forms of rational recreation under the benevolent gaze of parson and squire, the

Edwardian artisan donning collar, tie and best suit to watch a football match, and so on to the inter-war unskilled labourer exercising his last remaining freedom – the filling in of a pools coupon – and the post-war alienated proletarian diverting his class consciousness into the humble and vicarious partisanships offered by television Olympics and the 'match of the day'.

This picture is not simply the result of a scarcity of sources, nor is it simply a consequence of expecting too much from an early stage of research. The problem is primarily a conceptual one. Historians have made some real gains by being forced to address themselves to problems raised by sociologists and anthropologists. The result has been an immense broadening of the scope of history. But it is surely time that historians began to pay more critical attention to the concepts which sociology has placed at their disposal. Too often these concepts are passively accepted as if they were no more than harmless heuristic devices without any consequence beyond the meaning conveyed by the words themselves.

In fact, this is usually not the case. A loose commonsense usage of a sociological term tends, on closer scrutiny, to be circular or strictly meaningless: a mere well-intentioned gesture in the direction of a non-existent rigour. On the other hand, any attempt at a systematic usage will entail a definite interpretative explanatory framework which cannot be manipulated at will. When historians, on the lookout for some grander conceptual framework within which to situate their research, move out from a narrow empiricism into a theoretical eclecticism, they may easily find themselves tumbling down all manner of slippery paths, which they had had no prior intention of descending.

One obvious example of this has been the frequent resort to notions of 'social control'. It is a phrase conveying an obvious and plausible meaning. It would appear to stand to reason that those with power and authority in society have an interest in imposing, maintaining or reimposing 'social control', and it is in this loose commonsense form that many have used the idea of 'social control'. Sometimes it seems almost to be assumed that the concept is of Marxist provenance – social control being something which by definition a bourgeoisie continually administers, and in increasingly heavy doses, to an errant but gradually domesticated proletariat.

It is not difficult to demonstrate that a casual usage of 'social control' metaphors leads to non-explanation and incoherence. There is no political or ideological institution which could not in some way be interpreted as an agency of social control. There is no indication in the phrase of who the agents or instigators of social control may be; no indication of any common mechanism whereby social control is enforced; no constant criterion whereby we may judge whether social control has broken down – certainly not conflict, for this may ultimately, or even inherently, be a means of reinforcing conformity. Nor finally is there any fixed yardstick whereby we may know when social control has been reimposed. Since capitalism is still with us, we can with impunity suppose, if we wish to, that at any time in the last three hundred years the mechanisms of social control were operating effectively.

If a casual allusion to 'social control' turns out to be vacuous, it is equally clear that social control cannot merely be added on to a Marxist interpretation. The phrase social control suggests a static metaphor of equilibrium, which might be disturbed and then reasserted on a new basis. It suggests therefore three successive states – a prior functioning, a period of breakdown, and a renewed state of functioning. Even stopping at this point we can see a basic incompatibility with any Marxist interpretation. For if we seriously wish to adopt a Marxist explanation, it is impossible to operate this mechanical separation of periods of control and breakdown. A mode of production is irreducibly a contradictory unity of forces and relations of production. Just as, in order to survive, the relations of production must be continually reproduced, so is the contradiction embodied within those relations of production continually reproduced. Contradiction is not episodically, but continually, present; the antagonism, between the producers of the surplus and the owners and controllers of the means of production extracting the surplus, is a structural and permanent feature. Thus class conflict is a permanent feature, not a sign of breakdown, and the conditions in which class conflict may assume explosive or revolutionary forms bear only the emptiest of resemblances to a crude notion conveyed by the phrase 'breakdown of social control'.

Perhaps one simple illustration will indicate this difference. In some interpretations of the emergence and growth of rational recreation, the nineteenth century railway network is presented unproblematically as an agent of material and moral improvement, transporting temperate workers to the seaside, arousing harmless wonder at the beauties of nature, lessening the temptations of drink and gambling and so on. If it is true, in other words, that reformers of manners progressed from coercion to a 'strategy of counter-attraction', then this success was the achievement of the entrepreneur whose pursuit of profit had resulted in the creation of a magnificent technology of moral improvement. But that is only one way of looking at the railways. For the building of stations and cutting of new lines by these same entrepreneurs involved the arbitrary demolition of vast tracts of poor housing and the peremptory eviction of tens of thousands. Thus if the development of the railways was in one sense a reinforcement of new 'forms of social control', it was at the same moment an agent creating new problems of 'social control'.

More pertinent perhaps to the confusion caused by mixing Marxist concepts with notions of social control is the argument which runs: moral reformers, sabbatarians, methodists, temperance enthusiasts and charity organizers in the end were not the real agents responsible for imposing the new forms of social control. For all their efforts, they remained the purveyors of minority causes, distasteful not only to workers but to the bulk of the middle class. The real instigator of new and more effective forms of social control was the capitalist of leisure. The domestication of the new industrial working class was the accomplishment not of Wesley, Wilberforce, Samuel Smiles or Octavia Hill, but of Charles Morton, Lord Northcliffe and Alfred Littlewood. Despite the avowedly anti-capitalist intention of this argument – the conviction that class harmony is an unnatural and undesirable state of affairs – it seems to me to resemble a revamped version of Adam Smith's 'unseen hand'. The greed and private vices of capitalists, unbeknownst to them, create increasingly effective mechanisms of dousing, channelling or diverting the class consciousness of workers, since the most effective agency of social control is the capitalization of the leisure market. Whatever the status of this argument, it is certainly not Marxist for, like Adam Smith, it restricts capitalism to the market place; and it assumes that ideologies prevalent within the working class will not, in any fundamental sense, be articulations of their productive relationships within capitalism, but the result of their position as consumers of leisure.

Before going any further in an analysis of the consequences of employing even a loose commonsense notion of social control in combination with other concepts finally incompatible with it, we should look at the systematic sociological uses of the term, for this should make us even more wary of the dangers of borrowing a term of whose credentials and genealogy and implications we are unaware.

The difficulties for the historian attempting to give some meaning merely to the phrase are more than confirmed by examining the theory. The concept was first popularized in American sociology by Edward A. Ross who, in 1901, produced a book called *Social Control, a Survey of the Foundations of Order*. Its inspiration was an attempt to sociologize Darwin in a social Darwinist direction. For the interaction between the organism and nature, Ross substituted one between the individual and society. What, in this theory, a society has to control, is the animal nature of 'Man'. 'Man's' tendency to pursue his self-interest to the point of a war of all against all must be limited through learning or selection. The operation of Ross's concept was rather similar to that of Durkheim's *conscience collective*, which was also capable of constraining men's 'animal spirits' with a power directly proportional to the intensity of interaction around its specific forms. Family, marriage and religion were accorded this power at a primary level while, at the secondary level, professional associations would act in a similar way to counteract the anomie endemic in economic life.

Ross's notion of social control – a constraining social element which held in check Man's darker animal side – was taken up by Robert Park and the Chicago sociologists of the beginning of the twentieth century. The triadic state which, I have suggested, is implied by the word itself, was indeed the way in which the concept was developed. There was first the state of 'natural order', defined by Ross as derived from the spontaneous meshing of men's personalities and sociability on the one hand and from their sense of justice and capacity for resentment on the other. This 'natural order' was similar to what another American sociologist, Charles Horton Cooley, described in 1909 as the 'primary group'. If this was stage one, stage two was breakdown, a state which, the Chicago sociologists believed, was brought about by urbanization, immigration, the breakdown of the small community into competing groups and a decline in the efficacy of natural selection (which, by the way, was held to have been accountable for the growing number of 'moral idiots or lunatics' – people who according to Ross, 'can no more put themselves in the place of another than the beast can enter into the anguish of its prey'). Stage three, of course, is the re-creation of a moral rational order to replace the natural order rendered inviable by greater population density and heterogeneity: a process which Park saw as the shift from primary means of social control such as family, neighbourhood and community to secondary means of control such as police, political machine and courts.

If this first form of the concept of social control is not found very appealing, the second version popularized by Talcott Parsons is scarcely more attractive. His notion of social control is a derivation from a systematic theory of deviance. Here again there is a three-stage process, but this time of a psychological rather than biological kind. Stage one is the normal functioning of role expectations. Deviance (stage two) results not from 'animal spirits' but learning derived from past interaction, specific personality factors or the pressures and opportunities of immediate interactional situations. When role expectations are frustrated, the motivation of the actor is likely to develop ambivalence which can lead to (a) loss of attachment to any object or pattern, (b) compulsive expression of only one side of the ambivalence or, more usually, (c) a slightly schizoid state in which the acting out of both the conforming and alienated sides are segregated in time and place.

Deviance may be a danger to society, especially when deviants group together, but Parsons sees an ultimate source of social control in their ambivalence, and in the bridges that link utopian or radical groups to the main value pattern. These bridges, according to Parsons, enable many members to sell out after a longer or shorter stay in a deviant organization. An alternative way back to stage three (normal functioning) is by allowing partial deviance – the secondary institution, like youth culture or organized gambling, which allows some deviance from the dominant value pattern yet keeps the participants integrated within the dominant value pattern. By permitting the expression of some alienated feelings they may bring the 'actors' back to conformity.

This psychotherapeutic model can be applied to any process of social behaviour. Normally there will be structural arrangements for 'draining off' tensions which might trigger deviant behaviour. Primary groups like the family normally fulfil this role. Other modes include institutions of entertainment and play through which the catharsis of antisocial desires can be secured. The party, the carnival or mass entertainment are cited in this sense. I will not carry on with an analysis of these sociological models of social control. Suffice it to say that both are functionalist models, whose primary reference remains the interaction between individuals and a social organism. The thought is not of an antagonistic class system based upon exploitation, but, for example, of an urban community and a working-class sub-culture. Contradiction is not the normal state of this system, since it is a *community*. Breakdown is analysed in terms of biologistic or psychologistic pathology. Hence it can be seen that an attempt to link the idea of social control with some Marxist or semi-Marxist theory of capitalist development will have unhappy results.

Few historians are committed functionalists, but it is not uncommon for social historians to fall unconsciously into the functionalist models I have described. This is partly the result of the technical problems of writing history. The historian's problem is generally that he or she knows a great deal about one period, which blurs into a relative ignorance of what came before and what came afterwards. Thus, there is a very strong temptation to begin with something called 'traditional society', as Malcolmson does in his very interesting book on popular leisure-time pursuits, or as Edward Thompson implied when he wrote about the moral economy of the eighteenth century crowd. In this context, it is very useful to know from Keith Wrightson's research that many of the generally cited attributes of the eighteenth century village were not traditional, but new creations of the century following 1640. But it makes one wonder how traditional the traditional customs, which he describes as coming under attack from 1552 onwards, really were. The legal historian T. F. T. Plucknett once showed that the medieval term, 'custom from time immemorial', need only mean twenty-one years. Clearly the historian should refrain from calling the history he does not know 'traditional society'. This bad habit, it seems to me, has been one of the many unfortunate spin-offs from sociological theories of modernization.

Historians are also at the mercy of their ignorance of what comes after their special period of expertise. Here again there is a spontaneous tendency to think in terms of a new equilibrium having been established, one which, again, it is tempting to consider to be the result of the successful imposition of social control.

Here, it seems to me, the terrain is even more dangerous than the notion of 'traditional society'. For what social control invites us to think of is a process of 'incorporation', 'accommodation', 'bourgeoisification'; or, if one wishes to stress some revolutionary credential, one might call it 'bourgeois hegemony', the re-establishment of 'false consciousness', or even 'repressive desublimation'. The point about these terms is that, although they may register some moral distance from the apologetic complacency of functionalist theory, they in no way break from its theoretical linkages. To say that a functional totality is based on alienation, is only to add an epithet of moral or political disapproval. It does not change the causal relationship between terms within this functional totality. The plus signs are simply turned into minuses. We may think of sport, for example, as a healthy release for spontaneity and freedom, like the sociologist Eric Dunning; or we may think of it as a diversionary use of leisure time reinforcing the alienated consciousness engendered by the workplace. But there is no challenge here to the functionalist analysis of sport.

This overestimate of the operation of social control – by which is usually meant, ideological control – is often accompanied by another commonly encountered strand in sociological thinking: the use of 'ideal types' derived from Weber, or, if again one wants to claim a Marxist ancestry, the approach to class consciousness associated with Lukacs. Just as Weber gives us idealized, not to say fantasized pictures of the *rational* capitalist, so Lukacs provides us with a homologous idealization of the *revolutionary* proletarian. In the latter case, the result is a surreal model of revolutionary proletarian class consciousness, which has nowhere been observed to occur in real history. The problem for advocates of this model is to discover why history has deviated from it, and the answer is often the resort to the notion of hegemony, a concept which in some of its more recent usages works in a similar way to the functionalist notion of social control, but with a class terminology added. Gramsci's idea of hegemony is certainly useful in so far as it makes us look at the institutions through which the ruling ideology is transmitted. But it can only give a tautological answer to a false question if it is used to explain the absence of a revolutionary proletarian class consciousness in the sense envisaged by Lukacs. In Lukacs himself, the working class either has a revolutionary class consciousness or no consciousness at all (i.e. it inhabits the world of reification and possesses only 'false consciousness'). It is not therefore a large step for his latter-day sociological followers to translate this juxtaposition of terms into a historical process of transition in which originally revolutionary proletarians are 'incorporated' through the mechanisms of 'social control' or bourgeois hegemony.

In an analysis of leisure time, the results of this sort of approach are particularly absurd: but for the effective maintenance of social control, the hegemony of the bourgeoisie, the capitalist confiscation of leisure time, or whatever other ideological instrument is assigned this function by the analyst, we might expect workers to be singing revolutionary songs and preparing the uprising. The reason why they do not do so is because their putative class consciousness has been confiscated from them and diverted into some system-maintaining channel – chauvinism, sport or consumerism, for instance.

The question, which we must pose to such theories, is what can they actually explain. A long time ago, the historian Elie Halévy argued that a revolution in early nineteenth century England had been prevented by the hold exercised by methodism over the working class. Detailed examination of the evidence since this thesis was first put forward has shown that it explains neither the periodicity of revolutionary feeling, nor its geography. Halévy's thesis was by no means absurd, since methodism was a very plausible candidate for the role he assigned it. But if methodism can't be shown in any wholly convincing fashion to have prevented revolution, what are we to say about football? Interestingly enough, it emerges from John Hutchinson's research on football crowds before 1914 that Glasgow was one of the earliest centres of football as a mass spectator sport. We might, on the assumptions of the argument above, expect to find that its workers were particularly docile. But we certainly would not have expected to find that, a few years later, the city had become the most militant and even insurrectionary centre during the First World War.

It is very important to develop research into non-work time and the different ways in which workers have used it. But it would be a fundamental mistake to develop it into a subject in its own right. The greatest 'social control', if one wants to use the word, available to capitalism is the wage relationship itself – the fact that, in order to live and reproduce, the worker must perpetually resell his or her labour power. The necessity to obtain work, to remain fit enough for work, and to make ends meet is far more important than any packaged consumerist ideology which succeeds in intruding upon the worker's weekly or nightly period of rest and recuperation. Leisure time is clearly constricted by type and hours of work. To study leisure on its own is dangerous in two ways at least.

Firstly, many of the struggles fought around leisure in the first half of the nineteenth century were no more than the epilogues of struggles being fought out in the course of the working week. The introduction of a new work process often changed the hours and intensity of work, and its seasonality. If trade unionist or other forms of resistance failed, it is not surprising that the struggle to maintain an old pattern of leisure, built around a previous work process, quickly lost its point. It is interesting that most of the struggles over the transformation of popular recreation so far researched were one-off affairs. Even the fighting over street football in Derby in the early 1840s seems only to have lasted three or four years. Characteristically, while strikes are usually solid, struggles over popular recreation are divided. The very fact that so little verbal defence was made of traditional popular recreation, is not merely because rational recreationists monopolized the means of communication. It was because workers themselves were very divided on whether traditional forms of recreation were worthy of defence. Generally, the most politically articulate sector of the local workforce did not come out strongly in its defence. Unless we think industrialization was a mistake, we need not find this attitude particularly surprising. Owenites and Chartists did not challenge the steam engine itself, but the capitalist's control over the steam engine and his use of it systematically to overwork his employees. The answer was to end the capitalist control of work, or to capture the state that sustained the capitalist. Traditional recreations not only occupied a subordinate place in this battle, but many political activists saw these traditional pastimes as positively counter-productive in the formation of a working class capable of fighting this struggle. Some must have seen these traditional pursuits in the way that black-power militants regarded often celebrated aspects of traditional black culture in the 1960s as features injurious to the dignity of black people, as part of the syndrome symbolized by 'Uncle Tom'.

The second danger of studying leisure on its own is again related to the primacy of work, and the social relations within which it is carried on, in the determination of class position, and in the articulation of class attitudes. To study leisure and popular recreation as a distinct subject – particularly if we try to think of it in terms of a polarity between 'class expression and social control' – leads to a real danger of overpoliticizing leisure as an arena of struggle. Leisure institutions which remained essential to workers – pubs for example – were strongly defended. But others were given up with little resistance, because they had ceased to have a point. It is really dangerous to interpret the disappearance of pre-industrial recreations simply as a huge defeat. Some historians have drawn parallels between strikes and struggles over popular recreation. Their fundamental dissimilarity must also be stressed. The struggle in the factory is a struggle inherent in the relations of production. Any argument about incorporation finds itself on weak ground here. Struggles over leisure time do not have this inherent antagonism built into them. The primary point of a holiday is not political: it is to enjoy yourself, for tomorrow you must work. To write into recreations a symbolic form of class conflict – or its reverse, a channelling or diversion of class consciousness – leads precisely to the inrush of theories of incorporation to explain why workers have appeared to accept the capitalization of leisure with apparent passivity. Of course, carnivals, fairs or football matches may become the occasion of major social struggles. They have in fact often been so. But in nearly all instances we would find that they acted as the occasion or the catalyst of the events they triggered and not as the cause. Lastly, we should find that the further we pursued those causes, the further we should find ourselves from the tempting but tautological couplet – class expression/social control.

3

RETHINKING CHARTISM

Who were the Chartists? The Chartists' own view was stated by Thomas Duncombe, introducing the 1842 Petition: 'those who were originally called radicals and afterwards reformers, are called Chartists'.[1] But this was never accepted by the great bulk of contemporary opinion. From the moment that Chartism first emerged as a public movement, what seized the imagination of contemporaries were not the formally radical aims and rhetoric of its spokesmen, but the novel and threatening social character of the movement. A nation-wide independent movement of the 'working classes' brandishing pikes in torchlight meetings in pursuit of its 'rights' was an unprecedented event and, whatever Chartism's official self-identity, contemporary observers could not refrain from projecting onto it deeper, unavowed motives and sentiments. Thomas Carlyle's distinction between the 'distracted incoherent embodiment of Chartism' and its 'living essence ... the bitter discontent grown fierce and mad, the wrong condition

I should like especially to thank Sally Alexander, Istvan Hont and Raphael Samuel for the critical help and encouragement they have given me in the development of this essay. I would also like to thank Dorothy Thompson for generously putting at my disposal her own work and knowledge about Chartist history.

[1] Hansard, 3rd series, LXIII, 13–91; cf. O'Connor's observation: 'The movement party was known, had become strong and and united under the political term Radical, when, lo! – and to shew there is much in a name, our political opponents rebaptised us, giving us the name of Chartists. Now although there was no earthly difference between the principles of a Radical and of a Chartist, yet did the press of both parties ... contrive to alarm the prejudices of the weak, the timid and the unsuspecting, until at length they accomplished their desired object – a split between parties seeking one and the same end.' *The Trial of Feargus O'Connor* (1843), ix. The left wing of the movement tended to describe itself as 'democrat' rather than 'radical', see J. Bennett, 'The Democratic Association 1837–41: A Study in London Radicalism', in J. Epstein and D. Thompson (eds.), *The Chartist Experience, Studies in Working Class Radicalism and Culture 1830–1860* (1982).

therefore or the wrong disposition, of the Working Classes of England', with its implied gulf between the real and formal definition of Chartism, set the terms of the predominant response, whatever the precise definition given to these terms.[2] Chartists in vain protested their respect for property.[3] Macaulay, debating the 1842 Petition, deduced the Chartist position on property from the social composition of its constituency. To accept the Petition would be to commit government to a class which would be induced 'to commit great and systematic inroads against the security of property. How is it possible that according to the principles of human nature, if you give them this power, it would not be used to its fullest extent?'[4] Even the more sympathetic middle-class observers virtually ignored the political case of the Chartists. Mrs Gaskell's novel, *Mary Barton*, for instance, analysed Chartism solely in terms of anger, distress and the breakdown of social relationships. Thus, from the beginning, there was virtual unanimity among outside observers that Chartism was to be understood not as a political movement, but as a social phenomenon.

From the continental communist left, the young Engels, also deeply impressed by Carlyle's depiction of the 'Condition of England' problem, made a similar assumption. 'The middle class and property are dominant; the poor man has no rights, is oppressed and fleeced, the constitution repudiates him and the law mistreats him.' Thus, in Engels' view, the form of democracy represented by Chartism was not that 'of the French Revolution whose antithesis was monarchy and feudalism, but *the* democracy whose antithesis is the middle class and property ... The struggle of democracy against aristo-

[2] T. Carlyle, *Chartism* (1839), Ch. 1.

[3] '*Mr Doubtful*. But where is the clause for the redistribution of property? Have you forgotten that?

    Radical. That is a base and slanderous calumny which those who profit by things as they are have forged to damage our cause. There never was the slightest foundation for such a charge, although judges on the benches and parsons in the pulpit have not scrupled to give currency to the falsehood.'

'The Question "What is a Chartist?" Answered', Finsbury Tract Society (1839), reprinted in D. Thompson (ed.), *The Early Chartists* (1971), 92. Given the Chartist definition of property, however, it is not surprising that the propertied classes should feel threatened.

[4] Hansard, 3rd series.

cracy in England is the struggle of the poor against the rich. The democracy towards which England is moving is a *social democracy*.'[5] Engels' picture of Chartism, developed in 'The Condition of the English Working Class in 1844', was seen retrospectively as a major empirical confirmation of the later Marxist conception of 'class consciousness', elaborated in such works as the *German Ideology*, the *Poverty of Philosophy* and the *Communist Manifesto*. The premiss of this position was, in Marx's words, that 'the struggle' against 'capital in its developed modern form, in its decisive aspect' is 'the struggle of the industrial wage worker against the industrial bourgeois'.[6] Thus, applied to Chartism, whatever its formal professions, its living essence was that of a class movement of the proletariat born of the new relations of production engendered by modern industry. Its real enemy was the bourgeoisie, and the revolution it would have to effect would amount to the overthrow of this class. As Chartism disencumbered itself of its middle-class allies – a process which Engels considered to have culminated in 1842[7] – the proletarian character of the struggle would assume an ever more conscious form.

While Engels' optimistic conclusions have, for obvious reasons, not been accepted, many of his basic ways of seeing this period have been incorporated into the subsequent historiography of Chartism. The relationship between Chartism, modern industry and class consciousness has remained a prominent theme of labour and socialist historians. His contrast between Manchester and Birmingham, between the class relations of the factory town and that of a city of small workshops, has been amply developed by social historians and sociologists. But it is important to insist that Engels' emphasis upon the social character of Chartism, however brilliantly argued, was – as the testimony of Carlyle and Macaulay suggests – in no sense the peculiar property of a proto-Marxist position. The social interpretation represented the predomin-

[5] F. Engels, 'The Condition of England, The English Constitution', in K. Marx and F. Engels, *Collected Works* (1973), vol. 3, 513.

[6] K. Marx, 'The Class Struggles in France, 1848 to 1850', *Collected Works*, vol. 10, 57.

[7] F. Engels, 'The Condition of the Working Class in England', *Collected Works*, vol. 4, 523.

ant approach of contemporaries. The analysis of the young Engels represented one particular variant of it – that which interpreted Chartism as the political expression of the new industrial proletariat. Another variant, elements of which could also be traced back to liberal commentators at the time, has been equally, if not more, influential in the subsequent historiography of Chartism: that which locates Chartism not as the expression of modern factory workers, but of handloom weavers and other declining 'pre-industrial' groups. The period since the Second World War has yielded further and equally distinctive variants of the social approach – the correlation between Chartism and the trade cycle, associated with Rostow, and the identification of Chartism with atavistic responses to modernization, associated with Smelser.[8] Indeed, in nearly all writings on Chartism, except that of Chartists themselves, it has been the movement's class character, social composition, or more simply the hunger and distress of which it was thought to be the manifestation, rather than its platform or programme which have formed the focal point of enquiry.

It is not surprising that historians have placed these themes at the centre of their studies of Chartism. But it is surprising that there has not been more recognition of the interpretative costs of such an approach. Generally, doubts that have been expressed about particular versions of a social approach, have not extended to the limitations of the social approach as such. The prevalent mode of criticism has been as resolutely social in its assumptions as that of the interpretation to be opposed. Critical discussion has mainly clustered around such questions as the exploitative character of industrialization itself, the reality of the threat to living standards and the real extent or depth of class hostilities. The difficulty of this form of criticism is that pressed to its conclusions it makes the very existence of a combative mass movement difficult to explain, irrespective of its precise character. Far more problematic, yet barely touched upon by the critics of the various social interpretations of Chartism, is the general neglect of the specific political and ideological form within which this mass

[8] W. R. Rostow, *The British Economy of the 19th Century*, Oxford (1948); N.J. Smelser, *Social Change in the Industrial Revolution* (1959).

discontent was expressed and the consequent tendency to elide the Chartist language of class with a range of Marxist or sociological notions of class consciousness. What has not been sufficiently questioned is whether this language can simply be analysed in terms of its expression of, or correspondence to, the putative consciousness of a particular class or social or occupational group. If an analysis of this language does not confirm such a relation of direct manifestation or correspondence, what implication does this have for the interpretation of Chartism as a whole? The language itself has seldom been subjected to detailed examination.[9] But even in cases where it has been, the gravitational pull exercised by the social interpretation has generally been powerful enough to inhibit any major revision of the conventional picture of the movement.

The intention of this essay is to suggest the rudiments of such a reinterpretation. In contrast to the prevalent social–historical approach to Chartism, whose starting point is some conception of class or occupational consciousness, it argues that the ideology of Chartism cannot be constructed in abstraction from its linguistic form. An analysis of Chartist ideology must start from what Chartists actually said or wrote, the terms in which they addressed each other or their opponents. It cannot simply be inferred – with the aid of decontextualized quotation – from the supposed exigencies, however plausible, of the material situation of a particular class or social group. Nor is it adequate, as an alternative, to adopt a more subjective approach and to treat Chartist language as a more or less immediate rendition of experience into words. This way of interpreting Chartism possesses the virtue of paying more serious attention to what Chartists said. But it too ultimately resolves problems posed by the form of Chartism into problems of its supposed content. Against this approach, it is suggested that the analysis of the language itself precludes such a directly referential theory of meaning. What is proposed instead is an approach which attempts to

---

[9] For two analyses which do illuminatingly focus upon the language and politics of radicalism during this period, see T. M. Parssinen, "Association Convention and Anti-Parliament in British Radical Politics, 1771–1848', *English Historical Review*, LXXXVII(1973); Iorwerth Prothero, 'William Benbow and the Concept of the "General Strike"', *Past and Present*, 63 (1974).

identify and situate the place of language and form, and which resists the temptation to collapse questions posed by the form of Chartism into questions of its assumed substance. It is argued that, if the interpretation of the language and politics is freed from a priori social inferences, it then becomes possible to establish a far closer and more precise relationship between ideology and activity than is conveyed in the standard picture of the movement.

In adopting this approach, however, it is not intended to imply that the analysis of language can provide an exhaustive account of Chartism, or that the social conditions of existence of this language were arbitrary.[10] It is not a question of replacing a social interpretation by a linguistic interpretation, but rather it is how the two relate, that must be rethought. Abstractly, the matter determines the possibility of the form, but the form conditions the development of the matter. Historically, there are good reasons for thinking that Chartism could not have been a movement except of the working class, for the discontents which the movement addressed were overwhelmingly, if not exclusively, those of wage earners, and the solidarities upon which the movement counted were in fact also those between wage earners. But the form in which these discontents were addressed cannot be understood in terms of the consciousness of a particular social class, since the form pre-existed any independent action by such a class and did not significantly change in response to it. Moreover, the form was not, as is sometimes implied in the social interpretation, a mere shell within which a class movement developed. For it was what informed the political activity of the movement, it defined the terms in which oppression was understood, and it was what provided the vision of an alternative. It was further what defined the *political* crisis from which Chartism emerged and it fashioned the political means

[10] Nor is it intended to suggest that what is being offered here is an exhaustive analysis of the language of Chartism. The language analysed here is largely taken from radical literature and speeches reported in the radical press. Quite apart from the fact that such reported speech took no account of accent or dialect, I am not arguing that this is the only language Chartists employed. What is examined here is only the public political language of the movement. Much further research would be required before a full account of the language of Chartism could be produced.

by which that crisis was resolved. The type of explanation which ascribes the movement to distress or the social changes accompanying the Industrial Revolution never confronts the fact that the growth and decline of Chartism was a function of its capacity to persuade its constituency to interpret their distress or discontent within the terms of its political language. Chartism was a political movement and political movements cannot satisfactorily be defined in terms of the anger and disgruntlement of disaffected social groups or even the consciousness of a particular class. A political movement is not simply a manifestation of distress and pain, its existence is distinguished by a shared conviction articulating a political solution to distress and a political diagnosis of its causes. To be successful, that is, to embed itself in the assumptions of masses of people, a particular political vocabulary must convey a practicable hope of a general alternative and a believable means of realizing it, such that potential recruits can think within its terms. It must be sufficiently broad and appropriate to enable its adherents to inhabit its language in confronting day to day problems of political and social experience, to elaborate tactics and slogans upon its basis, and to resist the attempts of opposing movements to encroach upon, reinterpret or replace it. Thus the history of Chartism cannot satisfactorily be written in terms of the social and economic grievances of which it is argued to be the expression. Such an approach does not explain why these discontents should have taken a Chartist form, nor why Chartism should not have continued to express the changing fears and aspirations of its social constituency in new circumstances. It is with these questions that this essay is concerned. But before embarking upon such a discussion, we must first attempt to demonstrate more concretely what the interpretative costs of the social approach have been.

One major consequence of the social interpretation of Chartism is that when the actual demands of the movement have been discussed, they have been treated more as a legacy from its prehistory than as a real focal point of activity. Given the assumption that Chartism represented the first manifestation of a modern working-class movement, there has appeared something paradoxical in the fact that such a movement could have come together behind a series of radical constitutional demands first put forward over half a century before. But, even in works in which no strong assumptions are made about the modernity or class character of Chartism, little effort is made to explain why distress and unemployment should find expression in a movement for universal suffrage rather than more immediate pressure for relief from the state. Instead, ever since 1913 when Edouard Dolléans first suggested that the cause of Chartism was to be discovered in the working-class reaction against the Industrial Revolution,[11] historians have tended to downplay the political programme of the Chartists as merely expressive of discontents whose true sources and remedies lay elsewhere.

Such an approach has been compounded by another emphasis in Chartist historiography, originally unconnected to the social interpretation, but which in the course of the twentieth century has increasingly coalesced with it. From the time when Chartism first began to be written about, attention was focussed on the divided nature of the movement. The first generation of Chartist historians, embittered ex-Chartists like Gammage, Lovett and Cooper, concentrated disproportionately upon rifts in organization and the angry and divisive battles between leading personalities.[12] In subsequent historiography, concentration upon the social character of the movement lent itself easily to the analysis of these divisions in social and economic terms. Divergencies of personality and cultural formation were now made to correspond to divergencies of economic situation and locality. The antagonism between Lovett and O'Connor was given a sociological coloration. It became a symbol of the supposed incompatibility between the non-industrialized constitutionally-minded artisans of London and Birmingham – followers of Lovett, Attwood and Sturge, inclined to class alliance and moral force – and northern factory workers or declining handloom weavers – followers of O'Connor, hostile to the middle class, ill-educated and quasi-

---

[11] E. Dolléans, *Le Chartisme, 1831–1848*, rev. edn, Paris (1949), Ch. 1 and 319.

[12] R. G. Gammage, *The History of the Chartist Movement* (1854); facsimile reprint of 1894 edn (1976); W. Lovett, *Life and Struggles of William Lovett, in his pursuit of Bread, Knowledge and Freedom* (1876); T. Cooper, *Life of Thomas Cooper, Written by Himself* (1872).

insurrectionary.[13] Later and more sophisticated versions of this approach, freed from some of the Fabian assumptions which had originally structured it, shifted arguments about Chartism even further from the battles and ideas of the leaders to the differing social textures of protest in different regions, and these regions themselves were arranged along a scale of progressive class polarization determined by the extent of industrialization.[14] Such polarities, however, have been weakened by more recent research. Despite Birmingham's well-publicized reputation for harmonious inter-class radicalism in the nineteenth century, its Chartists rejected the BPU (Birmingham Political Union) leadership and for four years after 1838 looked mainly to O'Connor and stressed class independence.[15] It has similarly been shown that London Chartism in the 1840s was neither particularly weak, nor particularly moderate, as the old interpretation supposed. By 1848, it had become one of Chartism's most militant centres.[16] Conversely, factory and heavy industrial areas like south Lancashire and the north-east, distinctly militant centres in the early years of Chartism, were far less prominent in 1848.[17] Moreover recent occupational analysis of Chartist adherence in its early years appears to suggest that the extent to which certain trades were disproportionately represented – shoe-makers or handloom weavers, for instance – has been exaggerated, and that Chartism attracted a more representative cross-section of the main trades in each locality than has usually been assumed.[18] If this is the case, it implies that too

---

[13] See, in particular, M. Hovell, *The Chartist Movement*, Manchester (1918).

[14] See, for instance, Asa Briggs, 'The Local Background of Chartism', in Asa Briggs (ed.), *Chartist Studies* (1959).

[15] See C. Behagg, 'An Alliance with the Middle Class: The Birmingham Political Union and Early Chartism', in Epstein and Thompson, *The Chartist Experience*; and see also T. Tholfsen, 'The Chartist Crisis in Birmingham', *International Review of Social History*, III (1958).

[16] See Iorwerth Prothero, 'Chartism in London', *Past and Present*, 44 (1969); D. Goodway, 'Chartism in London', *Bulletin for the Society for the Study of Labour History*, 20 (1970).

[17] On the north-east, see W.H. Maehl, 'Chartist Disturbances in Northeastern England, 1839', *International Review of Social History*, VIII (1963); on south Lancashire, see R. Sykes, 'Early Chartism and Trade Unionism in South East Lancashire', in Epstein and Thompson, *The Chartist Experience*; and see also, John Foster, *Class Struggle and the Industrial Revolution, Early Industrial Capitalism in Three English Towns* (1974); P. Joyce, *Work, Society and Politics*, Brighton (1980).

[18] D. Thompson, 'The Geography of Chartism', Unpublished MS; and see also her remarks on this in the 'Introduction' to her *Early Chartists*.

much attention to local or occupational peculiarities can obscure the extent to which Chartism was *not* a local or sectional movement. Chartism was a national movement. Yet this more suprising phenomenon – the extent of unity in the early Chartist movement and the enduring loyalty of a sizeable minority over more than a decade to the remedies of the Charter, despite all disagreement and difference – has been left in the realm of commonsense assumption.

Thus the stress upon division and local differences has tended to accentuate the weak points in the social interpretation of Chartism: its tendency to neglect the political form of the movement and thus to render obscure and inconsequential the reasoning that underlay the demand for the Charter. Mark Hovell, still perhaps the most influential historian of Chartism, set the terms of the predominant approach when he argued that 'by 1838 the Radical Programme was recognized no longer as an end in itself, but as the means to an end, and the end was the social and economic regeneration of society'.[19] This was a seemingly unexceptionable statement and something like it had been said on occasion by Chartists themselves. But Hovell's amplification of it betrayed a basic misunderstanding, which rendered the Charter an oddity and the 'end' incoherent. 'The most optimistic of Chartist enthusiasts', he wrote, 'could hardly have believed that a new heaven and a new earth would be brought about by mere improvements of political machinery.' 'But', he continued, 'social Chartism was a protest against what existed, not a reasoned policy to set up anything in its place. Apart from machinery, Chartism was largely a passionate negation.'[20] Subsequent landmarks in the historiography of Chartism have, if anything, only strengthened the impression of incoherence at the core of the movement. For G. D. H. Cole, 'the Chartist movement was essentially an economic movement with a purely political programme'.[21] 'A common idea might have held them together; the Charter, a mere common programme, was not enough to prevent them from giving their

---

[19] M. Hovell, *The Chartist Movement* (1970 edn), 7.
[20] Ibid., 303.
[21] G. D. H. Cole, *A Short History of the British Working Class Movement, 1789–1947* (1948), 94.

mutual dislikes free rein.'[22] For Asa Briggs, writing in *Chartist Studies* in 1959, the Charter was not so much a focus as 'a symbol of unity'. But 'it concealed as much as it proclaimed – the diversity of local social pressures, the variety of local leaderships, the relative sense of urgency among different people and different groups'.[23]

In the face of this interpretative consensus, it is worth citing the position of the first historian of Chartism, R. G. Gammage, writing in 1854. Gammage certainly did not deny the social origins of political discontent in the sense that 'in times of prosperity there is scarce a ripple to be observed on the ocean of politics'.[24] Nor did he deny that the people, once victorious, would adopt 'social measures' to improve their condition. But, significantly, he does not talk of 'political machinery', 'a mere common programme' or 'a symbol'. He states, on the contrary, that 'it is the existence of great social wrongs which principally teaches the masses the value of political rights'; and his explanation of the thinking behind the Charter places the emphasis quite differently from Hovell and the historians who have followed him. In a 'period of adversity', he wrote:

> The masses look on the enfranchised classes, whom they behold reposing on their couch of opulence, and contrast that opulence with the misery of their own condition. Reasoning from effect to cause there is no marvel that they arrive at the conclusion – that their exclusion from political power is the cause of our social anomalies.[25]

Political Power is the cause. *Opulence* is the effect. But to subsequent historians, whether liberal, social democratic or Marxist, it has been axiomatic that economic power is the cause, political power the effect. If this axiom is read back into the political programme of the Chartists, there is no marvel that that programme should have appeared incoherent.

Not all historians have assumed that Chartists must have meant the economic and social, when they spoke about the political. The underestimation of the political character and context of the popular struggles in the pre-Chartist period has

[22] Ibid., 120.
[23] Briggs, *Chartist Studies*, 26.
[24] Gammage, *History of the Chartist Movement*, 9.
[25] Ibid.

been magnificently remedied by Edward Thompson's *The Making of the English Working Class*. As he demonstrates, the experience of the plebeian movement between 1780 and 1830 was not simply that of intensified economic exploitation, but also of sharp and semi-permanent political repression. Moreover, the attitude of the government and the unreformed Parliament to customary trade practices often seemed yet more cavalier than that to be found in the localities. Thus he can argue with some force that 'the line from 1832 to Chartism is not a haphazard pendulum alternation of "political" and "economic" agitation, but a direct progression, in which simultaneous and related movements converge towards a single point. This point was the vote.'[26]

The great achievement of Thompson's book is to have freed the concept of class consciousness from any simple reduction to the development of productive forces measured by the progress of large-scale industry and to have linked it to the development of a political movement which cannot be reduced to the terminology of incoherent protest. To have established this connection is a vital advance. But we must go further. Thompson's concept of class consciousness still assumes a relatively direct relationship between 'social being' and 'social consciousness' which leaves little independent space to the ideological context within which the coherence of a particular language of class can be reconstituted. A simple dialectic between consciousness and experience cannot explain the precise form assumed by Chartist ideology. A highlighting of the experience of exploitation and political oppression would not in itself account for Gammage's statement. It was not simply experience, but rather a particular linguistic ordering of experience which could lead the masses to believe that 'their exclusion from political power is the cause of our social anomalies' and that 'political power' was the cause of 'opulence'. Consciousness cannot be related to experience except through the interposition of a particular language which organizes the understanding of experience, and it is important to stress that more than one language is capable of articulating the same set of experiences. The

---

[26] E. P. Thompson, *The Making of the English Working Class* (1963), 826.

language of class was not simply a verbalization of perception or the rising to consciousness of an existential fact, as Marxist and sociological traditions have assumed. But neither was it simply the articulation of a cumulative experience of a particular form of class relations. It was constructed and inscribed within a complex rhetoric of metaphorical association, causal inference and imaginative construction. Class consciousness – 'a consciousness of identity of interests between working men of the most diverse occupations and levels of attainment' and 'consciousness of the identity of interests of the working class or productive classes as against those of other classes', as Thompson defines it[27] – formed part of a language whose systematic linkages were supplied by the assumptions of radicalism: a vision and analysis of social and political evils which certainly long predated the advent of class consciousness, however defined.

In England, radicalism first surfaced as a coherent programme in the 1770s, and first became a vehicle of plebeian political aspirations from the 1790s. Its strength, indeed its definition, was a critique of the corrupting effects of the concentration of political power and its corrosive influence upon a society deprived of proper means of political representation. As such, in variant forms, it could provide the vocabulary of grievance to a succession of political and social groups.[28] Elements of this vocabulary

[27] Ibid., 807.
[28] For sources on country party ideology in the eighteenth century and its connection with radicalism, see the following: C. Hill, 'James Harrington and the People', in *Puritanism and Revolution* (1958); P. Zagorin, *The Court and the Country, the Beginning of the English Revolution* (1969); D. Rubini, *Court and Country, 1688–1702* (1967); C. Robins, *The Eighteenth-Century Commonwealth Man*, New York (1968); I. Kramnick, *Bolingbroke and His Circle, the Politics of Nostalgia in the Age of Walpole*, Cambridge, Mass. (1968); J. G. A. Pocock, *The Machiavellian Moment*, Princeton, NJ (1975); J. G. A. Pocock, 'Virtue and Commerce in the 18th Century', *Journal of Interdisciplinary History*, 3 (1972); M. Peters, 'The "Monitor" on the Constitution, 1755–1765: New Light on the Ideological Origins of English Radicalism', *English Historical Review*, LXXXVI(1971); J. Brewer, *Party Ideology and Popular Politics at the Accession of George III*, Cambridge (1976); J. Brewer, 'English Radicalism in the Age of George III', in J. G. A. Pocock, (ed.), *Three British Revolutions*, Princeton, NJ (1980); I. Kramnick, 'Religion and Radicalism: English Political Theory in the Age of Revolution', *Political Theory*, 5 (1977); C. H. Hay, 'The Making of a Radical: The Case of James Burgh', *Journal of British Studies*, 18 (1979); M. Canovan, 'Two Concepts of Liberty: Eighteenth Century Style', *Price–Priestley Newsletter*, 2 (1978); I. Hampshire-Monk, 'Civic Humanism and Parliamentary

went back to the revolutions of the seventeenth century and were reforged by those who felt excluded by the settlements of 1688 or 1714 or by the so-called 'country party' during the years of Walpolean or Pelhamite dominance. The particular resonance, still alive in the Chartist period, of words like 'patriot' or 'independent', and the demonological associations of fundholding and stock-jobbing, dated back to this time. From the 1760s, the tenancy of this language tended to pass from right to left. Country Toryism receded – though it never disappeared – in the face of radical Whiggery. New components of the vocabulary were added by the Americans and their English supporters, and echoes of a less decorous seventeenth century radicalism could again be detected. With the Wilkesite controversy, a radical movement in a full sense began. The focus was no longer simply upon court and city coteries and the corruption of patronage and place, but more consistently and determinedly upon the constitution and the means of representation. The unbalanced and disordered constitution could only be restored to health by drawing upon the 'people', and at the same time the definition of the people was widened, with a shift of emphasis from property to person. In the 1790s, radicalism became plebeian and democratic and successes in America, Ireland and, above all, France lent it a revolutionary edge. It was accordingly repressed, a condition which, given its survival, bestowed upon it a yet more intransigent sense of its righteousness and the accuracy of its diagnosis. After the end of the Napoleonic Wars, radicalism found itself forced to stretch its vocabulary to encompass new sources of distress and discontent within its terms. For not only did it find itself confronted by a new economic situation, it also found its nostrums challenged, though in quite different ways, by the novel emphases of political economy and Owenism, both of which cut across its premises. In response, radicalism attributed a growing

Reform: The Case of the Society of the Friends of the People', *Journal of British Studies*, 18 (1979); J. M. Murrin, 'The Great Inversion, or Court Versus Country: A Comparison of the Revolution Settlements in England (1688–1721) and America (1776–1813)', in Pocock, *Three British Revolutions*; D. O. Thomas, 'Richard Price and the Tradition of Civic Humanism', Unpublished Paper (1980) given to the 'Political Economy and Society Seminar', Research Centre, King's College, Cambridge.

number of economic evils to a political source and in the following thirty years managed to withstand these rival analyses with some success. It accommodated many of the preoccupations of the Owenites, while rejecting with less and less equivocation any compromise with political economy. The cost of this process was an increasing distance from the bulk of its former middle-class constituency. But however much radicalism extended its scope during this period, it could never be the ideology of a specific class. It was first and foremost a vocabulary of political exclusion whatever the social character of those excluded. Thus if it became *de facto* more and more the exclusive property of the 'working classes' in the 1830s and 1840s, this did not lead to a basic restructuring of the ideology itself. The self-identity of radicalism was not that of any specific group, but of the 'people' or the 'nation' against the monopolizers of political representation and power *and hence* financial or economic power.

It is in this sense that the growing political hostility between the middle and working classes after 1832 must be understood. In radical terms, in 1832, the 'people' became the 'working classes'. Explaining the emergence of Chartism in 1838, for instance, the *Northern Star* considered:

The attention of the labouring classes – the real 'people' – has been successively (and yet to a certain degree simultaneously) aroused by the injuries they have sustained by the operation of a corrupt system of patronage hanging around their necks a host of locusts, in the shape of idle and useless pensioners and a swarm of hornets, in the form of mischievous placemen and commissioners to support whom they are weighed to the earth by the pressures of taxation; by the operation of the Corn Laws which made rents high and bread dear; by the iniquitous protection of the fundholders which made money dear and labour cheap; by the horrors of the factory system which immolates their progeny and coins the blood of their children into gold, for merciless grasping ruffians and by the abominations of the poor law act which virtually and practically denies them the right to live. All these and one hundred minor grievances, subservient to the same grand end (of making the working classes beasts of burden – hewers of wood and drawers of water – to the aristocracy, Jewocracy, Millocracy, Shopocracy, and every other Ocracy which feeds on human vitals) have roused the feelings of the people and prompted the respective parties to seek a remedy for the smarting of their wounds.[29]

By the same token, as a group, the middle classes had ceased to

[29] *Northern Star*, 4 Aug. 1838.

be part of the 'people'. For they had joined the system of oppressors and were henceforth answerable for the actions of the legislature. Indeed, rigorously speaking, government now became that of the 'middle classes'. Speaking of the Reform Bill, the *Poor Man's Guardian* wrote a year later: 'By that Bill, the government of the country is essentially lodged in the hands of the middle classes; we say the middle classes – for though the aristocracy have their share of authority, it is virtually absorbed in that of the middlemen who form the great majority of the constituency.'[30]

Now, if it is true that the language of class – at least in its usage by the popular movement – was the language of radicalism, then a number of consequences follow. The most obvious one is that the political demands of the popular movement should be placed at the centre of the story of Chartism, rather than treated as symbolic or anachronistic; and not only the demands, but also the presuppositions which underlay them. For these were neither the superficial encasement of proletarian class consciousness, nor a simple medium of translation between experience and programme. If the history of Chartism is re-analysed in this manner, then the chronology of its rise and decline can be made more precise. The central tenet of radicalism – the attribution of evil and misery to a political source – clearly differentiated it both from a Malthusian-based popular political economy which placed the source of dissonance in nature itself,[31] and from Owenite

[30] *Poor Man's Guardian*, 17 Aug. 1833.

[31] Malthus' *Essay on the Principle of Population* began, and continued to be seen by Malthus himself, as a polemic against radical egalitarianism, in the first instance, William Godwin's *Enquiry Concerning Political Justice*. The directness and pointedness of Malthus' attack was strongly reinforced by his intimacy with the radical dissenting and 'country' tradition, from which Godwin's work in large part sprang. It was a tradition in which he himself had been brought up, and the *Essay* of 1798 represented the moment at which he decisively rejected it. The bitter hostility of radicals against Malthus and the isolated position of those like Francis Place who attempted to combine Malthusianism and radicalism is scarcely surprising. On this, see B. Fontana, I. Hont and M. Ignatieff, 'The Politics of Malthus' First Essay and the Scottish Tradition', Paper given to the Malthus Colloque, Paris (May 1980). The incorporation of Malthusian propositions into the emerging discipline of political economy, at least by some of its best-known practitioners, also explains, more than any other single factor, the anathema in which political economy was held by the great majority of the radical movement. By the late 1830s those who combined radicalism and Malthus were generally referred to as 'sham radicals'. Adam Smith was not included in this hostility. For the use of Smith to buttress Chartist arguments, see the remarks of Peter Bussey, *Northern Star*, 16 Feb. 1839, and William Lovett, *Northern Star*, 31 March 1838.

socialism which located evil in false ideas which dominated state and civil society alike.[32] But it also suggested that the success of radicalism as the ideology of a mass movement would depend upon specific conditions, those in which the state and the propertied classes in their *political and legal capacity* could be perceived as the source of all oppression. The programme of Chartism remained believable so long as unemployment, low wages, economic insecurity and other material afflictions could convincingly be assigned political causes. If, for instance, lack of political representation and a corrupt system of power rather than economic phenomena were responsible for the misery of the working classes, then it followed from this that partial reforms like the Ten Hours Bill or the repeal of the Corn Law could not bring real improvement, indeed were more likely to hasten deterioration, since they left the system intact. Nor could trade unionism be considered a realistic alternative since, if the labour market was politically determined, then differences of bargaining power between different groups within the working classes were largely illusory. So long as the empirical forecasts which followed from radical premises appeared to be borne out, Chartists had little reason to expect widespread defections from their ranks. Once, however, the evidence suggested that real reform was possible within the unreformed system, that the state did not wholly correspond to the radical picture and conditions changed in such a way that differences in the fortunes of various trades became clearly visible, despite the identity of their political situation, then radical ideology could be expected to lose purchase over large parts of its mass following. Such an approach suggests a different way of looking at the period of mid-Victorian stabilization from that prevalent among social historians.[33] In radical discourse the dividing line between classes was not that between employer and employed, but that between the represented and the unrepresented. Thus hostility to the middle classes was not

[32] For an analysis of the defining features of a 'socialist' position in the period up to 1848, see G. Stedman Jones, 'Utopian Socialism Reconsidered', in I. Hont (ed.), *After Adam Smith* (forthcoming).

[33] See, for example, H. J. Perkin, *The Origins of Modern English Society, 1780–1880* (1969); Smelser, *Social Change*; T. Tholfsen, *Working Class Radicalism in Mid-Victorian England* (1976); Foster, *Class Struggle*.

ascribed to their role in production, but to their participation in a corrupt and unrepresentative political system, and it was through this political system that the producers of wealth were conceived to be deprived of the fruits of their labour. Once therefore the conviction of the totally evil character of the political system itself began to fade and distress became less pervasive, there was no independent rationale within radical ideology for antagonism towards the middle class as such. If this is the case, there is then little need to introduce ambitious sociological explanations, such as the emergence of a labour aristocracy, co-option by the middle class or the invention of new and subtle means of social control, in order to explain the disappearance of Chartism. Such approaches ignore the more elementary point that, as a system of beliefs, Chartism began to fail when a gulf opened up between its premisses and the perceptions of its constituency. Local and everyday awareness of difference of social position, of course, remained, but it was no longer linked across the country through the language of radicalism to a shared conviction of a realizable institutional and political alternative. Thus, if expressed hostility to the middle classes declined, despite the continuation of capitalist relations of production, this should be no occasion for surprise. For it was the product of the decline of a political movement whose expressed reasons for hostility to the middle class had had little to do with the character of the productive system in itself.

We have so far argued for an analysis of Chartism which assigns some autonomous weight to the language within which it was conceived. If the language of Chartism is interpreted not as a passive medium through which new class aspirations could find expression, but rather as a complex rhetoric binding together, in a systematic way, shared premisses, analytical routines, strategic options and programmatic demands, we can then introduce some notion of a limit beyond which radical analysis could not be stretched without abandoning its basic tenets and thus losing coherence as an interrelated set of assumptions. But before attempting to suggest some of the points at which these limits were reached, we must first explore what were the interrelated assumptions of post-1830 radicalism and Chartism and show how the language of class was tied to radical premises.

It is best to begin with the simple question: why was the Charter considered desirable? According to Lovett who framed the Charter, 'the end and object of all despotism being to uphold monopolies, there can be no escape from it, so long as the exclusive power of law making shall be suffered to abide with the monopolists'.[34] From the ultra-left of the movement, although the vocabulary certainly differs, the mode of reasoning is similar. According to the Manifesto of the London Democratic Association, which aspired to emulate the Jacobins in the coming revolution, 'because the institutions of the country are in the hands of the oppressors, because the oppressed have no voice in the formation of the laws that rule their destiny – the masses are socially – because they are politically slaves. To put an end to the present cannibal system – we must! We will!! have universal suffrage.'[35] Hetherington similarly attributed the major cause of poverty to the 'monopoly of the power of legislation in the hands of the few'. The monopoly of land and the monopoly of machinery as instruments of production were basically attributable to 'the still more glaring injustice of the monopoly of law making as an instrument of distribution'.[36] For law-making, as O'Brien put it, was a 'monopoly by virtue of which property owners are enabled to keep continually augmenting their property out of the labourer's plundered wages'.[37] The case for universal suffrage was not generally argued on an abstract plane as a universal right inhering in every citizen. The case was more usually put in practical and corporate terms and closely tied to the Chartist analysis of the cause of the condition of the working classes. While outside observers often regarded Chartism as an assault on the propertied by the propertyless, Chartists did not regard the working classes as propertyless. For since the only legitimate source of property was labour, labourers were therefore in possession of the most fundamental form of all property. As Cobbett had stated in his *Address to*

---

[34] *London Mercury*, 4 March 1837, reprinted in Thompson, *Early Chartists*, 58.
[35] *Northern Star*, 13 Oct. 1838.
[36] Ibid., 20 April 1839.
[37] Ibid., 6 Oct. 1838.

the Journeymen and Labourers of England in 1817, 'whatever the pride of rank, or riches or of scholarship may have induced some men to believe, or affect to believe, the real strength and all the resources of the country, have ever sprung and ever must spring from the labour of its people'.[38] The aim therefore was not an expropriation of the rich by the poor, but the ending of a monopoly situation in which all other forms of property were afforded political and legal support, while that of labour was left at the mercy of those who monopolized the state and the law. As John Crabtree of Barnsley observed:

It had once been observed that without the Suffrage their property could not be protected; but the working class were told they had no need of the suffrage as they had no property to protect. They had indeed none save that which was in the strength of their arms; and from that property, every description of property arose, and therefore, theirs was the only property of real value and ought to be the first in the world to have legislative protection. If they would not endeavour to attain such laws as would procure the protection of their only property, they could not wonder at seeing mansions spring up at the corners of every field they passed and the aristocracy feeding on their labour more than ever.[39]

Or as O'Brien put it:

'Knaves will tell you that it is because you have no property, you are unrepresented. I tell you on the contrary, it is because you are unrepresented that you have no property ... your poverty is the result not the cause of your being unrepresented.[40]

In the absence of any legislative protection for labour, those who possessed political power could simply engross property by legislative fiat. Not only could they impose taxes at will, they could also manipulate the money supply to enrich themselves. Thus, just as the 1815 Corn Law was defined as a 'starvation law' for the benefit of the landed interest, so the resumption of cash payments in 1819 was a law made for the benefit of the fundholders, through which millions were thought to have been transferred from debtors into the pockets of creditors.[41] The property amassed by these measures was

[38] *Cobbett's Weekly Political Register*, 2 Nov. 1816, 545–6; see also on this, Thompson, *Making*, 772; Prothero, 'Benbow', 158.
[39] *Northern Star*, 19 June 1839.
[40] Cited in A. Plummer, *Bronterre, A Political Biography of Bronterre O'Brien* (1971), 177–8.
[41] See, for instance, O'Connor's speech in Glasgow, *Northern Star*, 28 July 1838.

'artificial'. It was not the product of labour, but literally the creation of law. The growing polarity between the poverty of the working classes and this 'artificial wealth' could therefore be seen as the result of a process of legal robbery, made possible by the monopoly of law-making. It was in this sense that O'Connor argued that all such laws were a fiction, 'because they have been made for the protection of fictitious money, which represents nothing but the produce of your wealth while in a state of transition from one pack of moneymongers to another pack of speculators'.[42] It is certainly possible to discover differences of tone and emphasis between Chartist spokesmen in the discussions of these issues, but what emerges most clearly in the late 1830s was the remarkable unanimity of reasoning that lay behind the demand for the Charter. There was no dissension on this score between O'Connor, Lovett, Harney and the countless speakers up and down the country reported in the *Northern Star*. Poverty and oppression could only be removed with the abolition of the monopoly of law-making or, as O'Connor put it, 'there was no vice in the people for which he could not assign a legal reason'.[43] The spectrum of positions between moderate and extreme lay *within* radicalism, not *between* radicalism and something else.

If this was the general sense in which Chartists could concur in attributing the oppression of the working classes to their exclusion from political representation, it suggests a far greater continuity between Chartism and preceding forms of radicalism than most historians have admitted. For if oppression was conceived as legal and political in character, then the Charter became far more than a symbol or a mere means to an end. To support this argument, however, it is necessary to ask whether there were no other arguments of a more recognizably class conscious character which had emerged from the experience of movements supported by the 'working classes' between 1815 and 1837, and which might have formed the real, if not explicit, basis of working-class support for Chartism. Such an inference can be drawn, for instance, from all those interpretations of the period, whose material is

[42] *Northern Star*, 22 June 1839.
[43] Ibid., 15 Sept. 1838.

organized around the twin themes of the Industrial Revolution and the growth of a working-class movement. In this scenario, the period between 1815 and 1832 can be viewed as one in which the popular movement became a working-class movement with distinctively working-class ways of looking at politics and society. Trade unionism, co-operation, Owenism, 'Ricardian socialism', the unstamped press and the experience of the parliamentary reform movement can then be viewed as stepping-stones in a learning process through which class consciousness was formed. Confirmation at an ideological level can be provided by the argument that Painite or Cobbettite radicalism, which placed its emphasis upon the state and taxation as the sole source of oppression, gave way to a more class-based conception of exploitation of workers in their role as producers rather than consumers, and thereby to an emphasis upon the class character of the popular movement. Thus radicalism in its initial form is conceived as receding as class consciousness advances, and the political division between the middle and working class established in 1832 is seen as ratifying a process that had already been long in maturation.

Whatever the validity of this picture, it will be argued here that, at least at the level of utterance, it is not confirmed by evidence of ideological change of an appropriate kind. Certainly, changes took place in radicalism between 1815 and 1840 and Chartism incorporated many of the new themes which became prominent in the 1820s, but not in such a way as to breach its basic presuppositions, nor necessarily in directions which drew it closer towards a later class-based language of socialism. We shall argue that the evidence of the 1820s suggests that radicalism in a strict sense remained the predominant ideology of the popular movement, defining both the understanding of oppression and the popular vocabulary of class, and further that rival perspectives, so far as they could be situated beyond the horizons of radicalism, offered if anything a less class-oriented mode of viewing society and politics than the radicalism to which they were counterposed. In order to test the argument, we shall look at the social and political conceptions developed within trade unionism, Owenism and 'Ricardian socialism', and attempt to suggest in what ways they did inflect the radicalism of the post-1832 period.

The first and most obvious place where one might expect to find some kind of challenge to radical analysis is in the arguments and pronouncements that accompanied the development of trade unionism in the 1820s. The implication of a Painite or Cobbettite radicalism was that civil society and the relations between masters and men would function harmoniously, but for the parasitic plundering of the state and its beneficiaries. Yet in the post-1815 period, expressions of discontent by members of the working classes arose most directly from their experiences as wage earners – overwork, falling wages, unemployment, the threat of machinery and new forms of the divisions of labour which affronted customary expectations. Furthermore, these afflictions were accompanied by the rise to prominence of a new type of employer, principally, as it seemed, attuned to the foreign market rather than home consumption and hostile to, or contemptuous of, traditional workshop practices and the informal moral economy which had actually or allegedly underpinned them. In this situation, in which behaviour originally associated with particularly 'grinding' employers was apparently becoming the norm in whole trades, journeymen were impelled to formalize their unofficial practices and assumptions, to form unions and even make alliances across different trades, different districts and different gradations of skill.

How could these developments be considered compatible with the assumptions of radicalism, in which the political system rather than civil society was conceived to be the original source of oppression? The fate of the rural cottager, evicted or expropriated by the process of enclosure could easily enough be attributed to the arbitrary legal and political violence of the ruling aristocracy and thus could fill without difficulty a pre-prepared place within radical rhetoric. But the situation of the artisan, the outworker and the factory operative fell under no such obvious entry in the radical lexicon. It was a state of affairs which had apparently grown up *within* the people, rather than *between* the people and the engines of 'force and fraud' or the machinations of 'old corruption'.

The trade unionist press and trade unionist speeches were certainly full of complaints about the new situation which had developed from the time of the Napoleonic wars, but it is difficult to discover the development of either a trade union practice or a trade union theory which contradicted or went beyond radical assumptions (except in so far as they derived from Owenite positions, which will be discussed separately). In a strict sense trade union practice by its very nature posed a potential challenge to radicalism in that it presupposed that trade organization could maintain customary wage levels and work conditions despite the arbitrary and oppressive character of the law-making class. But in the period before 1833–4 this difference never became very explicit because virtually all active trade unionists were also radicals. Nor was the development of trade unions in this period as novel as it was once thought. The attempt to establish a general union of all trades was not a quasi-syndicalist deduction from ideas to be found in Owenism or 'Ricardian socialism', nor was it an invention of the 1829–34 period. There had been previous attempts in Manchester and London in 1818 and 1825. The practice of inter-trade co-operation in a particular district was a well established one. What was new, was the formalization of this idea combined with a growing sense of similarity of position in different trades and different places, made possible by the diffusion of a newly legalized trade union press.[44]

Moreover, the context of the development of the idea of a general union was not that of an offensive drive to capture the whole product of labour, as was once thought, but a heightened sense of vulnerability among weaker trades in the face of the encroachments of a hostile economic environment. The General Association of London Trades in 1827, associated with the shipwright, John Gast, emerged from the threat of a reimposition of the Combination Laws in 1825–6. The Manchester based National Association for the Protection of Labour (NAPL), associated with the spinners' leader, John Doherty, was formed after the defeat of his union in the strike of 1829. The formation of the Grand National Consolidated

---

[44] On the development of trade unionism in the 1820s and early 1830s, see in particular, R. G. Kirby and A. E. Musson, *Voice of the People, John Doherty 1798–1854, Trade Unionist, Radical and Factory Reformer*, Manchester (1976); Iorwerth Prothero, *Artisans and Politics in Early Nineteenth Century London*, Folkestone (1979). I am heavily indebted to these two studies of Doherty and Gast respectively for my picture of trade unionism in this period.

Trades' Union (GNCTU) in London in 1833 arose from the
tailors' preparations for an all-out struggle to halt the decline
of their trade after the failure of their strikes in 1827 and
1830.[45] It is indicative that the constitution of the NAPL
allowed support to affiliated unions only in the case of strikes
against *reductions* in wages. 'The object they ought to obtain',
Doherty stated, 'was that freedom and independence which
had long been the characteristic of Englishmen, but of which
at present only a small remnant was left.'[46] Gast thought
similarly that 'the "bold peasant" must again become his
"country's pride", pauperism become hateful in the minds of
labourers, the dead weight cut adrift, then (and not till then)
England will again be a pattern for the world and the envy of
surrounding nations'.[47] In answer to radicals, Owenites and
followers of political economy, all of whom were for different
reasons sceptical of the capacity of trade societies to affect
wage levels and working conditions, trade unionists at this
time had little answer beyond the desirability of re-estab-
lishing a world governed by customary expectations and just
agreements regulating the conduct of masters and men.

Just as developments in trade union practice developed
mainly out of the exigencies of the situation, so perforce did a
trade union stance on the economy develop in response to the
offensive of popular political economy. The crucial factor here
was the growth of a trade union press, made possible by the
repeal of the Combination Laws and the attempts of utilitarian radicals like Francis Place to win over the trade societies
to the teaching of political economy. Thus, in the London
Trades Newspaper and the NAPL's *United Trades Cooperative
Journal* and its successor, *Voice of the People*, a specifically trade
society position on problems of economics and politics began
to be formulated. But here again there were no ideas which
went beyond radical conceptions of the relationship between

---

[45] See T. M. Parssinen and Iorwerth Prothero, 'The London Tailors' Strike of 1834
and the Collapse of the Grand National Consolidated Trades' Union: A Police
Spy's Report', *International Review of Social History*, xxii (1977); B. Taylor, '"The
Men are as Bad as their Masters ... "': Socialism, Feminism and Sexual
Antagonism in the London Tailoring Trade in the Early 1830s', *Feminist Studies*,
5,1 (1979).
[46] Kirby and Musson, *Voice of the People*, 163.
[47] Prothero, *Artisans*, 227.

employer and employed. Indeed the basic stance was in fact
identical to that espoused by radicals and Chartists through to
the end of the 1840s. Although the *Trades Newspaper* attempted
to popularize Hodgskin's *Labour Defended*, and Doherty's
journals reprinted extracts from William Thompson, the most
popular and widely diffused position was that enunciated by
trade unionists themselves – a straightforward belief that
increased home consumption would remedy the evils of
unemployment, fortified by the conviction of the right of every
operative to good wages and a constantly reiterated alarm
about the development of a 'new aristocracy of wealth' and
the progressive deterioration of the condition of the producers
of that wealth. 'Malthusian' first became an abusive epithet,
both among trade unionists and radicals in the 1820s, and a
position which was to become standard – connecting excessive
competition, abuse of machinery, overwork, declining wages
and unemployment with the mushroom growth of large
capitalists and the promotion of the export trade – was well
established by the end of the decade. A characteristic
statement of this view was put forward by Thomas Single in
the *Trades Newspaper*:

Were we, at once, to leave off some of our machinery, and lose some (nay
almost all) of our foreign trade, and give working men the necessaries of life
for a day's labour, our home trade would increase, quite as much, or more,
than our foreign trade decreased. At all events, we should not then be living
in the midst of starvation in a land of plenty ... What! are thousands and
millions in this country to starve for the sake of commerce – for the sake of
enabling a few great capitalists to carry on a system of trading with
foreigners by machinery, which has no other earthly tendency than to enrich
hundreds and starve millions?[48]

The evil role of foreign trade remained a constant feature of
the Chartist analysis of the deterioration of the condition of
the working classes and a significant portion of the middle
classes. It had led to the destruction of any natural relationship between production and consumption and its replacement by a gambling speculative system which gave large
capitalists excessive profits at the expense of small capitalists
and produced a constant lowering of wages. Its origin was to

[48] Ibid., 228.

be derived from the lack of taxation on machinery. According to the *Northern Star* in 1839:

Our modern foreign trade owes its existence to the privilege, accorded to manufacturing capitalists of lessening gradually and unceasingly, by the agency of untaxed machinery, the value of human labour – the honest profits of all trades depending for their returns on the home market – as well as the value of the soil of England.[49]

Or as it had written a year before:

Thus labour, which ought to be the regulator of commerce has been subjected, for want of laws to regulate the profits on machinery, to a parcel of gambling speculators, who have glutted the foreign market with the proceeds of cheap labour, till at length we have lived to see the English labourer's produce, stored in foreign countries, and offered by the gambler at a less price than the same article can be had for at home.[50]

The Chartist solution was the same as that offered by trade unionists and radicals in the 1820s. According to Lovett, writing on behalf of the London Working Men's Association:

We would urge them not to forget the superior advantage of a profitable home consumption. For if wages are to be continually reduced to meet foreign competition there will be a gradual lessening of our home trade; the respectable class of shopkeepers and tradesmen, who are somewhat prosperous by reasons of the present wages of the working classes – if these wages were reduced down or anyways approximating to those of our unfortunate Irish brethren – would soon be driven from the country, or sink into some degraded class we would all be reduced to – the mere starving conductors of the splendid machinery of England.[51]

And it was basically the same case that was put to shop-keepers and the uncorrupt part of the middle classes by O'Connor, McDouall and Jones in the months leading up to the presentation of the third Chartist Petition in 1848.[52]

Trade unionism, therefore, was certainly indicative of divisions that had grown up within the people, but it did not contradict the notion of the people as radicalism envisaged it. Gast blamed the shipwright's position upon the national debt

---

[49] *Northern Star*, 2 March 1839.
[50] Ibid., 12 May 1838.
[51] Ibid., 31 March 1838.
[52] See J. Belcham, 'Fergus O'Connor and the Collapse of the Mass Platform', in Epstein and Thompson, *The Chartist Experience*.

and taxation. Doherty considered that support for the NAPL should not bring operatives into conflict with honourable employers, since the latter pressed down by excessive taxation and the Corn Laws were the creatures of circumstance as much as their workmen. Even in 1834 he hoped that masters could be weaned from dependence on the 'infernal philosophy' of the 'high priests', Malthus and MacCulloch, teaching them that distress was the result of overpopulation and monopolies, rather than taxation, paper money and excessive competition.[53] Political economy was not seen as the ideology of a class, but a false, selfish and inhuman view of human nature which had captured the support of many masters, but which the journeymen's counter-case might successfully undermine. Similarly, in strikes themselves and the battle for public opinion that surrounded them, the enemy was not the employers as a class, but rather the grinding and tyrannical employers in contrast to their honourable associates. A strong trade society maintaining an agreed rate of wages for agreed stints of work would be a benefit to masters by preventing excessive competition between them. High wages would stimulate home demand and hence secure a fair rate of profit. In unorganized trades, on the other hand, good masters were forced to follow bad masters in lowering wages, since competition left them no option. There was certainly a consistent hostility expressed towards 'capitalists'. But they, unlike masters, tended, as we shall see, to be thought of as part of the political system rather than the class structure, for they were the engrossers of what radicals considered to be 'artificial' wealth.

If trade unionism did not represent an extraneous alternative to radicalism in its conception of class and oppression, what about Owenism, which was so clearly connected to trade union and co-operative activity between 1829 and 1834? In general, it may be suggested that Owenites certainly broadened the conception of oppression prevalent in the radical movement through their critique of distribution and the competitive system, but that their position remained fundamentally incompatible with any development of a

---

[53] Kirby and Musson, *Voice of the People*, 283–4.

language of class since it contradicted the presuppositions upon which it was based. Historians, approaching Owenism as a phase in the history of the labour movement or the development of the working class, have tended, however, to discount the formal assumptions of Owenites and to suggest that working-class activists reshaped Owenism into a class-oriented position of a novel kind. Each of these points will be examined in turn.

There can be no doubt about the part played by Owenism and the co-operative movement in a wider sense in broadening the notion of oppression as it had been understood by Paine, Cobbett and Richard Carlisle. Owenism focussed upon those problems which in any case preoccupied the depresssd trades – low wages, machinery, surplus labour and the growing polarity between wealth and poverty – and placed them in a systematic context. If labour was the source of all wealth, then growing disparities of income could not simply be ascribed to the evils of aristocracy, monopoly, taxes and corruption, as had been the predominant theme of the radical platform of 1819[54] The difference between what labour produced and its actual receipts could not be wholly accounted for by the plunder of 'the tax-makers, the pensioners, the placemen and the tax-eaters in general'. John Gray of the London Co-operative Society, whose *Lecture on Human Happiness* of 1825 became a standard text of the co-operative movement, provided a vivid and concrete image of a class of non-productive property owners living off the labour of others through his dramatization of Colquhoun's national income statistics of 1814. Paine had thought that more than one quarter of the labour of mankind was swallowed up in taxes.[55] But from Colquhoun's tables it could be deduced that while the average annual product of the producer amounted to £54, his average receipts in wages only amounted to £11, and therefore that 'by the present arrangements of society, the productive classes are deprived of nearly four-fifths of the

[54] For an illuminating examination of changes in radical ideology between the period after the Napoleonic wars and the 1830s, see P. Hollis, *The Pauper Press, A Study in Working-Class Radicalism of the 1830s*, Oxford (1970). Her analysis of the importance of these changes, however, differs significantly from the interpretation advanced here.

[55] T. Paine, *The Rights of Man*, Everyman edn (1969), 213.

produce of their labour'.[56] The real income of the country, he concluded, 'is taken from its producers, chiefly by the rent of land, by the rent of houses, by the interest of money, and by the profit obtained by persons who buy their labour from them at one price and sell it at another'.[57] This notion or something like it cropped up frequently in the next twenty years. Doherty supposed that three-quarters of the produce of agricultural and manufacturing labour was taken by the government and the employers.[58] 'One of the Oppressed' wrote from Manchester to the *Poor Man's Guardian* in March 1832:

I have told you that the evils under which you labour are not produced by taxation. I have shown you that the whole expense of the government, from the king to the common soldier, does not amount to more than one halfpenny a day upon each individual in the two kingdoms; and that the abolition of the whole of the government would relieve you to the amount of only one halfpenny a day ... and I have told you that the *immediate* cause of your poverty is the exorbitant rents, tithes, interests on money, profits on labour, and profits on trade, which are imposed on you by laws made by the landstealers, the merchants, the manufacturers, and the tradesmen in that house from which you are excluded, and by which exclusion you are prevented from making laws to regulate your wages.[59]

The *Poor Man's Guardian* itself thought taxes were a 'mere bagatelle',[60] while the idea that the productive classes received only one-fifth of their earnings became part of the standard repertoire of the speeches and articles of Bronterre O'Brien in the early Chartist period.[61] O'Connor thought that labourers consumed only one-quarter of their earnings,[62] and even Attwood, introducing the 1839 Chartist Petition of Parliament, stated that:

The first thing sought for by these honest men, everyone of whom produced by his labour four times more to the country than they asked for in exchange, was a fair subsistence – and yet their country refused them one fourth the values of their labour.[63]

This broadening of the conception of the evils faced by the

[56] J. Gray, *A Lecture on Human Happiness* (1825), 20.
[57] Ibid., 70.
[58] Kirby and Musson, *Voice of the People*, 422.
[59] *Poor Man's Guardian*, 14 April 1832; the letter was dated Manchester, 19 March.
[60] Ibid., 22 March 1834.
[61] See, for instance, *Northern Star*, 6 April 1839.
[62] Ibid., 29 Sept. 1838.
[63] Ibid., 22 June 1839.

producer was generally accompanied in Owenite literature by the notion of a rise to prominence of 'capitalists' or a new 'aristocracy of wealth'. Such an idea was not so much a theoretical innovation as a systematization of an idea which was anyway becoming common currency. Doherty, for example, talked about the master spinners as Cobbett had talked about farmers. In the beginning they had been 'plain industrious men' disposed to mix socially with their workmen, but they had been transformed by massive profits into a 'new race' of 'cotton lords';[64] and his *Voice of the People* considered that the gulf between rich and poor had never been wider since the aristocracy of title had been replaced by an aristocracy of wealth which had 'established a slavery more hideous in its effects and has ground down its victims to the extreme verge of poverty'.[65] Or, again, more formally, Thomas Hodgskin considered that capital and capitalists:

> have long since reduced the ancient tyrant of the soil to comparative insignificance, while they have inherited his power over all the labouring classes. It is, therefore, now time that the reproaches so long cast on the feudal aristocracy should be heaped on capital and the capitalists; or on that still more oppressive aristocracy which is founded on wealth, and which is nourished by profit.[66]

William Thompson, on the other hand, thought that it was not so much that one class had reduced the other, but rather that:

> The feudal aristocracy and the aristocracy of wealth have coalesced; and those last admitted into the unholy coalition against the happiness of the great majority of their fellow creatures, are frequently the most bitter enemies – like slaves selected for slave drivers in the slave-polluted districts – of the Industrious Classes, of whose hardships they so lately partook.[67]

What the Owenite and co-operative movements, in particular, contributed to these ideas, was to interpret this process of broadening oppression and growing polarization as products of a system of competition. As John Gray put it:

> There is not a man in this country who depends, in any way, on commerce for subsistence, who has not a thousand commercial enemies. The labourer who seeks employment, frequently finds enemies to his interest even among

---

[64] Kirby and Musson, *Voice of the People*, 370.
[65] Ibid., 219.
[66] T. Hodgskin, *Labour Defended* (1825); reprint of 1922 edn, New York (1969), 67.
[67] W. Thompson, 'One of the Idle Classes', in W. Thompson, *Labour Rewarded* (1827); reprinted New York (1969), 9.

those who would otherwise be his friends ... The merchant, the wholesale dealer, the retail tradesman, the mechanic, each of these finds an enemy to his commercial interest in every individual engaged in the same line of business as himself.[68]

'The present system of human affairs', he concluded, 'is calculated, in almost all its parts, to bring the principle of self-love into competition with benevolence.'[69]

It was above all William Thompson, a co-operator who accepted the desirability of universal suffrage, who put the co-operative argument about competition in a form which radicals and trade unionists were most likely to accept. For, unlike Owen, he used Painite or Godwinite imagery to put the case. The language of corruption and deceit which had developed in the early eighteenth century as a response to the new financial practices associated with parliamentary parties and the growth of public debt, and which had been broadened by Paine and Cobbett into a juxtaposition between the people and 'old corruption' or the forces of 'force and fraud', was now extended into the fabric of civil society itself. 'In former times', wrote Thompson:

The feudal and theological systems, the systems of force and fraud, sometimes at war, sometimes at peace with each other, ruled the affairs of men, and consumed all the products of labour that were not necessary to keep the labourers in existence and in working condition. In the midst of these contentions of force and fraud, the system of Industry working on knowledge has been gradually working its way. In every part of Europe the system of Industry is partly established. In no part of Europe, or of the world, is the system of Industry, as it ought everywhere to be, predominant over the systems of force and fraud. Wars were formerly waged for rapine or superstition. During the latter ages they have frequently been waged under the sincere ignorant belief of procuring commercial advantages by them. So much, however, are the old systems of force and fraud interwoven in our present social arrangements, that there is scarcely a transaction of life in which even at the present day, force and fraud do not take a share.[70]

---

[68] Gray, *Human Happiness*, 45. It should be noted, however, that there were gradations of position on competition within the Owenite movement, as well as outside it. Owen himself was the most totally opposed to competition but William Thompson, for instance, was more concerned with elimination of force from exchange than with the effects of competition as such – an emphasis which he derived from Godwin. For a discussion of these issues, see G. Claeys, 'The Owenite Theory of Exchange', Unpublished MS (1980).

[69] *Ibid.*, 46.

[70] Thompson, 'Idle Classes', 11.

And, after discussing taxes and tithes, he went on:

From the intricacies of production, the difficulties of ascertaining value and quality, from the inequalities of knowledge and skill, there is scarcely a transaction of barter or exchange in which the over-reaching spirit of competition does not mingle fraud, whether by an affected indifference to the exchange, or by undervaluing the thing to be acquired, or by overvaluing the thing to be given. By unjust *exchanges*, then, supported by force or fraud, whether by direct operation of law, or by indirect operation of unwise social arrangements, are the products of the labour of the industrious classes taken out of their hands. The field for chicane is unbounded as the exercise of human faculties.[71]

Engels considered in 1844 that incompatible attitudes towards competition lay at the root of the split between middle-class and working-class radicals.[72] So far as this was true, Owenism and co-operation had played an important part in sharpening this division. The older radicalism of the pre-1820 period had tended to juxtapose competition to monopoly. Those who accepted the teachings of political economy could still articulate their radicalism in these terms. Owenism and co-operation, on the other hand, like some strands of romanticism current in middle-class circles juxtaposed competition to community, with the contrast between competition and association as an important intermediate stage. This notion of competition as an *unnatural* force which imposed itself upon men from the outside – rather than the later Marxist idea of competition as the result of a contradiction within the system of production itself – could easily accommodate and make sense of the trade unionist's perception of good masters reluctantly having to follow bad in lowering wages, and the radical's belief that corruption and oppression were alien intrusions upon a natural order of things, in which the master, the mechanic, the merchant and the shopkeeper would each receive his proper share. Moreover, the emphasis upon association as a transitional step enabled a junction to be established between Owenism and the preoccupations of trade unionists. It was thus a modified form of the Owenite view rather than the liberal belief in competition as a beneficent and natural force which became

[71] Ibid., 12.
[72] Marx and Engels, *Collected Works*, vol. 4, 523.

predominant in trade union and radical circles. Thinking in terms of the effects of competition became an integral part of the Chartist analysis in the 1830s and 1840s, with destructive effects upon important planks in the older common radical platform. On taxes, for instance, the *Poor Man's Guardian* in 1833, while agreeing with Cobbettites about the desirability of repealing tithes and taxes on consumption, stated:

We are bound in sincerity to state our conviction that the poor labouring man would derive little or no benefit from these measures, were Reform to stop there. The necessaries of life would doubtless be greatly cheapened for him, but the ever growing glut of the labour market would soon bring down his wages in a corresponding degree. The commercial classes would engross the entire advantage, and to the producing slave what difference would it make whether his earnings went to the parson or to the ravenous slave driving shopocrat.[73]

And on the repeal of the Corn Laws, another old radical war-cry, O'Connor stated alongside other arguments:

Free trade is but a substitute for landed monopoly at home, and free trade is but chaunted as a means of creating a competitive power for the task-master, and a new source of commercial speculation for gamblers with fictitious money for real labour – have you store houses abroad, and you have a wholesale market for the money mongers, and your necessities will form the standard of retail prices.[74]

Nevertheless, for all that radicals had absorbed from the Owenite critique of competition, there remained an important difference between the two positions. Owenism was of great importance in highlighting a view of competition, not as the particular misfortune of this or that trade, but as a pervasive system extending oppression beyond the sphere directly attributable to the activities of the state. It thereby rendered problematic Tom Paine's view that, 'when in countries that are called civilised, we see age going to the workhouse and youth the gallows, something must be wrong in the system of government'.[75] But the radical and Chartist position remained nearer to Paine than to Owen. For what radicals and trade unionists most usually condemned was not competition, but excessive competition; and, as the *Poor Man's Guardian*

[73] *Poor Man's Guardian*, 26 Oct. 1833.
[74] *Northern Star*, 3 Nov. 1838.
[75] Paine, *Rights of Man*, 221.

stated, what was wrong was 'not so much the competitive principle of which Mr Owen complains, as the illicit direction given to it by cannibal civilisation'.[76]

Indeed, the fundamental incompatibility between Owenism and radicalism should not be underestimated.[77] Owenism, in a strict sense, was quite consistent in considering political change irrelevant to its basic diagnosis. The source of competition and 'antipathy' was not political, but ideological. False ideas about human nature, inscribed in religious, political and economic theory, and institutionalized in education and upbringing, were responsible for the evils of competitive society and the unnecessary polarity between wealth and poverty. Change could only result from a recognition of this truth, through a process of enlightenment and conversion. In the absence of this moral revolution, political change would be in vain; the example of the United States, a country with democratic institutions where competition ruled supreme, could be and frequently was cited to prove the point. Secondly, if the source of evil was ideological, then Owenism was also consistent in making no particular appeal to one class at the expense of another. In its analysis of the immorality of competition, Owenism made no distinction in principle between the competition of the unhappy rich for senseless luxury and that of the unhappy poor for employment. All were equally afflicted by the war of all against all. So it made as much sense to appeal to the governors as the governed. Of course, it was an elementary principle of propaganda to couch the appeal to different social groups in different terms. Thus the rich could be promised security and true happiness, while the poor could be shown the legitimate means of securing the full fruits of labour. Therefore, despite its association with this latter aspiration, Owenism was always careful to distance itself from any ambition couched in class terms. Indeed, class vocabulary itself was thought to be one of the evil results of competition, promoted in particular by its cruellest exponents. William Thompson blamed 'the class of *competitive* political economists' for the currency of such terms as 'the

---

[76] *Poor Man's Guardian*, 19 Oct. 1833.

[77] For a more elaborate presentation of the argument advanced here, see my 'Utopian Socialism Reconsidered'.

working or labouring classes' to describe the 'industrious' – 'as if they ought never to do or think of anything else but working or labouring'.[78] It was for similar reasons that Owenism rejected on the whole a language of rights and preferred a language of utility. The changes advocated were those which would secure the greatest happiness of all, once rationally understood. Historic or natural rights and the claims of particular social groups were shunned because they formed part of the divisions and pretensions of the old competitive world. Man possessed not natural rights, but rather a natural propensity to pursue happiness. It was not therefore the abrogation of rights, but rather the false consciousness engendered by 'antipathy' which prevented man from reaching his goal. What Owenism offered 'the industrious' was not class identity, but 'a science', a true knowledge of the general causes of unhappiness, in comparison with which particular forms of government, oppressions of the rich or the past wrongs of the English people were simply irrelevant since they were all products of the false and selfish beliefs of the old world.

It was because of this theory of the possibility of a 'new moral world', not in spite of it, that Owenism attracted groups of artisans in London, Birmingham and other centres and, through them, contributed more than any other single source to the enlargement of the scope and language of aspiration within the radical movement itself. From the days of the London Corresponding Society, and throughout the bulk of the campaigning years of Cobbett and Hunt, the dominant language of radicals had been a form of constitutionalist rhetoric, which had used precedent to justify images of an organic community and elaborated a mythical history of saxon or medieval England to reclaim rights which historically belonged to the English people. Even the purest disciples of Paine, like Richard Carlile, saw nothing incongruous in switching back and forth between Cobbettite attacks on 'old corruption' and Painite attacks on 'Kingcraft, Lordcraft and Priestcraft' in the name of the Rights of Man.[79] Discussing the

[78] Thompson, 'Idle Classes', 94.
[79] On this point, see E. Yeo, 'Social Science and Social Change: A Social History of Some Aspects of Social Science and Social Investigation in Britain, 1830–1890', Sussex University Ph.D. (1972), 18–19.

limitations of this constitutionalist radical rhetoric in the eighteenth century, Edward Thompson has written:

> It implied the absolute sanctity of certain conventions: respect for the institutions of monarchy, for the hereditary principle, for the traditional rights of the great landowners and the established church, and for the representation, not of human rights, but property rights. Once enmeshed in constitutionalist arguments – even where these were used to advance the claims of manhood suffrage – reformers became caught up in the trivia of piecemeal constitutionalist renovation. For a plebeian movement to arise, it was essential to escape from these categories altogether and set forward for wider democratic claims.[80]

The plebeian movement never did 'escape these categories altogether', for radicalism, as we have seen in the reasoning behind the demand for the Charter, determined the form taken by the democratic movement, both before and after 1832, and the language of radicalism was structured in terms of a vocabulary of property, whether in the form of fictive history or natural rights. This remained the case, even when it was stretched to encompass the claims of a class whose only property lay in 'the strength of their arms'. But so far as a more consistently humanist and universalist tone was present in the claim for democratic rights made by large numbers of Chartists than had been present among the advocates of manhood suffrage in the 1790s or the 1810s, it was the Owenite movement rather than Paine that had accomplished this transformation. It should not be forgotten that the Charter was originally drawn up by an ex-Owenite, William Lovett, and that in its first formulation he not only, like Paine, forcefully rejected any claim based on historical precedent, but mixed a language of rights with an Owenite language of utility and also included women within its scope. Whatever the limits of Owen's law that 'man's character is made for him, not by him', it was of enormous importance for those who came into contact with it, in clearing the ground for a belief in natural and universal equality, human perfectibility, the malleability of social and political institutions and a movement which looked unambiguously to the future rather than the past. In place of the wrongs of the 'free born Englishman', in place of a limited vocabulary appropriate to

[80] Thompson, *Making*, 88.

the redress of particular grievances, Owen offered his adherents a universal and historically unencumbered language in which to express their demands and aspirations. It was the form in which the popular movement inherited the rationalist and scientistic strand of enlightenment thinking. In the words of George Holyoake, Owen enabled 'working men to reason on their conditions'[81] and this represented a permanent gain even for those who, like Lovett, came to reject many specific features of Owenite analysis or Owenite strategy. Some sense of the lasting impact made by Owen upon working men's moral beliefs and vocabulary for interpreting the world can be gained from the last will and testament of Henry Hetherington, veteran publisher of the unstamped and chartist press, who had long since parted company with the orthodox Owenite movement. He hoped that the address given at his funeral in 1849 would point with equal frankness to the good and bad points of his character so that 'none may avow just and rational principles without endeavouring to purge themselves of those errors that result from bad habits, previously contracted, and which tarnish the lustre of their benign and glorious principles'. And he continued:

These are my views and feelings in quitting an existence that has been chequered with the plagues and pleasures of a competitive, scrambling, selfish system by which the moral and social aspirations of the noblest human beings are nullified by incessant toil and physical deprivations; by which, indeed, all men are trained to be either slaves, hypocrites, or criminals. Hence my ardent attachment to the principles of that great and good man – Robert Owen.[82]

---

[81] G. J. Holyoake, *Sixty Years of an Agitator's Life*, 2 vols. (1893), vol. I, 19; and see on this aspect of Owenism, Yeo, 'Social Science and Social Change', Ch. 2.

[82] *Democratic Review*, Sept. 1849, 159; see also an earlier comment in the *Poor Man's Guardian* on Owen: 'His lectures on the Organisation of Industry, and the Formation of Character, have done a world of good. They have made men's minds familiar with the importance of labour, and consequently of the labouring classes. They have taught the latter to see in themselves what they really are – the lords of creation. Every working man who reads Mr Owen's essays becomes a new being in his own estimation. He no longer feels himself a mere lump of living mechanism, predestined for the use and abuse of others. He sees that, however degraded he has been made to be, it is possible for him, under new arrangements, to become the equal of those that look down upon him. He sees that Nature has stamped no inferiority upon him – that Providence has been equally bountiful to him, as to others, in all the essentials of human happiness; and that, in short, whatever inferiority belongs to him is SOLELY THE WORK OF MAN, *and by man therefore remediable.*' *Poor Man's Guardian*, 4 April 1835.

Was there then no current among the working classes which put together the experiences of the radical, co-operative and trade union movements to produce a more distinctively working-class strategy transcending the radical conception of class? In order to test this idea, at least at the level of utterance, we shall look briefly at the particular merger between radicalism and Owenism established in the early years of the National Union of the Working Classes (NUWC) and, from the trade union side, at the analysis to be found in the *Crisis* and the *Pioneer* in 1833–4, since it has sometimes been argued to represent a syndicalist position.

The NUWC, founded in 1831, has been considered of importance to historians of socialism and the labour movement for several reasons. Its title has been taken as a milestone in the consciousness of a separate working-class identity. Some of its most prominent members, Hetherington, Hibbert, Benbow and O'Brien, together with Huntite working-class radicals in Manchester, represented the earliest and most intransigeant opposition to the 1832 Reform Bill and its enfranchisement of the middle class. It was the organization to which Benbow first proposed his strategy of a general holiday: another conventional landmark in the formation of working-class consciousness. Finally, the NUWC also included some of the most prominent artisan advocates of co-operation and could thus be seen as one of the first junctions between socialism and working-class politics.

None of these points, however, will bear the weight of interpretation which has been placed upon them. The NUWC's conception of class remained wholly within radical parameters. The justification for its name was the egalitarian premiss that all should work, and thus the intended polarity was not that between 'working classes' and 'middle classes', but between the working classes and the idle classes. It was the same reasoning which led the Working Men's Association a little later to inscribe on its membership card: 'The man who evades his share of useful labour diminishes the public stock of wealth, and throws his own burden upon his neighbour.'[83] Similarly, the opposition to the 1832 Reform Bill was not because of its enfranchisement of a middle-class enemy, but

---

[83] Gammage, *History of the Chartist Movement*, 9.

because it compromised the principle of manhood suffrage, which had been the starting point of the radical platform since 1819.[84] While the majority of radicals, initially at least, supported 1832 as the first step towards universal (male) suffrage, Hetherington and the group around him, like Hunt, saw it as a ploy to strengthen 'old corruption'. As Hetherington recalled a few years later, he had seen that the aim of the Bill had been 'to detach the middle from the working classes, and to unite the former with the aristocracy, in common league against the producers'.[85] So far as Benbow's general holiday proposal is concerned, Iorwerth Prothero has convincingly demonstrated that it should be understood wholly in terms of an ultra-radical position which went back to the insurrectionary schemes of 1816 and 1817. Moreover, his political position owed nothing to Owen: his advocacy of the strike strategy and his interest in co-operative schemes were framed in a perspective governed by his heroes, Paine and Cobbett. The 'general holiday' was not premissed upon the idea that the working class should use its industrial muscle against the capitalist state, but rather that the industrious – including employers and employed – should cease from their labours and thereby provoke the idlers into a violent confrontation with the people.[86] Such a conception explains why O'Connor and O'Brien should advise Chartists against implementing the 1839 Convention's approval of a 'sacred month' on the grounds that the people were not armed.[87] Finally, so far as Owenite and radical positions were welded together in the NUWC, the form in which it occurred does not support any contention of a working-class position which transcended both. It suggests, on the contrary, the continuing hegemony of radical assumptions, even among those artisans who had been most deeply impressed by Owen's ideas and who accepted the ideal of co-operation. This was evident, for example, in a debate of the NUWC in December 1831, when interest in co-operation was still at its height. The NUWC passed a resolution put forward by the Owenite radical, William Lovett, that:

[84] See, Prothero, *Artisans*, Ch. 14.
[85] *Poor Man's Guardian*, 24 May 1834.
[86] Prothero, 'Benbow'.
[87] *Northern Star*, 3 Aug. 1839.

This meeting is of opinion, that most of the present evils of Society, are to be attributed to corrupt legislation, coupled with uncontrolled machinery, and individual competition; and that the only permanent remedy will be found in a new system in which there shall be equal laws and equal justice – when machinery shall be turned to the advantage of the whole people, and where individual competition in the pursuit of riches, shall be unknown.[88]

The implication of this position was that the causes of competition were not ideological, but political. Landowners and capitalists lived off the fruits of labour expropriated from the producers. They did not suffer, but benefited from the present system. Co-operation could only become a real possibility once the people had obtained their political rights. Such a position was explicitly stated around the same time by Henry Hetherington, commenting on Owen's scheme 'to employ beneficially and educate usefully, all who are unemployed and uneducated in the British Empire', launched with a panoply of appeals to the titled and respectable at the Royal Bazaar in Gray's Inn Road:

The Chronicle thinks that the *views* of the Society are too Utopian to be realised. – Quite the reverse they are essentially practicable and beneficial, if the people had a free stage and no favour. When the people have EQUAL RIGHTS, and their consequent EQUAL LAWS, the superiority of Mr Owen's principles will admit of demonstration, but not till then. To attempt to establish even partially, upon independent grounds, any of Mr Owen's philanthropic views in the present state of the country, and before the working classes are politically emancipated, is only putting the cart before the horse, and will end in an abortion . . . It is quite clear that the Association cannot be popular with honest working men with a grain of sense in their heads, as all the public robbers of the country, from the king downwards, are requested to afford it protection.[89]

Thus Owenism entered the strategy of the NUWC, so far as it did so, not only subordinated to the demand for universal suffrage, but also to the radical analysis which underlay it.

A different test case is that provided by an analysis of the position expressed in the *Crisis* and the *Pioneer*, the official papers of the Builders' Union and the GNCTU in the upsurge of 1833–4. These journals have been held to represent a 'syndicalist' Owenite alternative to radicalism, with the implication of a society divided between classes in economic rather than political terms. Both journals pushed for the

[88] *Poor Man's Guardian*, 24 Dec. 1831.
[89] Ibid.

strategy of one large union and, during the period of mounting trade union repression in 1834, advocated a general strike as the only means of eliminating competition and securing the triumph of 'regeneration' and co-operative production. It is certainly true that both the *Crisis* and the *Pioneer* developed a strikingly non-constitutionalist definition of universal suffrage. According to Smith of the *Crisis*, for instance:

The immediate consequences of any attempt to crush the efforts of the popular mind at this present juncture will be a most resolute determination on the part of the people to legislate for themselves. This will be the result. We have never yet had a House of Commons. The only House of Commons is a House of Trades, and that is only just beginning to be formed.[90]

But, despite this substantial difference in strategy, the analysis of the divide between the 'working classes' and its oppressors was not very different from that to be found in the working-class radical press. The *Pioneer*, for instance, divided society into agriculturalists, manufacturers, governors and idlers. Present society was characterized by 'vast numbers' who 'live on the produce of the labour of others, whilst they themselves do nothing'. The way to achieve the emancipation of the industrious was 'simply by the union of those who do labour declaring that those who produce nothing shall not consume the produce of others, whilst they themselves do nothing':[91] a perspective not markedly different from the vision of change outlined in Volney's *Ruins of Empire*.[92] Moreover, such a union, at least as it was initially and ideally conceived, was to incorporate both masters and men – such was the plan of membership, for example, of the Builders' Guild of September 1833.[93] In accordance with its Owenite inspiration, the *Pioneer* also considered competition to be the cause of low wages.[94] 'It

90 *Crisis*, 12 April 1834; and see also, *Pioneer*, 31 May and 7 June 1834.
91 *Pioneer*, 5 Oct. 1833.
92 See C. F. Volney, *The Ruins, or A Survey of the Revolutions of Empires* (1881 edn), 52–5.
93 See *Pioneer*, 14 Sept. 1833.
94 At a delegate meeting in London in October 1833, a draft plan for a General Union of the Productive Classes was discussed. In his speech announcing the programme, Owen stated. 'The Members of this Union have discovered that competition in the sale of their productions is the chief and immediate cause of their poverty and degradation, and that they can never overcome either as long as they shall conduct their affairs individually, and in opposition to each other.' *Crisis*, 19 Oct. 1833.

is the bane of the condition of the middle man as well as of the working man; both are set by the ears together to play a savage game of self-destruction, for the benefit of Jews and money-jobbers.'[95] But, unlike the Owenite schema, in which competition was conceived to be the result of ignorance, the *Pioneer* considered that competition was actively encouraged by the idle to benefit themselves. The means by which the idle were able to promote the competitive battle was through their control of money. 'Money alone is the thing which gives the unproductive classes their power over the producer and which enables the idle to abstract from the industrious the fruits of their toil.'[96] It was because of this belief that Morrison, the editor of the *Pioneer*, could conceive the labour exchange and labour note scheme in 1833 as an alternative to the radical strategy of universal suffrage and declare that 'our object is not political'.[97] For, by abstaining from participation in the employment of the circulatory medium devised by the idle and unproductive, the people were armed with a short-cut solution to their oppression. Turning, however, to the origins and causes of this usurped control of money, the *Pioneer* couched its analysis in the same political terms as those of the radicals:

Q. How has it originated that society has become divided into labourers and idlers?
A. In the infancy of society every man exerted himself to supply his own wants and for the common good; but in the process of time one man assumed power over others and compelled others to keep him in idleness; and thus the natural state of society was destroyed.
Q. Was this the case in Britain?
A. It was – A vile plunderer (called William the Conqueror) about 1000 years ago overran Britain and divided the soil amongst his followers; and they in succession to the present time have found the labouring class to supply their wants.[98]

Finally, if it cannot be maintained that the *Pioneer* signified a fundamental breach with radicalism in the direction of

---

[95] *Pioneer*, 23 Nov. 1833.
[96] Ibid., 30 Nov. 1833.
[97] Ibid., 12 Oct. 1833.
[98] Ibid., 5 Oct. 1833.

syndicalism or social democracy, there still remains the phenomenon which historians have incorrectly termed 'Ricardian socialism' and the arguments that were either thought to derive from it or developed in parallel with it in some sectors of the post-1830 radical press.[99] Here if anywhere, one might assume, there emerged forms of argument which articulated an independently developing working-class conception of capitalism and exploitation in the years between Peterloo and Chartism. For in the work of Hodgskin, Gray, Thompson and Bray and in the analyses sometimes found in the *Poor Man's Guardian* and the *Northern Star*, the older radical focus on 'kingcraft and priestcraft', and upon taxation as the main source of oppression, gave way to attacks upon capitalists, property and the middle class. Older histories of socialism connected the emergence of this 'Ricardian socialist' theory with a period in which, 'Great Britain cast off its agricultural character and passed over to industrialism on a large scale.'[100] Hodgskin's proposition that 'not rent, but the compound interest of the capitalist keeps the labourer poor' could thus be taken as a corresponding breakthrough to a class-based theory of exploitation, no longer simply comparing what labour produced with what it consumed, but comparing the value and rewards of labour with the value and rewards of the employer, and thus disrupting or transcending the radical conception of the productive classes. There has been some dispute about the extent to which this 'new analysis' displaced the assumptions of the older radical platform dating from around 1819.[101] There are also those who are sceptical about the extent to which the new political stance of the 1830s could have derived from working-class reading of 'Ricardian socialist' literature.[102] They substitute for the impact of 'Ricardian

---

[99] See H. S. Foxwell, 'Introduction' in Anton Menger, *The Right to the Whole Produce of Labour* (1899); E. Lowenthal, *The Ricardian Socialists*, New York (1911); M. Beer, *A History of British Socialism*, 2 vols. (1919); G. D. H. Cole, *Socialist Thought, The Forerunners 1789–1850* (1967).

[100] Beer, *British Socialism*, vol. 1, 283.

[101] See Hollis, *Pauper Press*, Ch. VII.

[102] This difficulty arises partly from disagreements about the reliability of Francis Place. Place wrote of Owen and Hodgskin, 'the present mischief these two men have in some respects done is incalculable'. Older historians of this period tended to accept Place's picture, without criticism. According to Hovell, for instance, 'the new Unionism

socialism' the implicit hypothesis that it was the logic of events that pushed working-class radicals in a social democratic direction. The concept of the general strike, for instance, while originating in a purely radical framework around 1831–2, is thought to have developed into a more recognizable proletarian industrial strategy as a result of employer and state hostility to trade union aspirations in 1834.

All these interpretations, however, underestimate the basic similarities between the 'old' analysis and the 'new', and the basic continuity of the radical political position. If we scrutinize the picture of the capitalist and the process of unequal exchange, both as it was developed in so-called 'Ricardian socialist' literature and as it was expressed in the press, it will be possible to see why the focus on capital and capitalists neither disturbed basic radical assumptions, nor sanctioned a class hostility towards the employer, but rather, if anything, reinforced hostility to the traditional radical foes, the landlords and the money lords. We may begin by examining the position of Thomas Hodgskin, since his analysis – that of a neo-Godwinite rather than an orthodox political radical – can be taken as a limit case of new conceptions of 'capitalist' exploitation in the 1820s and 1830s, and because it has sometimes been regarded as a prime source of an alternative 'working-class political economy' which allegedly developed after 1832.[103]

In fact, Hodgskin's conception of 'capitalist' exploitation has nothing specific to say about the form of exploitation associated with industrial capitalism, nor can it be said to engage in any serious way with the economic reasoning of Ricardo. His picture of the 'capitalist' was of a middleman:

Betwixt him who produces food and him who produces clothing, betwixt him who makes instruments and him who uses them, in steps the capitalist,

derived its economics from Hodgskin and its inspiration from Robert Owen' (Hovell, *The Chartist Movement*, 45). Prothero argues, however, that Place had particular reasons to exaggerate the importance of Hodgskin and Owen, and therefore that his assessment of their impact upon the views of working men should be treated sceptically. See Prothero, *Artisans*, 208 and Ch. 10 *passim*. But Hodgskinite views certainly found their way into the *Poor Man's Guardian* through the medium of O'Brien.

[103] See on Hodgskin, E. Halévy, *Thomas Hodgskin*, trans. A. J. Taylor (1956).

who neither makes nor uses them and appropriates to himself the produce of both. With as niggard a hand as possible he transfers to each a part of the produce of the other, keeping to himself the larger share. Gradually and successfully has he insinuated himself betwixt them, expanding in bulk as he has been nourished by their increasingly productive labours, and separating them so widely from each other that neither can see whence that supply is drawn which each receives through the capitalist. While he despoils both, so completely does he exclude one from the view of the other that both believe they are endebted to him for subsistence. He is the middleman of all labourers.[104]

How then did the capitalist come into possession of this power? Since as a follower of Locke and Adam Smith, viewed through the eyes of Godwin, Hodgskin regarded production as a natural process and nature to be harmonious, the source of unequal exchange was to be sought not in the economic process itself, but in artificial laws and political power.[105] The condition of the labourer was in fact to be attributed to a divergence between the natural and artificial rights to property. 'Property itself', wrote Hodgskin, 'or man's right to the free use of his own mind and limbs, and to appropriate whatever he creates by his own labour, is the result of natural laws.'[106] Nature provides man with a given object in exchange for a certain quantity of labour: this is the real or natural price of an object. The capitalist, however, to surrender the same object to the labourer, demands from him, in addition to the quantity exacted by nature, a still greater quantity of labour.[107] The ability of the capitalist to extract this extra labour is derived from his possession of property — for circulating capital is nothing but the power to command the labour of another man. This property of the capitalist was defined as 'the privilege given him by the laws of society to which he belongs, of deducting a portion of the produce of labour'.[108] Since the laws of nature are benevolent, there is a natural tendency for knowledge and productive power to

---

[104] Hodgskin, *Labour Defended*, 71–2.
[105] For Hodgskin's reading of Locke, see T. Hodgskin, *The Natural and Artificial Right of Property Contrasted* (1832), 11–27 and *passim*.
[106] T. Hodgskin, *Popular Political Economy* (1827), 236.
[107] Hodgskin, *Labour Defended*, 75.
[108] Halévy, *Thomas Hodgskin*, 101.

outstrip population. Poverty is therefore not the result of nature, but the artificial law-maintained monopolization of property. Thus, although there is a natural increase of productivity and men should have to work less, the capitalist, through his control of the law, pockets all the increase in productivity for himself, and gives to the labourer no more than a subsistence wage. The laws which sustain the capitalist are the work of those who first obtained a monopoly of power, men 'who had no profession but war and knew no trade but robbery and pillage'.[109] In the original state of European society, the natural progress of agriculture had meant that the amount of land needed by each individual was growing progressively smaller. But this natural process was interrupted by the invasion of Barbarian hordes, pastoral people who, by right of conquest, divided the soil into larger and more primitive units of ownership.[110] From this date arose the conflict between the natural and legal rights of ownership. Capitalism was the result of conquest and monopolization of the land. 'Mr R. has found labour rewarded in our society as if the labourer were a slave and he has assumed this as his natural condition.'[111]

What should be stressed is that the 'capitalist' was defined solely by his role of parasitic oppressor and, as in William Thompson, despite their important differences, his power is conceived as an extension of the system of force and fraud. Even the owner of fixed capital was simply conceived as a type of usurer who hires out the means of production to labourers at a rate of compound interest. Thus, in one of Hodgskin's examples, over and above the natural cost of production the maker of clothing is conceived as having to pay interest to the owner of the sheep, the buyer of the wool, the owner of the spinning mill, the owner of the weaving shed, the cloth merchant and the master of the tailoring shop.[112] The difference between Hodgskin's position and any later social democratic analysis emerges clearly in his conception of the manufacturer. 'Masters, it is evident', he wrote, 'are *labourers*

---

[109] Ibid., 120; and see Hodgskin, *Natural and Artificial*, 73.
[110] Hodgskin, *Natural and Artificial*, 70–3.
[111] Hodgskin to Place, 28 May 1820, cited in Halévy, *Thomas Hodgskin*, 72.
[112] Hodgskin, *Labour Defended*, 75–6.

as well as their journeymen. In this character their interest is precisely the same as that of their men. But they are also either capitalists or the agents of capitalists, and in this respect their interest is decidedly opposed to the interests of their workmen.'[113] Like John Gray, who included a certain proportion of manufacturers in his 'useful class', Hodgskin conceived the labouring role of the manufacturers to be the useful work of management and supervision. It was only in their role as middlemen, possessing a political monopoly over the exchange system, that they were to be opposed as capitalists. What we have here, therefore, is not a picture of two opposed classes thrown up by a new system of production, in which the role of the employer as manager and controller of the process is a crucial feature of its exploitative character, but rather a harmonious world of production inhabited by masters and men, degraded by the artificial imposition of a political system which sanctions and sustains the extraction of exorbitant interest payments to a purely parasitic class of capitalists who garrison every point of exchange.

In the unstamped and radical press of the 1830s, the stress upon the political domination of the exchange process is equally pronounced. Moreover, the basic constancy of assumption that underlay the differences between the 'old' and the 'new' analyses is suggested by the way in which rents, tithes, interest and profit were all conceived as politically maintained imposts, not separated by any sharp conceptual distinction from the official taxation imposed by the state. The rate of profit, for instance, was conceived not primarily as an index of the state of economic activity, but rather of the extent of the political power of the law-making class. According to 'One of the Know-Nothings' writing in 1831:

I do not say that any individual has the power to increase his profits at pleasure: but I do say that any particular body or class of individuals, having the privilege to make the laws themselves, can increase their profits to any extent they please; and by increasing their own, they must increase the profits of all others in the same line of business with themselves, and as a proof of which, I say again, look at the landholders.[114]

[113] Ibid., 80.
[114] *Poor Man's Guardian*, 24 Dec. 1831.

And, according to another correspondent, writing to the *Poor Man's Guardian* in 1834:

By the term 'remunerating profit' the writer probably means twenty per cent, which is perhaps the ordinary rate of profit on fleeting capital. But he is much mistaken if he imagines that it is so moderate a profit as this which is wanting to create a demand for labour. The true state of things is, that no labourer can yield any profit to his employer who cannot produce commodities three times more valuable than what he consumes. No capitalist can employ labour which will not pay a tax of 200% to the main body of capitalists.[115]

Fair exchange resembled Smith's picture of the aboriginal exchange between the hunter of the beaver and the hunter of the deer in Book II of the *Wealth of Nations*, in which each received in exchange an equivalence in labour expended. The natural right to the fruits of labour could be derived from Locke's *Second Treatise*.[116] The difference between equitable

---

[115] Ibid., 30 Aug. 1834.

[116] 'Read Paine, Locke, Puffendorf, and a host of others and they will tell you that labour is the only genuine property', O'Brien, *True Scotsman*, 6 July 1839; see especially, J. Locke, *Second Treatise on Government*, Ch. 5. The appeal of Locke to late eighteenth and early nineteenth century radicals is difficult to reconcile with the picture of his thought as a legitimation of specifically capitalist property relations, as it is presented in C. B. MacPherson, *The Political Theory of Possessive Individualism*, Oxford (1962). It is much easier to understand if Locke's theory is situated instead in a puritan, scriptural and natural law context, see J. Dunn, *The Political Thought of John Locke*, Cambridge (1969). The best single discussion of Locke's labour theory of property is to be found in J. Tully, *A Discourse on Property*, Cambridge (1980), which strongly reinforces this latter position; on the preceding history of natural rights theories, see R. Tuck, *Natural Rights Theories*, Cambridge (1979); for an examination and explanation of the general lack of serious interest in Locke's theory of political obligation before the 1760s, see J. Dunn, 'The Politics of Locke in England and America in the Eighteenth Century', in J. Dunn, *Political Obligation in its Historical Context*, Cambridge (1980), 53–81. The process by which Locke's labour theory of property came in the course of the eighteenth century to be employed as a radical axiom still remains fully to be researched. It seems that the possibilities of a radical interpretation of the text were not appreciated, or at least not prominently exploited, before the 1760s and 1770s. Locke's conception of the land as originally the common property of mankind was appealed to by Spence. The use of Locke specifically to defend the labourer's right to his produce and an explanation of the pauperization of labour as a consequence of the usurpation of this right is to be found in J. Thelwall, *The Rights of Nature Against the Usurpations of Establishments* (1796). The connections between Locke's theory and early nineteenth century radicalism are briefly touched upon in C. H. Driver, 'John Locke', in F. J. C. Hearnshaw (ed.), *The Social and Political Ideas of Some English Thinkers of the Augustan Age 1650–1750* (1928); see also I. Hampshire Monk, 'Thelwall's Critique of England', Unpublished MS (1980).

exchange and the present state of affairs was ascribable to political monopoly:

The object and right of the labourer is to get an equivalent for his labour, alias the full value of his produce in money. Whatever prevents him getting this value is, *to him*, robbery. The important question to him then is, what is it that prevents his getting that value? The answer is (and there is but one) the INSTITUTIONS OF THE COUNTRY. These institutions give one portion of his earnings to the landlord, another to the parson, a third to the tax gatherer, a fourth to the lawyer, a fifth to the money lender, a sixth to the man of income (not included in the preceding classes) and a seventh (which is by far the largest share) to the capitalist – alias, to the parties who grow rich by setting him to work for them, or by exchanging and selling his produce. Now, whatever is given to, or rather taken by, these parties, beyond a fair equivalent for their respective services, is *to him* (the labourer) so much downright robbery.[117]

One way – sometimes, as in the *Pioneer*, the main way – in which the natural reciprocity of exchanges was conceived to have been subverted by monopoly political power, was through the introduction of money as a general medium of exchange. Money permitted the accumulation of unconsumed surplus wealth, it was controlled by the law-making class, it was manipulable and it facilitated the official or unofficial taxation of every exchange transaction at the expense of the producers. Thus, while for Ricardo, commodities did exchange in the long run according to the amount of labour necessary to produce them, for radicals price formation was a politically determined phenomenon in which the relationship between value and price was, in economic terms, arbitrary. According to O'Connor, for instance, speaking in 1839:

The majority of the middle classes live, not upon trade, not upon fair dealing, but upon the fictitious prices which the taxes allow them to charge for their commodities. The small shopkeepers and all persons with small and especially real capital, are equally with the operatives, oppressed by taxation; but pride as yet has induced them to prefer their social distinction to political improvement.[118]

Or, as Shelley had put it:

---

[117] *Poor Man's Guardian*, 14 Feb. 1835.
[118] *Northern Star*, 8 June 1839.

> Paper coin – that forgery
> Of the title deeds which ye
> Hold to something of the worth
> Of the inheritance of the earth.[119]

The political domination of the exchange process had also led to the warped development of the division of labour itself. Frequently stressed by those radicals who had adopted some of the emphases of Owenism, was the creation by the system of an unnecessary proliferation of 'distributors' who interposed themselves between the direct producers of useful goods. O'Brien, for instance, looked back to a time:

when profits were little more than a fair remuneration for the time, skill and superintending care of the master – and when there were certain great annual fairs in various parts of the country, to which the producer used to take his produce direct, and sell it himself instead of selling his labour to an employer who sells it again to the factor or merchant who sells it again to the retailer and so on till it reaches the consumer, with an accumulation of profits upon it far greater than the original cost of the manufactured article.[120]

For, as the *Poor Man's Guardian* put it in 1831:

The present mode of making the distributors the employers and the producers the employed is an inversion of the natural order of things, and is equally injurious to the consumer and the producers. Its consequence is that the labour of the producers is made an article of commerce, and as such liable to all the consequences of competition.[121]

Or again in 1833:

The exchange and distribution of wealth, which, intrinsically, is only a secondary employment, is made of the highest importance, while the production of it which is first in consequence, as it is in the order of nature, is rendered the least profitable, the most laborious and consequently the most degraded in public estimation.[122]

Universal suffrage, it continued, would abolish mere consumers and reduce exchangers to one-tenth of their present number. Indeed, in the most extreme version of this position,

---

[119] Shelley, *Queen Mab*.
[120] *Northern Star*, 28 July 1838.
[121] *Poor Man's Guardian*, 17 Sept. 1831.
[122] Ibid., 23 Nov. 1833.

it might transform distributors into the salaried assistants of co-operatives of the producers.[123]

This Owenite and co-operative stress upon the evils of the distributive system certainly contributed something to the composite image of the 'shopocrat' that emerged in post-1830 radicalism. In co-operative literature itself, the multiplication of shopkeepers and retailers was treated as a symbol of the competitive irrationality of society. According to John Gray:

Certain it is, that these men are not unproductive, for never, upon the face of the earth, was there anything half so productive of deception and falsehood, folly and extravagance, slavery of the corporeal and prostitution of the intellectual faculties of man, as the present system of retail trade ... And that they do not give to society an equivalent for which they consume is certain. A fourth or fifth part of their time is expended in decorating their shopwindows, that is in spoiling goods, and at least half of it in waiting about for their customers, or doing nothing useful. If any man will walk through London streets and use his eyes, he will want no arguments to convince him, that there are, at least two thirds more of this class than there is any necessity for ... How much longer will mankind be so wilfully blind as not to know that all trades people from the merchant to the apple woman, are mere *distributors of wealth, who are paid for their trouble by the labour of those who create it?*[124]

These evils of the distribution system were intimately linked to the distortion of the division of labour, once geared to meet the meretricious needs of the idle consumer. As Gray again put it:

Are we for ever to be told, that the man who is spending thousands in the gratification of some absurd whim, is doing good, because he circulates money amongst tradesmen, and because he furnishes employment for a number of labouring men? Every labouring man so employed, is a useless member of society, for the produce of his labour is useless; and the effect is a direct tax on the productive labourer usefully employed.[125]

Radicals, unlike Owenites, were more circumspect in their attitudes to shopkeepers. As in their reaction to competition, it was not the existence of the private retailer as such, but rather the undue preponderance of retailers – the product of the 'cannibalism of artificial society' – that was the object of their critique. The point of convergence between radicals and

---

[123] A position stated in W. Thompson, *Inquiry into the Principles of the Distribution of Wealth Most Conducive to Human Happiness* (1824), 167. This ideal was espoused on a number of occasions in the *Poor Man's Guardian*, see, for instance, 31 Aug. 1833.

[124] Gray, *Human Happiness*, 26–7.

[125] Ibid., 30.

Owenites in this area lay mainly in the critique of luxury and the luxury trade.[126] There was, however, little that was novel in this stance. Praise of simplicity of wants and condemnation of the spendthrift opulence of urban, monied society had been a well-worn theme of eighteenth century country sentiment. The accentuation of such notions in radicalism and 'Ricardian socialism' suggests, once again, the inappositeness of conceiving the positions developed there as components of an alternative or specifically working-class political economy. A theory of the emergence and dynamics of commercial society – the presupposition of a systematic political economy – differed in kind from an ethical or political critique of commercial society in the name of natural right or a rationalistic evaluation of needs. For the only position which could eventually be formalized into a political economy was that most notoriously dramatized by Mandeville's *Fable of the Bees*, premissed upon the acceptance, however ironical, of the randomness of the growth of needs associated with the development of the division of labour and the displacement of customary by fashion-oriented consumption. Thus, in Adam Smith's work, the development of the luxury trade played a crucial part in the breakdown of feudal society and its replacement by an economy based upon free labour.[127] For radicals and Owenites, on the other hand, the growth of luxury and the proliferation of middlemen was simply a symptom of the unnatural state of society and the artificiality of its wants.[128] Therefore, while they endorsed the progress of arts and manufactures, which the development of the division of labour had engendered, they put political domination or ignorance in the place of the unseen hand and envisaged a society in which, once these distortions had been removed, a

---

[126] See, for instance, for a characteristic position, *The Associate*, March 1829. 'Expensive luxuries (which have the effect of enlarging cupidity and diminishing our sympathies with others) will ... cease to be created when the producers of them shall have to weigh the trouble of producing them against the pleasure of displaying them in their own persons.' [I am grateful to Greg Claeys for this reference.]

[127] A. Smith, *The Wealth of Nations*, E. Cannan (ed.), Chicago (1976), Book III.

[128] Animus against 'factitious wants' and luxuries was the predominant form of approach to the question of needs in the radical and Owenite press, but not consistently or universally so. See, for instance, *Trades' Newspaper*, 28 Jan. 1827, for a defence of the unlimited character of desire and hence need.

high level of productive development might coexist in harmony with the primitive equity that had characterized the barter exchange between the hunter of the beaver and the hunter of the deer.

All this should help to explain why, for theorists of 'unequal exchange' and spokesmen of the new form of radicalism in the unstamped press, the fundamental conflict was not between employers and employed, but between the working classes and the idle classes. As the *Poor Man's Guardian* stated in 1833:

There are two great parties in the state – two great moving principles ... These parties are, 1 – those that are willing to work; and 2 – those that are not. The principles are labour and capital.[129]

The employer, like the shopkeeper, was subsumed under the category of the middleman. He literally occupied a middle or intermediate position between the labouring producer and the idle consumer and was subject to the conflicting pressures of both. As a middleman, whose interest was to buy cheap and sell dear, he certainly took up a position alongside other oppressors, but more as lackey than as controller of the system. He was thus attacked not as the ultimate beneficiary, but rather as the willing complier in the tyrannical rule of property. The 'Political Corrector' provided a characteristic picture of his role in the newer form of radicalism:

When the farmer sells his corn; instead of paying money to his workmen for doing the work, as he ought to do, he gives it to the idlers in the name of rent, tithe, usury, toll or retains it himself in the name of profit. The master in every useful branch of manufacture acts upon the same principle with the money he obtains for the produce of his workmen.[130]

And the point was made more explicitly by the *Poor Man's Guardian* in 1835:

The grand point to understand is this – that the tendency of the present system is to give the proprietors of *land* and *money* – of money especially – unlimited control over the productive power of the country. Under this system the producer receives not what he earns – not the equivalent of his

---

[129] *Poor Man's Guardian*, 3 Aug. 1833; cf. Hodgskin's remark: 'The contest now appears to be between masters and journeymen, or between one species of labour and another, but it will soon be displayed in its proper characters; and will stand confessed a war of honest industry against idle profligacy which has so long ruled the affairs of the political world with undisputed authority.' *Labour Defended*, 103–4.

[130] *Poor Man's Guardian*, 22 Feb. 1834.

services – not the value of his produce in money or other produce – but what these parties choose to give him. If he produces a pound's worth of goods, he does not receive a pound, or a pound's worth of other goods in exchange, as he ought to do, but only what his employer can induce him to take in preference to starving ... Not that his employer pockets the rest. We know that in the majority of cases he does not – nay, that he often gets less than the producer himself. But, then, in such cases the wealth is received by other parties, who claim it as rent, tithe, pension, annuity, or some such form ... As the employer, and the other parties alluded to, make the institutions by which this distribution is made, it is manifest that, inasmuch as they profit by them, they can have no interest in changing them.[131]

This conception of the employer as the middleman between the two principal contending classes is well illustrated by the discussion of the strategy of a general strike in 1834. Historians have rightly noted the novelty of the suggestion of a general strike mounted by trade unions – rather than simply the industrious classes, as in Benbow's original formulation. But it is also important to note the continuity of the radical conception that underlay it.[132] 'The capitalists will never increase wages except through fear of the physical force of the labourers', wrote a correspondent to the *Poor Man's Guardian*, 'let there be a universal strike for some minimum of wages in every trade'.[133] The rationale of this position, beyond the improvement of the position of the producer himself, was not the destruction of the class power of employers, but rather to strike a blow against the propertied idlers and their state. Either, it was thought that the result would be a rise in prices that would hit the idle consumer rather than the working classes or, it could be argued:

High wages involves low rents, low rates, low profits, low usury, low taxes, low everything that is levied on industry. Take for instance the agricultural labourer. You cannot raise *his* wages without reducing the farmer's profits. Do this and you compel the farmer to mulct the landlord and parson of a part of their rent and tithe; and these being reduced, it is plain the tax gatherer must go without a portion of his taxes. Thus to raise wages is to lower rents, tithes, taxes and every other impost on labour.[134]

Like the labour note scheme, this proposal clearly represented

[131] Ibid., 25 July 1835.
[132] See, for example, Prothero, 'Benbow', 166–71.
[133] *Poor Man's Guardian*, 30 Aug. 1834.
[134] Ibid., 22 Feb. 1834.

an alternative to the orthodox radical strategy, but like that scheme it operated within the same set of assumptions about the nature of power and class relations. It was therefore not difficult for radicals to reject the argument. 'How can we overthrow the present system?', wrote the *Poor Man's Guardian* immediately after the trade union demonstration against the Tolpuddle verdict. 'We say by employing the organization of the Unions to carry universal suffrage.' And it went on:

With the present system, the masters *could* not if they would, and *would* not if they could increase the wages of the men, for so unnatural is the position in which competition has placed them, that they cannot as a body do justice to the men, without doing injury to themselves. Thousands of employers can barely exist at the present rate of profits. Affect these profits by ever so slight an increase of wages, and they are ruined.[135]

On the other hand, it concluded, the master had no comparable reason to refuse universal suffrage. 'He can have no objection to urge against the labourer's enfranchisement, that is not founded upon ignorance and fraud.'[136]

The employer, like other middlemen, was criticized in this newer form of radicalism not on account of his economic role, but for his political beliefs and social attitudes. As Hetherington wrote:

No individual is blameable for accumulating all he can earn as employer, shopkeeper, pawnbroker, or otherwise, so long as the present system endures. That system leaves an individual no choice but to *live by it* or die.
    At all events, it leaves him no alternative but that of enslaving others or being a slave himself. The guilt, then, is not in living *by* the system or *according to it* – it is in supporting it.[137]

It was therefore quite consistent that the attitude of the radicals to employers, middlemen and the middle classes in general should fluctuate according to the attitude of the middle classes to the demands of the people. Now that the middle classes were enfranchised, their attitudes could reasonably be inferred from the actions of the legislature. The question therefore, for post-1832 radicals and later for the Chartists, was not how to overturn the middle classes, but

---

[135] Ibid., 26 April 1834.
[136] Ibid.
[137] Ibid., 14 Feb. 1835.

rather why, in the prevailing conditions, the middle classes did not support the demands of the people and how they could be persuaded or forced to do so. If the middle classes were not to be trusted, it was because their political actions demonstrated their base selfishness. As the *Poor Man's Guardian* noted in April 1833: 'Since their accession to the franchises conferred by the Reform Bill, the middle classes thought only of themselves ... the experience of the last three months convinces us that the spirit in which they desire to exercise the franchise is as exclusively selfish as the aristocratic spirit which gave them a monopoly of it was arbitrary and unjust.'[138] And this had been demonstrated by their narrow interest in house and window taxes, triennial parliaments and the ballot in contrast to their silence about taxes on bread, malt, hops, tobacco, sugar, glass, spirits and the newspaper stamp.

The reason for their debility and baseness related to the artificial position of the middleman in the property-dominated political system. Writing in the aftermath of the passing of measures for Irish coercion by the middle-class legislature, the *Poor Man's Guardian* gave the following characterization of their position:

Even the shopkeepers and master manufacturers, amounting (with their dependents) to more than six millions of the population, are more or less interested in the system – their business being to buy labour *cheap* from the poor, and sell it *dear* to the aristocracy, they are immediately dependent on the latter for support. Besides, taken as a body they are the basis of society, occupying an intermediate position between the workman and the aristocrat – employing the one and being employed by the other, they insensibly contract the vices of both tyrant and slave; tyrants to those below them – sycophants to those above them – and usurers from necessity and habit – they prey on the weakness of the workman, while they extort all they can from the vanity of the aristocrat. Indeed, the middle classes are the destroyers of liberty and happiness in all countries. It is their interest (under the present form of society) that the poor should be weak and the rich extravagant and vain; and this being the case, the man who expects from them any real opposition to despotism, from inclination, must be a fool or a madman.[139]

It was for the same sorts of reasons that 'PC' considered that 'the master of every useful working man is the greatest tyrant that man has to contend with':

[138] Ibid., 6 April 1833.
[139] Ibid., 23 March 1833.

He readily accedes to, and gives it to the idlers without a murmur, at the same time he calls in the aid of the constable, the police, the military and the law, to suppress the just demands of his workmen ... Why does he not resist the idlers instead of his workmen? Why the reason is this – because in giving the money to those idlers who have no right to it, he thereby obtains their sanction and protection in keeping in the name of *profit* much more than he has a right to himself, and of accumulating that profit into what he calls *property*, which soon enables him to become an *idler*, and live on rent and usury.[140]

But such attacks, based as they were upon inferences from middle-class political behaviour, could always in the light of changing evidence be contested within the radical framework. Allen Davenport, objecting to the attack in the *Poor Man's Guardian* upon middlemen, pointed to their support of the people, in the case of the Calthorp Street jury:

Had you launched your thunder against the great capitalist, and monopol-isers of every description, whether shopholders, fund-holders, landholders, or church-holders, I should have liked the article better; but your indiscriminate attack on the whole body of shopkeepers is badly timed, to say the least of it ... It appears to me that men act nearly alike under the same circumstances; therefore, as we cannot create a new race of men, we had better direct our efforts towards creating new circumstances.[141]

The radical position in relation to the middle classes was less inconsequential than is sometimes thought. There was general agreement that, given their contradictory position involving both servility and tyranny, the middle classes as a whole would only support the claims of the people when pressured by necessity. This was not a new discovery of the post-1832 period. As Cobbett recalled, 'hundreds of times did I tell major Cartwright that there never would be Reform to any extent as long as the paper money system remained unshaken', and he attributed the reform agitation of the Birmingham middle class to the pressure upon prices and credit resulting from Peel's resumption of cash payments in 1819.[142] The attempt to create such pressure remained a consistent radical strategy in the post-1832 and Chartist period. The predominant image of the middle classes was of a timid and fearful, as well as petty-tyrannical group, who

---

[140] Ibid., 1 March 1834.
[141] Ibid., 24 Aug. 1833.
[142] From Cobbett's *Register*, cited in *Poor Man's Guardian*, 29 Oct. 1831.

would only ally with the people out of necessity or expediency. Their natural sympathies within the prevailing artificial system lay with property and they themselves were thought to aspire to become idlers. To combat this situation, therefore, the *Poor Man's Guardian* thought that 'the democratic spirit' must be pushed 'upwards', as the 'aristocratic principle' was now pushed 'downwards'.[143] Moreover, the middle class, as the radicals conceived it, was not only amenable to pressure, it was already a split class:

The force of society is in their hands. They have the press – the house of Commons – the capital of the country – the weight of opinion – unlimited means of combination – in short the whole artillery of society. So irresistible is their power, that were they to act unitedly, destruction would be inevitable for any individual who would wag a jaw against them. Fortunately, however, they are not united; for, independently of their mutually conflicting interests, a large portion of them depend entirely on the custom or patronage of the poor, and another considerable portion are governed by humane feelings in despite of their selfish interests. These two portions, acting with the intelligent part of the working classes, offer a considerable counterpoise to the rest of their body, which is nevertheless a decided majority of the whole.[144]

This in turn was why radicals and Chartists, while supporting exclusive dealing, tended to oppose combined trade union action to secure higher wages rather than political change. Reflecting on trade union activity in 1834, the *Poor Man's Guardian* wrote:

You could easily, for instance, convince the clerk in a counting house with only £30 or £40 a year, that he might have a much better reward for his time and labour under institutions which did not bestow the rewards of industry upon aristocratic idlers or accumulating usurers; but you could never show him any advantage was to be gained by having the price of shoes and clothes, and bread, raised upon him by combinations to raise wages while no similar raise was to take place in his own. The trades began at the wrong end. They began by arousing against themselves the class that immediately pressed upon them, intead of involving the aid of that class against those laws and institutions which made both poor for the benefit of the aristocracy – landed and commercial. Almost all the small shopkeepers and small masters could be easily taught that they have a decided, an exalted and enduring interest in the changes, which we of the *Guardian* seek.[145]

---

[143] *Poor Man's Guardian*, 25 Oct. 1834.
[144] Ibid., 11 July 1835.
[145] Ibid., 30 May 1835.

This attempt to draw in the middle classes through threat or persuasion did not basically change during the Chartist period. In the light of the experience of the 1830s and as the depression deepened from 1837, the suspicion and indignation against the middle classes increased. All their basest characteristics within the existing system had been amply confirmed. But since the fundamental assumptions remained unchanged, the proneness to courting, threatening or ignoring the middle classes fluctuated according to the political situation, rather than moving in a unilinear direction.

Thus, after the withdrawal of the Birmingham middle-class leaders from the Convention in 1839, ostensibly in the face of the prospect of 'ulterior measures', O'Connor noted, 'the first note of the retreat of the timid middle classes, who, believe me, never intended joining you upon the question of universal suffrage without the understanding that they should say "thus shalt thou go and no further"'.[146] Anger was expressed at the middle-class desertion, all their basest qualities were paraded and the intrinsic difficulties of an alliance between 'the men who buy cheap and sell dear' and 'the men who sell cheap and buy dear' were emphasized. Already, at the end of 1838, O'Connor had stated his determination not to moderate the agitation at the behest of the 'money mongers' who considered the movement was going too far: 'Guard yourselves my friends, against all men who would attempt to throw dissension among you. I commence this battle with the fustian coats, unshorn chins and blistered hands.'[147] But this should not be regarded as an abandonment of the radical strategy; it was rather an attempt to pressurize the legislature by 'a strong portrayal of your moral power' on the part of the unrepresented working classes. As he told O'Connell in June 1839:

We do *not* exclude the middle classes from our ranks, but on the contrary we court them. The middle classes have *not* the same interests in good and cheap government that the operatives have; because the middle classes, many of them, live by bad, and prosper by dear government. The middle classes are the authors of all those sufferings which *they* experience at the hands of the aristocracy, while they are also the authors of all the miseries which the working classes experience from the middle classes, from the

[146] *Northern Star*, 30 March 1839.
[147] Ibid., 29 Dec. 1838.

aristocracy and dear and bad government; because the government emanates from a majority of the middle classes, and therefore we must look upon them as the authors of their own misery.[148]

The problem, as he told Chartists, was 'that they have no inheritance save in your labour, and they are not sufficiently sagacious to discover that upon your independence depends their prosperity'.[149] After the failure of the Convention and the ultra-radical plans of the summer and autumn of 1839, different tactics were tried. McDouall came out of prison in 1840 stating that 'nothing had been gained by attacking the middle classes';[150] O'Brien similarly moved to a more conciliatory strategy, after having stated in 1839 that 'the middle classes are not your friends. They never will be your friends as long as the present commercial system endures.'[151] O'Connor and most of the Chartist leadership backed the Conservatives in the 1841 election as another means of bringing pressure upon the middle classes by helping to throw out the Whigs.[152] Similarly the difficulties surrounding the possibilities of allying with Sturge and the Complete Suffrage Union in 1842 concerned not the desirability of attracting middle-class support, but agreeing the terms upon which it could be based. True middle-class friends of universal suffrage would declare for the Charter and, in the light of the political record of political organizations like the BPU and the Anti-Corn-Law League, any proposal to merge Chartism behind a middle-class organization was bound to meet with resistance. But ambition to recruit the middle classes to the standard of the Charter when times were propitious was not abandoned and in 1847–8, O'Connor, McDouall and Ernest Jones once again attempted to mobilize the middle classes against the money-crats.[153]

Undoubtedly, there was a shift of emphasis and imagery in the Chartist period. The campaign over factory slavery, the

---

[148] Ibid., 8 June 1839.
[149] Ibid., 30 March 1839.
[150] Ibid., 22 Aug. 1840.
[151] Ibid., 22 Sept. 1838.
[152] Chartists were only to back Conservative candidates, however, in the last resort, in the absence of any candidate supporting the extension of the suffrage.
[153] See, J. Belcham, 'Fergus O'Connor and the Collapse of the Mass Platform', in Epstein and Thompson, *The Chartist Experience*.

introduction of the New Poor Law in the north, the fate of the handloom weavers and the growth of cyclical and technological unemployment, all raised factory owners to a prominence which they had not possessed in 1832. According to the *Northern Star* in 1839:

The progress of machinery has been so rapid, so unchecked and so self-protecting in its course, that those who have been engaged in the pursuit, have, as if by magic, become the monied aristocracy of the country; and, as our rulers declare for, and our system sanctions a monied franchise as a proof of legislative fitness, it is not to be wondered at if the social rank of the money mongers becomes equal to their possessions; and if ere long we find that general, which has been progressive, namely a complete change of situation between the steam and landed aristocracy of the country.[154]

Similarly McDouall considered:

The factory system originated in robbery and was established in injustice ... The factory masters have destroyed a race of the best and most intelligent class – the handloom weavers ... English society has been so completely undermined and public confidence has been so destroyed by the accursed factory system that a despotic government can introduce any measure, whether poor law or centralisation among them.[155]

Such a position was greatly reinforced by the campaign of radicals of Tory provenance.[156] Summarizing Raynor Stephens' position, Mr Tong of Bury explained why he had been arrested:

It was because Mr Stephens had denounced the present system of government which made virtue a crime and rewarded vice (applause), because he had declared openly and candidly, that the children of the poor ought not to be called out to work long before the sun had risen above the horizon, and ground to dust long after he had set; because he had declared that women ought not to labour at all, but their duties ought to be confined to the household; that little boys ought to play about the country at 'hop, skip and jump' and girls ought to be brought up under the immediate control and instruction of their parents, to be taught to sew, knit, bake and brew, because he said that every Englishman ought to be in possession of as much wages as would make his family comfortable – (hear, hear) because he

[154] *Northern Star*, 16 March 1839; for the range of policies suggested to regulate the advance of machinery, see M. Berg, *The Machinery Question and the Making of Political Economy 1815–1848*, Cambridge (1980), esp. Pt 5.

[155] *Northern Star*, 23 March 1839.

[156] When the interconnections are traced between radicalism and eighteenth century country ideology, points of affinity between Tories like Oastler and leading radicals become easier to understand.

told the tyrants to their teeth that their money was blood money and that God almighty had sworn an oath that he would draw his sword of vengeance and slay the oppressors of the poor (great applause).[157]

The movement of the Chartist period incorporated a much broader cross-section of the working population than that of the early 1830s. It is not surprising that in the light of the experiences and agitations of the 1830s, the factory owners at the end of the 1830s should – in the north – be identified as the main tyrants. The degree of hostility towards this group was evident in the Chartist antagonism towards the Anti-Corn-Law League, which they saw as a diversionary ploy of the manufacturers or a means of intensifying their tyranny, although in fact that League was more characteristically a movement of the lower middle classes.[158] Similarly, the New Poor Law was unilaterally associated with the new industrial middle class, although in fact landowners had been more responsible than employers for getting the Bill through Parliament. And even more sinister schemes were attributed to their inspiration. Referring to the probably satirical ultra-Malthusian pamphlet of 'Marcus' in 1839, Harney told a Derby crowd:

The want of universal suffrage has allowed the horrors of the factory system so long to continue – that bloody system deforming the bodies and debauching the minds of our children. Oh! Ye millowners and factory lords! How will ye answer for the wholesale murders ye have committed – how will ye answer at God's judgement seat for your crimes against humanity ... With the bloody law of Marcus in force only one step more will be wanting to complete the system, and that will be a law to authorise the millowners, the Factory Lords and the shopocracy generally to put you to death when worn out.[159]

As the *Northern Star* put it, writing on factory legislation, in April 1839:

If they (the people), as they easily may, compel the tottering imbeciles who now hold the reins of government to restore their rights of universal suffrage – a parliament so chosen will soon teach these mill devils to dance a very different tune.[160]

[157] *Northern Star*, 16 March 1839.
[158] See V. A. C. Gattrell, 'The Commercial Middle Classes in Manchester 1820–57', Cambridge University Ph.D. (1972).
[159] *Northern Star*, 9 Feb. 1839.
[160] Ibid., 27 April 1839.

There can be no doubt about the intensity of the hostility towards factory owners in 1839, and it spilled over into rage against the middle classes in general, as William Benbow found when he addressed a meeting at Abbey Leigh near Gorton around the same time:

Mr Benbow said – I address myself to the working men, and also the middle class men of Gorton. I do it on the principle that there are good men as working men, and also good men as middle class men (here some in the meeting misunderstood the gentleman, which caused a few interruptions). Gentlemen – allow me, and I will set you right. I do not pretend to say that there are no middle class men who do not seek on all occasions to dock your wages.[161]

But, while the depth and extent of antagonism is not to be questioned, it should not therefore be assumed that the radical analysis that lay behind the Charter was in the course of displacement by a different and more class conscious mode of thought. James Leach, a factory worker, a future leader of the National Charter Association (NCA) and one of the Chartists most concerned with the factory question, addressing the same meeting as Benbow, stated: 'Not a working man in this vast assembly receives more than 5s to the pound of real value – (shame, shame) – the other fifteen are taken from him to support the aristocracy.'[162] The terminology – 'millocrat', 'cotton lord', 'steam aristocracy' – is indicative of some radical uncertainty about how to define factory owners in relation to landlords, money lords and the middle classes. But the belief that they had now displaced the old aristocracy did not weaken the conviction of the political origin and determination of oppression; and if anything it strengthened the idea that the politically enforced expropriation from the land remained the ultimate source of the condition of the working classes and the growing tyranny of the money and factory lords. Not only, as we have seen, were such assertions already being made in the 1820s, but since oppression was to be derived from the usurpation and monopolization of property, rather than a particular form of production, it was quite logical to continue to see the monopolization of land as the

[161] Ibid., 20 April 1839.
[162] Ibid.

prime cause of the misery of the worker, with the monopolization of money and machinery as secondary derivatives. Unlike
profit, which could be justified in moderation as the wages of
supervision, rent and interest were the product of no labour,
and there was therefore no natural right which could justify
them. According to John Gray, for example:

> The earth is the habitation, the natural inheritance of all mankind of ages
> present and to come; a habitation belonging to no man in particular, but to
> every man; and one in which all have an equal right to dwell ... There are
> but three ways in which it is possible to become rightly possessed of
> property. The first is by making it; the second by purchasing it; the third is
> by donation from another, whose property it was. Now it is clear that
> neither our present landowners, nor their ancestors ... can be the
> proprietors of an inch of it.[163]

The chain of reasoning was equally clear to Bray:

> individual possession of the soil has been one cause of inequality of wealth –
> that inequality of wealth necessarily gives rise to inequality of labour – and
> that inequality of wealth and labour and enjoyments, constitute the wrong
> as a whole.[164]

Moreover, although in the newer form of radicalism the
capitalist ownership of machinery was often stressed as the
reason for competition between labourers, low wages and the
existence of 'a reserve corps of labour', it remained true that
the usurpation of their natural rights to cultivate the soil had
made them 'landless' wage slaves in the first place, and that
the resumption of rights to the land would be the most
effective answer to the tyranny of the mill owner. As
O'Connor frequently observed, it was:

> The besetting sin – the great grievance under which the working classes
> labour, namely the living from hand to mouth, and being in a complete state
> of dependency upon their employers and hence the difference between
> English and Irish agitation. If every man had his month's provisions in the
> storehouse (which, with the blessing of God, universal suffrage will give
> him), there would be an end to your sophistry.[165]

Such a position was reinforced in the 1830s by the older

---

[163] Gray, *Human Happiness*, 35.
[164] J. F. Bray, *Labour's Wrongs and Labour's Remedies, or the Age of Might and The Age of Right*, Leeds (1839), 34.
[165] *Northern Star*, 8 June 1839.

critique of landed property made by the Spenceans. The *Northern Star* noted that 'the Spencean doctrine is not only preached, but details for its practical workings are brought prominently to public view'.[166] It connected the resurgence of interest in Spence with what was regarded as a further usurpation of the rights of the poor to a portion of the income from land enacted by the New Poor Law:

The people who never before that Reform Bill seriously canvassed the landlord's title to his share in the land, but who merely complained of his legislatorial interference with that proportion of its produce which belongs to the nation, now discover that so long as the title exists, so long will the prejudicial interference continue.[167]

Spenceans argued against all private property in land, basing their arguments not only upon natural right and biblical foundation but also upon the insistence that the land had historically belonged to the poor and that it had been stolen from them.[168] During the 1840s, the end to the monopolization of the land was in fact the main Chartist solution to the existence of industrial capitalism. According to James Leach:

If they would take away all chance of a working man being enabled to live by his labour as a mechanic, they ought, at least, to give him the means of falling back on the land as a security for liberty and life.[169]

There was no disagreement between O'Connor and more socialistic Chartists about the identification of the land as the centre point of a Chartist social programme. The argument, so far as it was political, was about whether land schemes should be inaugurated before the winning of the Charter, and about whether it should be divided between peasant proprietors or whether as Harney advocated, following the Spenceans, the land was to be the 'people's farm'.[170] Similarly, after 1848, in the period of 'Charter socialism', when Chartists were demanding 'the Charter and something more',

---

[166] Ibid., 16 June 1838.
[167] Ibid.
[168] On Spence and his doctrine, see T. R. Knox, 'Thomas Spence: The Trumpet of Jubilee', *Past and Present*, 76 (1977).
[169] Cited in D. Jones, *Chartism and the Chartists* (1975), 130.
[170] Cited in A. R. Schoyen, *The Chartist Challenge* (1958), 148.

nothing is more striking than the basic continuity of their analysis, despite the change of nomenclature. 'The feudal lords are doomed', wrote Harney:

> But the money-lords are full of life and energy, and resolutely resolved to establish their ascendancy on the ruins of the rule of their once masters, but now perishing rivals ... The feudal lords have scourged the proletarians with whips, but the money lords (if they prosper in their designs) will scourge them with scorpions ... The feudal aristocracy being doomed to expire, care should be taken that no new aristocracy be allowed to take their place. With that view THE LAND MUST BE MADE NATIONAL PROPERTY ... THE LAND BELONGS TO ALL, and the natural right of all is superior to the falsely asserted rights of conquest or purchase.[171]

It will be noticed that even in this last phase of Chartism, and even in a passage where the influence of Marx and Engels is directly detectable, a language of natural right still predominated. It was this language, and its residual but ineradicable individualist presuppositions, which lay at the centre of the English radical conception of classes, providing it with all the force of its militant convictions, but also firmly demarcating its analytical boundaries. Outside Owenism, the labour theory of property was inextricably tied to a theory of natural rights – the natural rights of the producer to his *property*, the fruits of his labour. After the rejection of the second Chartist Petition in May 1842, the *Northern Star* replied to Macaulay's attack in the House of Commons, 'the wretchedness, starvation and fearful despair of the operative classes loudly proclaim that *their property* – their labour and its fruits, are not secured to them, but on the other hand are the common prey of all the legal plunderers of society'.[172] The force and limits of the analysis appear similarly in O'Brien's argument about the land:

> It is assumed that land, mines, rivers &c., are fit and proper subjects of private property, like bales of cloth, pottery wares, or any other product of man's skill and industry; and that accordingly, the works of God's creation may be bought and sold in the market, the same as if they were the works of human hands. This is a principle so utterly abhorrent to common sense and reason – it is on the face of it so great a perversion of natural justice, that the rights of property cannot possibly be reconciled with it, nor coexist for a

[171] (Harney), 'The Charter and Something More', *Democratic Review*, Feb. 1850, 351.
[172] Cited in Schoyen, *The Chartist Challenge*, 117.

moment in the presence of it ... and for this simple reason, because the rights of labour and the rights of property, which ought to be really one and the same, are utterly irreconcilable under such a system.[173]

A thought not so dissimilar from that expressed by Thomas Spence over seventy years before:

> All Men, to Land, may lay an equal Claim;
> But Goods, and Gold, unequal Portions frame;
> The first, because, all Men on Land, must Live;
> The Second's the Reward Industry ought to give.[174]

If the land could be socialized, the national debt liquidated, and the bankers' monopoly control over the supply of money abolished, it was because all these forms of property shared the common characteristic of not being the product of labour. It was for this reason that the feature most strongly picked out in the ruling class was its idleness and parasitism. It was for this reason that Hodgskin, and those who followed him, excluded from condemnation all those features which distinguished the millocrat from the shopocrat. It is striking that, despite the intensity of hostility to the 'steam-producing class' in the Chartist period, no proposal was ever made to take over the mills and expropriate their owners.[175] The most that was proposed was that fixed capital should be purchased by the producers and paid in the form of labour bonds, and even this proposal – by Bray – remained strictly within the terms of the labour theory:

If a working man pay gold to a capitalist, or one capitalist pay gold to another, he merely gives a representative of the things which labour *has produced* – if he give a bond to pay at a future time, he merely promises to pay what Labour *will produce*. The past, the present and the future transactions of Capital all depend on Labour for their fulfilment. Such being the case, why should not Labour itself make a purchase?[176]

Compulsory purchase or even expropriation was the deserved fate of the *rentier*, the necessity to labour was to be the just deserts of the idler, henceforth the 'drones' would have to work as hard as the 'bees'. But high wages, short hours, a tax

[173] J. B. O'Brien, *The Rise, Progress and Phases of Human Slavery* (1885), 127–8.
[174] Cited in Knox, *Thomas Spence*, 87.
[175] For a characterization of the conflict within modern industry during this period, see Ch. 1 in this volume.
[176] Bray, *Labour's Wrongs*, 173.

on machinery and renewed access to land enforced by a democratic government was generally the most that was specifically advocated against the tyranny of the millocrat. Before anything further could be conceived, the whole labour theory based on natural right would have to be jettisoned.

We have attempted to demonstrate the interrelatedness of the presuppositions upon which the Charter could appear to be the remedy for the plight of the working classes in particular and the people in general. The hope that the Charter represented, as we have tried to show, was only comprehensible within the language of radicalism. Chartists could incorporate a discussion about competition and the power of 'capitalists', while still maintaining with Paine that the origins and basis of the system rested on the forces of force and fraud. As the *Poor Man's Guardian* stated, there was no objection to 'Paine's principles', only 'to his remedial measures as a practical reformer'.[177] We are also now in a better position to appreciate the strength of the Chartist position in the second half of the 1830s and to understand why the mounting discontent took a Chartist form. For radicalism was premised upon the active and oppressive role of monopoly political power and the state. The aggressive and interventionist activity of government and Parliament in the 1830s in restructuring institutions and forwarding the competitive system at the expense of the working classes therefore strongly vindicated the radical position. The measures for Irish coercion in 1833 could be seen as a dry run for an assault upon the producers in England. The treatment of the handloom weavers – in which radical and conservative proposals of a minimum wage enforced by trade boards was rejected in favour of leaving the workers to the forces of competition – confirmed the worst fears about a government of middle-men.[178] As the *Northern Star* wrote:

Let the poor handloom weaver bear in mind that the unrestricted use of machinery has thrown him completely out of the market and let those who are yet fortunate enough to be at work recollect that the said handloom

[177] *Poor Man's Guardian*, 14 Feb. 1835.
[178] See P. Richards, 'The State and Early Capitalism: The Case of the Handloom Weavers', *Past and Present*, 83 (1979).

weavers at all times serve as a corps of reserve to be cheaply purchased by the masters and hold those at work in submission.[179]

For, speaking of manufacturers, it went on:

The effect of the Reform Bill has been to throw power into the hands of the possessors of this description of property, and their support of the government is conditional upon the government's support of their claim to the unrestricted use of the labour of the country.[180]

It was for this reason that trade union alternatives to universal suffrage and Owenite schemes of 'regeneration' had foundered. Speaking of 1834, the *Poor Man's Guardian* stated:

The trade unions made an attempt last year to make a very partial change; and what was the consequence? Why they got transported and dispersed for their pains; and that, not satisfied with crushing them for the moment, the middlemen's government has taken effectual measures to prevent their revival again by passing a law to drive all applicants for parish relief into the workhouse or the grave ... We have here at a glance the history of the Dorsetshire convicts and of the murderous Poor Law Amendment Bill. They were both the work of the middle classes, through their tool the reformed Parliament.[181]

The completeness of the failure of the trade unions was also clear to John Bray, writing in 1837:

The capitalist and the employer have ultimately been too strong for them; and the trade unions have become, amongst the enemies of the working class, a bye word of caution or contempt – a record of the weakness of Labour when opposed to Capital – an indestructible memento of the evil working of the present system in regard to the two great classes which now compose society.[182]

The trial of the Glasgow cotton spinners in 1838 drove home the same lesson. It was pointless to expect effective reform when political power remained a monopoly of the propertied. The history of the 1833 Factory Act demonstrated that, and as O'Connor added:

If they were to work six hours a day with their present machinery they would even then have their markets overstocked with goods. It was impossible, therefore, even with a ten hours bill, unless they had the same control over their labour which the agriculturalist had over his produce,

---

[179] *Northern Star*, 23 June 1838.
[180] Ibid.
[181] *Poor Man's Guardian*, 21 March 1835.
[182] Bray, *Labour's Wrongs*, 100.

namely to send it into the markets when the supply was required. In all other instances, people could do this, and the capitalists knowing such was the case, endeavoured to throw their factory labourers out of their position by breaking down trade combinations.[183]

And the same was true *a fortiori* of the repeal of the Corn Laws. Even if the common suspicion that it was designed to lower wages was discounted, the *Northern Star* could still state:

We must repeat that we do not believe the oligarchy would permit even the repeal of the Corn Laws to work well for the community. If heaven were to rain down 'manna' – corn, wine and oil – the privileged class would still find a way to appropriate the bounty to themselves. While the aristocracy hold a monopoly of power, be sure they will never give up, unless nominally and collusively, any monopoly of profit.[184]

Above all, the sequence of legislation and government activity in the 1830s could convincingly be portrayed as forming a system. A tyranny was in process of construction, whose aim was to complete the enslavement of the producer. The advance of machinery and the enactment of the New Poor Law were intimately connected. 'We have repeatedly avowed our conviction', wrote the *Northern Star*:

that the spirit and tendency of this law was to enhance and make permanent the thraldom of the industrious classes by compelling them to give their labour on whatever terms the middle class moneymongers might choose to offer ... Its object and intention is to provide the means of at once sweeping from the face of the earth the shoals of population, which having been made redundant by a monopoly of the productive powers of machinery on the part of the rich, come to be regarded as a pecuniary burden by the villains who have robbed them of the means of independence.[185]

And answering the scepticism of southern radical journals about the vehemence of the Anti-Poor-Law campaign in the north, the *Northern Star* stated that it was not merely opposed to the measure, but saw it as 'the basis of a new constitution':

The auxiliaries of this infernal law are the factory scheme, the rural police, and the complete destruction of trade associations, which is the last remnant of power in the hands of the working classes and by which supply and

---

[183] *Northern Star*, 23 June 1838.
[184] Ibid., 9 Feb. 1839.
[185] Ibid., 3 March 1838.

demand could be wholesomely regulated. If the masters saw their own interests in a true light, they would encourage and not assist in suppressing trade associations.[186]

The great strength of the Charter in 1838–9, therefore, lay in its identification of political power as the source of social oppression, and thus in its ability to concentrate the discontent of the unrepresented working classes upon one common aim. As O'Connor put it, 'the Chartists of the present day, have what the radicals of 1819 had not, unity and a directing energy'.[187] But the great difficulty of radicalism, particularly in its Chartist form, was that the viability of its strategy depended not merely upon the mobilizing of the working classes but of the vast majority of the people. The petition and the 'General Convention of the Industrious Classes' were not premissed upon proletarian politics. They depended for their coherence upon the juxtaposition between the state and its parasitic supporters, landlords, money lords and capitalists on the one hand, and the industrious part of the nation, including a substantial portion of the middle classes, on the other. In other words, something like a repeat of 1832. Most of the 'ulterior measures' proposed in 1839, withdrawal from savings banks, abstention from excisable goods, tax refusal and even 'the sacred month', equally assumed the pressure of the industrious upon the idle. The problem was, however, that even in the radicals' own terms, such a scenario was highly problematic. For not only was there a general radical conviction that the middle class would only join the people when pressured by necessity, but from 1832 onwards the middle classes formed part of the legislative classes and had thus become the authors of the miseries of which the working classes complained. While a portion of middle-class opinion was prepared to support the Chartist Petition, there was no corresponding support for the Convention as a rival legislative body threatening Parliament. Thus, while many Chartist spokesmen remained sanguine in the first half of 1839 that, despite the withdrawal of the Birmingham leaders, 'as sure as the sun had set today, so surely must the middle classes join

---

[186] Ibid., 23 June 1838.
[187] Ibid., 3 Aug. 1839.

the ranks of the people',[188] the mounting evidence of lack of conclusive support from the people for the powers and measures of the Convention first shook the determination of the working classes in the localities and finally led to an ignominious dissolution of the Convention itself. As Parssinen has observed, the idea of an anti-parliamentary convention was conspicuously absent during the general strike of 1842, and was only half-heartedly believed in even by the delegates themselves in 1848.[189]

With the discrediting of the Convention idea by the events of 1839, however, one important rampart had been removed from the radical defence. It was a commonly cited radical assumption that 'for a nation to be free, it was sufficient that she wills it'. It had also been widely assumed that in countering this will violence would be initiated by the state, even before the coming together of the nation's representatives. As the *Poor Man's Guardian* had stated in 1834. 'The time will come (and it will come soon) when the usurers will drive you to resist the law, but not before they have first violated it themselves. By a rigid obedience of the law, you will drive them to that course.'[190] A middle class, pressured by material necessity and alienated by state violence, would then join the people in their justified resistance. However, the events of 1839 demonstrated that the radical picture of the state – based as it was on the period of the Napoleonic wars and the Six Acts – was already ceasing to be a reliable guide to action. For the government allowed the Convention to go ahead. It did not arrest the delegates *en bloc* and was confident enough of middle-class opinion to allow the Convention debates to proceed unimpeded. This placed the initiative unwelcomely in the hands of the delegates, producing demoralizing divisions over the issue of moral versus physical force. Attempts to provoke violence from the authorities only widened the splits between left and right and frightened off most of what middle-class support there was. The Monmouth rising completed the process of middle-class withdrawal and Chartist disarray, and the prudent decision to commute the sentence on Frost

---

[188] Speech of R. J. Richardson, *Northern Star*, 27 April 1839.
[189] Parssinen, 'Association Convention and Anti-Parliament', 530–1.
[190] *Poor Man's Guardian*, 12 April 1834.

removed the last potential focal point of unity.[191] Thus 1839 destroyed any simple notion of the unity of the people and the malignant predictability of the state.

If 1839 demonstrated the inadequacy of an inherited radical conception of political change, 1842 demonstrated radicalism's inability to gain any advantage from a new type of struggle. The difficulty of a radical strategy pursued – this time exclusively – by one class in society, was even more strikingly exemplified, and confusion was the result. In one sense, the 1842 strike represented a high point of radical success. In 1839, trade societies had not officially endorsed Chartism, they had played only a passive role in the agitation, and they had not even been consulted about the organization of the 'sacred month'. By 1842 on the other hand, in certain areas, trade societies had not only been convinced of the validity of the Chartist diagnosis, but they were prepared to take the lead in the movement for the Charter.[192] It represented a triumph for the strategy which the *Poor Man's Guardian* had advocated in 1834 and for which Chartists like McDouall and Leach had been pressing in the preceding two years. The declared aims of the strike in much of the Manchester area and many other regions were in strict accordance with Chartist analysis. As William Muirhouse told the 7 August Mottram Moor meeting, which initiated the turnouts in Lancashire, it was 'not a wage question', but 'a national question'.[193] The enemy was not employers as such, but 'class legislation'. As the Delegate Conference of Trades in Manchester resolved on 12 August:

We, the delegates representing the various trades of Manchester and its vicinities with delegates from various parts of Lancashire and Yorkshire, do most emphatically declare that it is our solemn and conscientious conviction that all the evils that afflict society, and which have prostrated the energies of the great body of the producing classes, arise solely from class legislation; and that the only remedy for the present alarming distress and widespread destitution is the immediate and unmutilated

---

[191] The importance of the commutation of Frost's sentence is emphasized in Thompson, *Early Chartists*, 21–2. The commutation was not the result of Whig government policy, however, but occurred because of the strong insistence of the Lord Chief Justice.

[192] See Sykes, 'Early Chartism and Trade Unionism'.

[193] Cited in M. Jenkins, *The General Strike of 1842* (1980), 68.

adoption and carrying into law, the document known as the people's Charter.[194]

Nor was the radical aim of carrying the whole of the people behind the movement dropped. The Manchester Delegates' Conference of 15 August declared:

The meeting proposes appointing delegates to wait upon and confer with shopkeepers, dissenting clergymen and the middle classes generally for the purpose of ascertaining how far they are prepared to assist and support the people in the struggle for the attainment of their political rights.[195]

Nor was there any simple division between those who wanted the Charter and those who wanted 'a fair day's wage for a fair day's work'. In many areas, the attainment of the one had come to be seen as the precondition for the attainment of the other. As the unemployed colliers of Hanley declared, 'it is the opinion of this meeting that nothing but the People's Charter can give us the power to have 'a fair day's wage for a fair day's work'.[196]

But, in other respects, the strike hastened the involution of Chartism. Without preparation or organization and without the prior mobilization of public opinion, it is difficult to conceive how the strike leaders thought the government might be induced to cave in. Nor, unlike 1839, was there any question of the government facing an armed people – an essential component of Benbow's original plan. The Chartist leadership was mainly taken by surprise and disunited. Well-grounded fears of government repression and the consequent absence of any proposal for a convention or political organization capable of focussing the demands of the strike, the inability of the trades' delegates to give leadership to the movement after the middle of August, and the effective refusal of the NCA to provide more than a passive endorsement of the demands of the turnout destroyed whatever slight chances of success the movement might have had.[197] The

---

[194] Ibid., 264.

[195] Ibid., 266.

[196] *Northern Star*, 20 Aug. 1842.

[197] Many aspects of the thinking behind the 1842 strike movement remain mysterious. For accounts of the strike, see A. G. Rose, 'The Plug Riots of 1842 in Lancashire and Cheshire', *Transactions of the Lancashire and Cheshire Antiquarian Society*, LXVII (1958); F. C. Mather, 'The General Strike of 1842: A Study in Leadership, Organisation and the Threat of Revolution during the Plug Plot Disturbances', in J. Stephenson and R. Quinault, *Popular Protest and Public Order* (1974); M. Jenkins, *General Strike*.

rationale of the strike was never made clear. Even Richard Pilling, generally recognized to have been one of the principal instigators of the movement, remained equivocal about the relation between the wage question and the Charter. On the one hand, he stated at his trial: 'it is not *me* that is the father of this movement; but that house. Our addresses have been laid before that house, and they have not redressed our grievances; and from there and there alone the cause comes.'[198] But, in his conclusion, he stated: 'Whatever it may have been with others it has been a wage question with me. And I do say that if Mr O'Connor has made it a chartist question, he has done wonders to make it extend through England, Ireland and Scotland. But it was always a wage question, and ten hours bill with me.'[199] So confused was the NCA's attitude to the strike, that its declaration of support could without embarrassment be treated by a prominent Chartist like Harney as an injunction to prevent the extension of the strike. The NCA in its declaration of 16 August pledged itself to disperse to the localities 'to give a proper direction to the people's efforts'.

Well, gentlemen, what was my conduct on my return to Sheffield? What was the direction I gave to the people's efforts. Why, I opposed the extension of the strike to that town, and prevented any strike or turnout taking place.[200]

The strike remained confined to operatives; middle-class opinion in those areas where the political aim of the strike was most clearcut was generally sharply divided from Chartism by the antagonism which had developed over the issue of the repeal of the Corn Laws. The effort by O'Connor and the bulk of the Chartist leadership to blame the strike upon the Anti-Corn-Law League or to claim that the strike was simply a wage struggle contradicted the radical premises of the operatives' demands. 1842 even more than 1839 dramatized the dissonance between the attempt to pursue a radical strategy and a movement almost exclusively working class in composition and increasingly debarred from exercising anything other than forceful pressure on middle-class opinion.

[198] *The Trial of Feargus O'Connor*, 249.
[199] Ibid., 254–5.
[200] Ibid., 235.

How far the strike produced a reorientation of government policy, rather than confirming it on a course of action it already intended to pursue, is uncertain.[201] What is certain, however, is that government policy became less and less vulnerable to radical critique as the 1840s wore on, while the coherence of radicalism became increasingly blurred. After the failure of the strike, the continued concentration of energy on the Charter proved impossible to sustain. The depression lifted and the Chartist solution – discredited by the experiment of 1842 – no longer attracted many trade societies, now more confident of exercising bargaining power within the system. Elements of the alternative language of popular political economy, held at bay for most of the decade between 1832 and 1842, crept into popular usage. There was certainly no simple capitulation to the liberal ideology of self-help and the identity of interest between employer and employed, as some historians have claimed.[202] But there was greater acceptance of determination by market forces and increasing usage of the terms 'labour' and 'capital' without reference to the political system in which, in the radicalism of the 1830s, these terms were inextricably inscribed. For committed Chartists, 1843 'was the year of slumber' and 1844 'scarce gave us breath to fill our sails'.[203] In the factory districts, even Chartist stalwarts found their interest deflected towards the campaign for the Ten Hours' Bill. As James Leach put it, 'he would stand second to no man in the advocacy of the Charter', but 'he did not think this a proper time for its introduction'.[204] The near success of the Ten Hours' measure in 1844 and the triumph of 1847 considerably strengthened the impetus

---

[201] The suggestion that the strike did cause a reorientation in government policy is put forward by John Foster in M. Jenkins, *General Strike*, 3–4. While a good case has been made out for the change of government tactics during the trial which followed the strike (see Jenkins, *General Strike*, Ch. 10) the larger claim remains doubtful. It is argued below that the state had already begun to retreat from the ideologically exposed position of the 1830s before the strike began. See also G. Kitson Clark, 'Hunger and Politics in 1842', *Journal of Modern History*, 25 (1953).

[202] See, for instance, Perkin, *Origins*; B. Harrison and P. Hollis, 'Chartism, Liberalism and the Life of Robert Lowery', *English Historical Review*, LXXXII (1967).

[203] Cited in J. T. Ward, *Chartism* (1973), 176.

[204] Ibid., 175; for Leach's thinking on the factory question, see W. Rashleigh, *Stubborn Facts from the Factories by a Manchester Operative* (1844).

towards reformism and single-issue campaigns – 'crotchets', as O'Connor had called them at the end of the 1830s – which deflected the people from the real cause of their miseries. The fact that a Factory Act could not only be passed, but within a few years be generally recognized as effective,[205] proved another blow to the radical conception of the corrupt, unrepresentative and self-interested state.

More immediately serious, however, for the coherence of the radical platform, was O'Connor's adoption of the land plan. It not only divided Chartists in their attitudes towards a policy for the land. It also represented a far more fundamental breach in the radicalism of the 1830s, since it implied that improvement was possible within the existing political system. As O'Brien remarked:

The strangest thing of all ... [is] ... that the philanthropic Feargus should have dragged millions of people after him to torchlight meetings, demonstrations, etc., all attended with great sacrifice of time and money, and caused the actual ruin of thousands through imprisonment, loss of employment and expatriation, when all the while he had only to establish a 'National Chartist Cooperative Land Society' to ensure social happiness for us all, and when, to use his own words ... he had discerned that 'political equality can only spring from social happiness'. Formerly, he taught us that social happiness was to proceed from political equality.[206]

Moreover, what O'Brien pinpointed as the disintegrative effect of the land plan upon the assumptions of radicalism was borne out by O'Connor's volte-face on the Corn Laws. Seen from the new perspectives of the land plan, the same disastrous consequences which Chartists had predicted from a repeal at the behest of the moneymongers were now seen as a benefit. As Gammage put it: 'When the League was in bad odour, nothing but ruin was predicted by O'Connor in case of its success. Now it would make the Land Plan triumphant by bringing down the price of land and thus enable the people more freely to purchase.'[207] All the old conviction and vehemence of the radical castigation of the state had gone. The interrelatedness of radical premises and the consequentiality of its arguments were now intersected with special cases

---

[205] See P. Joyce, *Work, Society and Politics*, Sussex (1980), 69–70.
[206] *National Reformer*, 15 and 22 May, 1847; cited in Gammage, *History of the Chartist Movement*, 269.
[207] Gammage, *History of the Chartist Movement*, 270.

and qualifying clauses. Commenting on Peel's repeal of the Corn Laws, the *Northern Star* wrote:

> Now had free trade been proposed in the Whig style – had it been granted as a boon to the increasing power of the League and a sop to the monied interest, unaccompanied with those wise, salutary and statesmanlike adjustments proposed by SIR ROBERT PEEL, not all the power at the disposal of the government could have averted the horrors of a revolution.[208]

There could be no more fitting testimony to Peel's achievement.

Interpretations of Chartism, as was noted at the beginning of this essay, have focussed overwhelmingly upon its working-class character. This emphasis has obscured some crucial dimensions of the character and timing of the movement. Historians in search of evidence of class consciousness are apt to miss the real preconditions of Chartist success and failure. For if Chartism became a movement of workers, it became so not out of choice, but from necessity – a result of its diminishing ability to convince any significant proportion of the middle classes of the feasibility of its position and the attractiveness of its social vision – and finally, of course, it ceased to hold the loyalty of any substantial portion of the working classes themselves. Viewed from this angle – as a form of radicalism and not simply as the movement of a class – Chartism can be situated in two different perspectives, the first long-term and secular, the second short-term and conjunctural.

As a secular phenomenon, Chartism was the last, most prominent and most desperate – though not perhaps the most revolutionary – version of a radical critique of society, which had enjoyed an almost continuous existence since the 1760s and 1770s. The vision which lay behind this critique was of a more or less egalitarian society, populated exclusively by the industrious, and needing minimal government. Political power, as Chartists conceived it, in line with eighteenth century radicals, was essentially a negative phenomenon, the freedom from present oppressions and the legal or legislative prevention of their recurrence. As Harney summarized even the ostensibly most Jacobin variant of this picture:

---

[208] *Northern Star*, 17 Jan. 1846.

The Charter was a means to an end – the means was their political rights, and the end was social equality. Did he mean that they all should have their food dressed alike, their houses built in parallelograms, their coats having one uniform cut? God bless you. No such thing. He only meant that all men should have what they earned, and that the man 'who did not work, neither should he eat' (Cheers).[209]

In such a society reward would be proportional to labour, dependence and clientage would be eliminated, there would be equal access to the land and the restoration of balance between town and country.[210] Corruption, tyranny and the polarity between wealth and poverty within existing society was ascribed to the political depredations of a parasitic class – landlords, tithe-holders, fundholders, bankers and, in the Chartist version, the aristocracy of wealth, middlemen and factory lords. From first to last, the contrast between the real and the artificial creation of wealth remained a constant feature of radical rhetoric, whatever the changes in the personnel catalogued or given salience under these respective headings. The distinction was not primarily between ruling and exploited classes in an economic sense, but rather between the beneficiaries and the victims of corruption and monopoly political power. The juxtaposition was in the first instance moral and political, and dividing lines could be drawn as much within classes as between them. In the eighteenth century, radicals like Wyvill, Price and Cartwright made a strong distinction between those dependent upon patronage and place and those who maintained their independence. Suspicion was directed not only at highly-placed pensioners, but also at the dependent poor.[211] At least into the 1870s radical rhetoric of a republican kind referred contemptuously to the inequality of treatment meted out to royal paupers at the top of society and workhouse paupers at the bottom.[212] A similar moral disdain for those who unwittingly or uncritically benefited from the present artificial system

[209] Ibid., 15 June 1839.
[210] For the way in which the predominantly urban 'middling sort' of the 1760s and 1770s adapted country ideology to their own purposes, see Brewer, 'English Radicalism'.
[211] See Prothero, *Artisans*, 26–7.
[212] On mid-Victorian republicanism, see R. Harrison, *Before the Socialists* (1965), Ch. v.

characterized the Chartist distrust of the enfranchised middle classes. Hence the admiration for those true 'patriots' who maintained their independence of judgement, irrespective of their economic roles. In this context, it is not surprising that John Fielden, one of the largest cotton manufacturers in the north, should have occupied such a revered place in the radical movement. His political stance was living proof that there was no inherent necessity in the association between employers and Malthusian political economy, the Anti-Corn-Law League or the Whiggery of a Brougham, Baines or Macaulay. His defence of the handloom weavers, his unwearying support of the factory movement and his advocacy of universal suffrage exemplified the type of support Chartists expected, but increasingly failed to obtain from the uncorrupted portion of the middle classes. Moreover, his picture of a more balanced relationship between land and industry closely resembled the alternative vision of the economy held by many Chartists. 'There is no natural cause for our distress', wrote Fielden:

We have fertile land, the finest herds and flocks in the world, and the most skilled herdsmen. We have rivers and ports, and shipping unequalled; and our ingenuity and industry have given us manufactures which ought to complete these blessings. I am a manufacturer; but I am not one of those who think it time we had dispensed with the land. I think that these interests are conducive to the prosperity of the nation, that all must go together and that the ruin of either will leave others comparatively insecure.[213]

There was always a minority of employers like Fielden, gentlemen like Duncombe, or local notables like Frost, even in this last phase of eighteenth century radicalism, to make its view of the polity and its class system credible. Even during the strike of 1842, there were evidently some employers who sympathized with the Chartist case. In Dundee, for instance, it was recorded:

Easson (first shop) – 33 men – went to master and asked rise – Mr E. stated he would give none, the trade could not afford it – He considered class legislation at the bottom of all their evils – 18 out of the 33 agreed to come out if the strike be national, the rest not to move.[214]

[213] J. Fielden, *The Curse of the Factory System* (1836), p. iii.
[214] *Dundee Warder*, August 1842, cited in C. Bebb, 'The Chartist Movement in Dundee', St Andrews B.Phil. (1977).

Conversely, it is noteworthy that in the 1842 strikes those singled out for aggressive attack were those noted for their obnoxious political views. In Manchester, it was the Birley mills, the owner of which being held primarily responsible for the Peterloo massacre. In the riots in the Potteries, as the researches of Robert Fyson shows, it was unpopular magistrates and Poor Law commissioners, not employers, who were the objects of violence – in particular the Rector of Longton, a man noted for the excellence of his wine cellar, who had advised the poor to use dock leaves as a substitute for coffee.[215]

Chartism has often been seen as a response to the Industrial Revolution and the changes in social relations that it engendered. But such an approach presupposes the observation of a social fact whose definition was common to contemporaries and later historians. The social aspects of the process which later historians were to call industrialization were envisaged by radicals and Chartists in terms which reproduced the emphases of eighteenth century radicalism, quite distinct from those of twentieth century social and economic historians. Thus, radical and Chartist politics make no sense if they are interpreted as a response to the emergence of an industrial capitalism conceived as an objective, inevitable and irreversible economic process. The radical picture was of a far more arbitrary and artificial development whose source was to be found not in the real workings of the economy, but in the acceleration and accentuation of a process of financial plunder made possible by the political developments of the preceding fifty years. The remote stepping-stones in this sequence could be traced back to the Norman Yoke, the loss of suffrage rights in medieval England or the dissolution of the monasteries, all of which had consolidated the monopoly of the landholders.[216] But the more immediate prehistory of the present began with the establishment of the national debt and the growth of new financial practices around the end of the seventeenth century,

---

[215] See R. Fyson, 'The Crisis of 1842: Chartism, the Colliers Strike and the Outbreak of 1842 in the Potteries', in Epstein and Thompson, *The Chartist Experience*.

[216] On the changing character of the argument about the Norman Yoke from the seventeenth to the nineteenth century, see C. Hill, 'The Norman Yoke', in *Puritanism and Revolution* (1958).

grew worse with the enclosures of the eighteenth century, and culminated in the enormous spoils reaped from speculation during the French wars. According to O'Brien, writing about the French revolutionary wars:

It was to open to the monied class of England, and the Continent, a new and inexhaustible field of investment for masses of fictitious or fraudulent capital which without such investment (i.e. war) would become a drug in the market and soon be of no more value than the same nominal amount of French assignats, or the Continental money of America in the last stage of depreciation ... The extension of trade, manufactures and machinery had engendered fresh swarms of capitalists who must also be enabled to convert their stagnant pools of rotten wealth into perennial streams of sound wealth. In plain English, after appropriating and consuming most of the produce of the then existing generation of labourers they must be enabled to appropriate also the produce of generations unborn to the use of their heirs, assigns and representatives, in all times to come. To accomplish this they lent upwards of £500 millions to our government to carry on the French revolutionary wars – thereby swelling our national debt from £280 millions to upwards of £800 millions, and thus, as it were killing two birds with one stone, that is to say, helping to destroy French Democrats and the Rights of Man on the one hand, and securing for themselves and their posterity the privilege of being everlasting pensioners on the nation on the other hand.[217]

But the infamy of the process did not stop with the French wars. It was compounded during the peace. According to John Fielden:

But when the war terminated, England returned to a gold currency, and restored the dealings of those within this country to an exchange in a metallic currency, subject to a debt contracted in paper; and out of this had arisen all those changes they had seen from that day to this. And we were now on the high road to tyranny at a quicker pace than we ever were before. The long and short of it was that this debt contracted in paper, could never be paid in gold.[218]

It was the French wars which had produced the vast expansion of foreign at the expense of home trade, the growth of machinery at the expense of operatives, the growth of paper

---

[217] J. B. O'Brien, *The Life and Character of Maximilian Robespierre, Proving by Facts and Arguments that that Much Calumniated Person was One of the Greatest Men and One of the Purest and Most Enlightened Reformers that Ever Existed in the World* (1838), vol. 1, 254–5.

[218] *Northern Star*, 9 June 1838.

speculation at the expense of real industry. The post-war situation had consolidated the position of these jumped-up speculators and gamblers at the expense of all other classes of society. As the *Northern Star* stated:

> Thus as the gambler who sits down at the gambling table with a bank of a million, is sure to gather unto himself at the long run all the small banks at the table, so is the present system sure to sacrifice both labourer, small capitalist and shopkeeper – to those who can command most money and the largest credit until at length the whole commercial speculations of the country will be vested in the hands of the most successful gambler.[219]

It was not least for these reasons that plebeian radicals and after them Chartists lived in hope of making an alliance with those disadvantaged classes to reverse the process.

What was peculiar to the Chartist phase of radicalism, therefore, was neither the abandonment of an inherited radical ambition to construct a broad popular alliance, nor a novel and class-specific way of looking at recent history in terms of what later historians were to describe as industrialization. In both these areas there existed a strong continuity between Chartism and preceding versions of radicalism. What was specific to Chartism was, firstly, the equation of the people with the working classes as a result of 1832 and, secondly, a corresponding shift of emphasis upon the relationship between the state and the working classes, dramatized by the Whig legislation which followed 1832. As a result of this shift, less emphasis was placed upon the state as a nest of self-interest and corruption – 'old corruption' in Cobbett's phrase; instead, it increasingly came to be viewed as the tyrannical harbinger of a dictatorship over the producers. As the 1830s progressed, the predominant image was no longer merely of placemen, sinecurists and fundholders principally interested in revenues derived from taxes on consumption to secure their unearned comforts, but was something more sinister and dynamic – a powerful and malevolent machine of repression, at the behest of capitalists and factory lords, essentially and actively dedicated to the lowering of the wages of the working classes through the removal of all residual protection at their command, whether trade societies, legal redress, poor relief or

[219] *Ibid.*, 12 May 1838.

what survived of the representation of the interests of the working classes in local government.[220] As a conjunctural phenomenon, Chartism represented the rapid upsurge and gradual ebbing away of this specific vision of the state.

The full dimensions of the activist and innovative character of the state in the 1830s have been somewhat obscured in recent years by the form of the debate about 'the 19th century revolution in government'.[221] Discussions of innovations in policy and administration have implied that the phenomenon can be summarized either in terms of the impact of Benthamite doctrines of efficiency and expertise, or as a series of pragmatic responses to new social problems. What is obscured is the importance of the political and ideological context in which such changes were made. To many contemporaries, the reforms which followed 1832 appeared to be of an alarming revolutionary character, and from a radical and Chartist perspective, as we have seen, the ominous political significance of the new policies is hard to underestimate. The New Poor Law, and the assisted migration of southern paupers to northern towns, both of which were considered part of a plot to lower wages by means of centralized non-representative state bodies, the Municipal Corporations Act and the extension of the police system, which effectively excluded the working classes from participation in local government, the refusal of factory legislation, the denial of protection to the handloom weavers, and the attack upon trade unions, could all be seen in Fielden's words as a part of 'the highroad to tyranny'; or, as Peter Bussey thought, speaking of the rural police, 'in effect another standing army – to make the people submit to all the insults and oppressions which government contemplates forcing upon them'.[222] The legislative record, from Peel's introduction of the Metropoli-

---

[220] The tension was exacerbated by the extent to which employers took over the magistracy in industrial regions in the 1830s; see D. Philips, 'The Black Country Magistracy 1835–60: A Changing Local Elite and the Exercise of its Power', *Midland History* (1976).

[221] The debate is summarized in A.J. Taylor, *Laissez-faire and State Intervention in Nineteenth Century Britain*, Economic History Society (1972); for a critique and suggested reinterpretation, see P. Richards, 'State Formation and Class Struggle, 1832–48', in P. Corrigan (ed.), *Capitalism, State Formation and Marxist Theory* (1980).

[222] *Northern Star*, 9 March 1839.

tan Police to the petering out of the Whig reform programme in the late 1830s, did indeed signify the most consequential attempt to dismantle or transform the decentralized treatment of problems of crime, poverty and social order characteristic of the eighteenth century state.[223] This apparently single-minded effort of the Whig government to create the coercive and administrative framework of a society wholly to be based on free competition proceeded at the expense of all those forces given voice by Chartism, 'Tory radicalism' and other still strong and diffuse forms of 'country' sentiment surviving from the previous century. The activity of the state could thus be seen as the brutal culmination of the ambitions of artificial wealth and monopoly power, which had been at work ever since 1688. The centralization of the powers of the state at the expense of local representation, combined with the apparent scheme to establish a tyranny over the producers in the context of the structural changes and cyclical difficulties experienced in the economy, created a potentially formidable opposition in the localities – both working and middle class, radical and Tory. The premises of radicalism were ideally suited to concentrate and focus this novel activity of the state. This is one reason why social discontent took a Chartist form. Chartism could not simply be said to have begun in 1832; it was the combined effect of 1832 and the gathering reaction to the legislative measures of the Whig government. The tendency of historians of the state to conceive 'the revolution in government' too narrowly as an administrative phenomenon, and of labour and socialist historians to treat Chartism as a social phenomenon, has obscured the closeness of interconnection between the two processes. The Chartist sentiment of 1837–9 was in large part a response to 'the revolution in government'.

But the very vehemence of opposition which these policies had provoked forced a change of course. At the end of the 1830s, the state was already beginning to withdraw from this exposed position. A policy of straightforward repression, such

---

[223] On the role and function of law in the eighteenth century state, see D. Hay, 'Property, Authority and the Criminal Law', in D. Hay, P. Lineburgh, J. Rule, E. P. Thompson and C. Winslow, *Albion's Fatal Tree* (1975); E. P. Thompson, *Whigs and Hunters* (1975).

as that which had been mounted by Sidmouth, was not repeated by Russell.[224] The apparently blatant 'class legislation' of the early 1830s was now beginning to be nuanced by moves of a less obviously sinister character – towards state-provided education, for instance, and the discussion of measures to improve the health of towns.[225] In such circumstances, Chartist agitation never had more than an outside chance of success, since the enfranchisement of the middle class in 1832 placed a major obstacle in the way of Chartist/middle-class alliance. There was no necessity for middle-class discontent to take a Chartist form. Some portion of middle-class opinion expressed its dissent from the doctrinaire policy of the Whigs in the 1830s by voting Conservative in the 1841 election. But fear and dislike of government extremism was counterbalanced by anxiety about the threatening and potentially insurrectionary character of Chartist discontent. The electorate therefore voted for a strong government promising to maintain and protect existing institutions. Peel made no political concessions to Chartism, but his avowed aim was to remove the material sources of popular discontent and to avoid identifying the state with any particular fraction or economic interest of the propertied class.[226] He followed the Scottish theologian, Thomas Chalmers, in believing that the competitive system was a theologically sanctioned system, in which the industrious would be rewarded and the profligate punished through the autonomous operation of its laws.[227] In order for such a moralized capitalism to exist, however, the legislature would have to ensure that unnecessary state interference in the operation of the economy was halted, that the burden upon industry and enterprise be removed, and that clear lines be drawn between the quick profits from specula-

---

[224] See F. C. Mather, *Public Order in the Age of the Chartists*, Manchester (1959).

[225] See, in connection with this, the shift in statistical societies from preoccupation with wages and employment to that of housing, health and education, Yeo, 'Social Science', Ch. 3; see also on education, Hollis, *Pauper Press*, Chs. I, III; R. Johnson, 'Educational Policy and Social Control in Early Victorian England', *Past and Present*, 49 (1970).

[226] See N. Gash, 'Peel and the Party System', *Transactions of the Royal Historical Society* (1951); N. Gash, *Reaction and Reconstruction in English Politics 1832–1852*, Oxford (1964), Ch. v.

[227] See B. Hilton, *Corn, Cash, Commerce*, Oxford (1977), 308–13; B. Hilton, 'Peel: A Reappraisal', *Historical Journal* (1979).

tion and the real gains of industry. A consistent object of his administration was to reduce taxes on consumption, even if this meant re-introducing the income tax, and in his banking and company legislation to regularize the operation of credit, whose maladjustment he considered responsible for the commercial crises which had periodically afflicted the country since the 'fatal' resort to paper money in 1797.[228] There were therefore significant areas of convergence between the priorities of the Peel government and the issues raised by the Chartist platform. But the intended effects of such reforms was precisely to remove the social disorder and disrespect for established institutions, of which Chartism and the Anti-Corn-Law League were thought to be the manifestations.

If Chartist rhetoric was ideally suited to concert the opposition to the Whig measures of the 1830s, by the same token it was ill-equipped to modify its position in response to the changed character of state activity in the 1840s. The Chartist critique of the state and the class oppression it had engendered was a totalizing critique. It was not suited to the discrimination between one legislative measure and another, since this would be to concede that not all measures pursued by the state were for obviously malign class purposes and that beneficial reforms might be carried by a selfish legislature in an unreformed system. Peel's reduction of taxes on consumption, continued with crusading zeal by Gladstone in the mid-Victorian period, his care however unrealistic to distinguish between moral and immoral economic activity, the high moral tone of the proceedings of the government and the effective raising of the state above the dictates of particular economic interests – whether landlords, financiers or manufacturers – was highlighted by the Mines Act of 1842, the 1842 Budget, the Joint Stock Company Act, the Bank Charter Act, and above all by the manner of the passing of the repeal of the Corn Laws. All this proved fatal to the conviction and self-certainty of the language of Chartism, especially in the period after 1842, when some real measure of prosperity returned to the economy. The unrepresentative House of Commons, the

---

[228] See Peel's speech introducing the Bank Charter Act, 6 May 1844, *Speeches of the late Rt Hon. Sir Robert Peel delivered in the House of Commons*, 4 vols. (1853), vol. IV, 349 ff.

aristocratic character of the Constitution, the privileged position of the Church, and the exclusion of the working classes from the legislature still remained evils about which all radicals could agree. Political power remained as concentrated as it had been before; bishops, lords and placemen were scarcely less entrenched.[229] But the tight link forged between the oppression of the working classes and the monopoly of political power exercised through the medium of 'class legislation' – the essence of Chartist rhetoric – began to loosen. The Chartist capitulation on the issue of repeal and free trade wholly undercut the emphasis upon the home market and underconsumption. The labour market and the fate of the producer could no longer be presented simply as politically determined phenomena. Economics and politics were increasingly sundered and the embryonic features of mid-Victorian liberalism began to emerge. Chartism was again to revive in 1847–8, but the staleness and anachronistic flavour of its rhetoric became apparent even to its strongest supporters.[230] That the stabilization of the economy and the mid-century boom finally killed off all but a few beleaguered Chartist outposts is a fact acknowledged by all historians of Chartism.[231] But as a coherent political language and a believable political vision, Chartism disintegrated in the early 1840s, not the early 1850s. Chartist decline was not initially the result of prosperity and economic stabilization, for it effectively preceded them. Attention to the language of Chartism suggests that its rise and fall is to be related in the first instance not to movements in the economy, divisions in the movement or an immature class consciousness, but to the changing character and policies of the state – the principal enemy upon whose actions radicals had always found that their credibility depended.

---

[229] For the changed character of radicalism in the post-Chartist period, see F. Gillespie, *Labour and Politics in England 1850–1867* (1927); F. M. Leventhal, *Respectable Radical, the Life of George Howell* (1971); Harrison, *Before the Socialists*.

[230] See Belcham, 'Fergus O'Connor'.

[231] What this stabilization involved is briefly discussed in Ch. 1 in this volume.

4

WORKING-CLASS CULTURE AND WORKING-CLASS POLITICS IN LONDON, 1870–1900: NOTES ON THE REMAKING OF A WORKING CLASS

In the London of the 1880s, Charles Masterman recalled, the future that all had foretold had been one of class war and the formation of a workers' party. But that future had not materialized. For, 'a wave of imperialism has swept over the country, and all these efforts, hopes and visions have vanished as if wiped out by a sponge'.[1] Masterman was writing in 1900, the year of the Mafeking celebrations. No one who saw the crowds on Mafeking night ever forgot them. 'Mafficking' entered the English language, and the memory was still vivid in the 1920s and 1930s when a growing literature of reminiscence comforted the dispirited inhabitants of servantless houses with the legend of a departed golden age. 'In those days', asserted one former stockbroker, 'East met West. And yet each "knew his place", the boast of the time ... You would see bevies of 'Arrys and 'Arriets in these national demonstrations burst out from the congestion of the pavements to jig themselves into forgetfulness of the sterner realities of Bermondsey and Bethnal Green as they "set" to one another in a saturnalia of howl and mouth organ.'[2] The strangeness of the occasion was strikingly recaptured by Thomas Burke, forty years afterwards: 'I was out at Armistice Night, but I don't recall that publicans went right off their heads and refused all day to take money from anybody. I don't remember any young men screwing up five-pounds notes and tossing them into the air for catch-who-can. I don't remember money-grubbing City men going so mad as to shower sovereigns and handfuls of silver among the crowd. I don't remember seeing

[1] C. Masterman, *The Heart of the Empire* (1901), 3.
[2] Shaw Desmond, *London Nights of Long Ago* (1927), 94–5.

179

men take off their hats and jump on them.'[3] The celebration was not confined to the central pleasure area or the middle-class suburbs. According to the report of the events in *The Times*, 'the news was received with extraordinary enthusiasm in East London and Saturday was generally observed as a holiday. The Whitechapel and Bow Roads were a mass of flags and bunting, while all the tramcars and omnibuses flew flags ... a large body of working men with flags and banners perambulated the Bow Road, singing patriotic airs, while hundreds of cyclists wearing photographs of Colonel Baden Powell formed into procession and paraded the principal thoroughfares of Poplar and Stepney.'[4] It is not surprising that startled liberals, like Masterman, should have imagined that they were witnessing the emergence of a 'new race ... the city type ... voluble, excitable, with little ballast, stamina or endurance – seeking stimulus in drink, in betting, in any unaccustomed conflicts at home or abroad'.[5]

This picture painted by anxious liberals and complacent conservatives must be somewhat modified. The predominant feeling on Mafeking night was not aggression but relief after the disasters of the 'black week'. There was little hooliganism or violence. It has recently been established that not workers but students and clerks formed the loutish jingo mobs which broke up pro-Boer meetings and ransacked the property of 'little Englanders'.[6] Recent research also suggests that the Boer War was not the main concern of working-class voters in the 'khaki election' of 1900. The poll was below average and the decisive issues in poorer London constituencies were local and material – high rents, job opportunities, Jewish immi-gration, the protection of declining trades and the im-provement of the water supply.[7] Finally, the recruitment figures show that workers did not volunteer to fight in the war in any significant numbers until the return of unemployment in 1901.[8]

[3] Thomas Burke, *The Streets of London* (1940), 136.
[4] *The Times*, 21 May 1900.
[5] Masterman, *Heart of the Empire*, 7–8.
[6] Richard Price, *An Imperial War and the British Working Class* (1972), Ch. IV.
[7] Price, *Imperial War*, Ch. III; Henry Pelling, *Social Geography of British Elections 1885–1910* (1967), 45, 47, 52, 57; id., *Popular Politics and Society in Late Victorian Britain* (1968), 94.
[8] Price, *Imperial War*, Ch. V.

These qualifications are important, but it is unlikely that they would have done much to assuage the anxiety felt by radicals and socialists at the time. For, if the working class did not actively promote the jingoism, there can be no doubt that it passively acquiesced to it. Certainly, the celebrations of Mafeking night were not highly politically defined. There is every reason to believe that they were an expression of admiration for the bravery of husbands, brothers and sons at the front, rather than a general endorsement of the war, and that this identification with the common soldier was the primary way in which London workers related to the South African campaign. But it is still important to remember that workers had not previously expressed such feelings by dancing in the streets and fraternizing with the rich.

Modern historians have tended to belittle the anxieties of Masterman and the perplexity of radicals and socialists. Standard interpretations of the period, 1870–1914, have tended to concentrate on the great waves of trade union expansion, the growth of socialism, the foundation of the Labour Party, the conversion of the working class from liberalism, the demand for social reform and the beginnings of the welfare state. Phenomena like Mafeking and the prevalence of conservatism among the working class in a large city like London, when discussed at all, have generally appeared as accidental or aberrant features of a period whose basic tendency was the rise of Labour and the mounting pressure for social reform. When attempts have been made to explain such deviations in the Boer War period, they have concentrated almost exclusively upon short-term causes and subjective factors: dissensions within the Liberal Party; the absence of a 'charismatic' figure like Gladstone or Bradlaugh capable of mobilizing an anti-war movement; the lack of any adequate theory of imperialism; and the inability of radicals or socialists to formulate an attractive alternative political programme.

Any form of historical explanation which is forced to resort to a theory of charisma immediately betrays its inadequacy. In reality, weakness of platform, absence of effective leadership and feeble organization were symptoms rather than causes of the lack of vitality in London working-class politics. The failure of radicals and socialists to make any deep impression on the London working class in the late Victorian and Edwardian period had deeper roots than subjective deficiency. Underlying it were longer term structural changes in the character of London working-class life which made attempts at political mobilization increasingly difficult. What Mafeking and other imperial celebrations portended was not so much the predominance of the wrong politics among the mass of London workers, but rather their estrangement from political activity as such. There was general agreement that the politically active working man of the time was a radical or a socialist. Loyalism was a product of apathy.

One of the features of this period which has generally received little attention from historians was the emergence of a distinctively new pattern of working-class culture in the years between 1870 and 1900: a type of culture which literary critics like Hoggart were to label 'traditional' in the 1950s.[9] One reason why the growth of this culture has been neglected is because indications of its presence are not generally to be found in Hansard, the political press or the records of trade unions. It might also be added that evidence of its growing ubiquity and strength is difficult to reconcile with prevailing general interpretations of the period which still largely derive from the work of Cole and the Webbs. But once the relevance of this information is admitted it becomes impossible to explain the behaviour and attitudes of the working class during this epoch outside the context of this culture and the material situation which it represented.

In this paper, I shall attempt – very tentatively – to trace the conditions of emergence of a new working-class culture in London and to delineate its characteristic institutions and ideology. Given this task, however, it must be borne in mind that nineteenth century London not only gave birth to a new working-class culture, but also to a new form of middle-class culture based upon an increasing convergence of outlook between the middle class and the aristocracy. Both these 'cultures' must be examined, for it is impossible to understand the one except in relation to the other. By juxtaposing the two,

[9] Richard Hoggart, *The Uses of Literacy* (1957). A pioneer historical exploration of the origins of this culture has been made by Eric Hobsbawm. See *Industry and Empire* (1968), 135–7.

I hope to explain the emergence of a working-class culture which showed itself staunchly impervious to middle-class attempts to guide it, but yet whose prevailing tone was not one of political combativity, but of an enclosed and defensive conservatism. In this way, I hope to open up a different line of approach to the problem of London politics in the age of imperialism and to go a little way towards reconciling the cultural, economic and political history of the working class.

In England today, the idea of working-class culture, of a distinct working-class way of life, is practically a cliché. It is still a major preoccupation of humour, of etiquette, of creative literature and of literary and sociological investigation. So pervasive has this theme become that class is almost invariably interpreted as a cultural rather than an economic or political category.

But it was only at the beginning of the twentieth century – in London at least – that middle-class observers began to realize that the working class was not simply *without* culture or morality, but in fact possessed a 'culture' of its own. Charles Booth's observation that the London working class was governed by 'strict rules of propriety', but that these rules did not necessarily coincide with 'the ordinary lines of legal or religious morality',[10] may appear bald and incurious when compared with the work of later connoisseurs like Orwell or Hoggart. Nevertheless, it signalled the beginnings of a new attitude towards the working class. Of course, there had been anticipations. Henry Mayhew, ahead of his time and class in so many respects, had gestured unsuccessfully towards this idea in his primitive anthropological distinctions between 'wandering' and 'civilized' tribes.[11] But Mayhew's approach found no echo in the slum-life literature of the ensuing forty years. London workers were 'heathen'. 'Civilization' had not reached them. The poor lived in inaccessible places, in 'dens', in 'swamps', in the 'deeps', in the 'wilds', or in the 'abyss'. The 'Light' of 'civilization' did not shine upon them because they dwelt in 'the shadows', 'the shade', 'the nether world', the 'darkest' regions. When missionaries from 'civilization'

---

[10] C. Booth, *Life and Labour of the People in London*, Religious Influences Series 3 (1902), vol. 2, 97.
[11] H. Mayhew, *London Labour and the London Poor* (1861), vol. 1, 1–2.

ventured into that 'Babylon', they were confronted by 'terrible sights', and if struck by guilt or fear, they recalled the stories of Dives and Lazarus or Jacob and Esau. The terms, 'working classes' or 'toiling masses' carried no positive cultural connotations, for they signified *ir*religion, *in*temperance, *im*providence or *im*morality. Indeed, it was often difficult for these strangers from the 'civilized' world to discover where the 'working classes' ended and where the 'dangerous classes' began. For crime, prostitution, disorder and sedition were also thought to lurk in these poor regions, hidden from the gaze of the well-to-do, and when left to fester in this 'nether world', could suddenly break out and threaten the town.[12] As the political economist, J. R. MacCulloch observed in 1851:

The lowest class of all, those whose means of existence are precarious, disreputable or dishonest, have peculiar habits. They care little for appearances and are all but unknown to the rest of the people, except when their wants and delinquencies intrude them on the public notice.[13]

The working class lacked 'civilization' because it was hidden away and removed from it. The imagery of this language and the situation which it represented was itself a novel product of the Victorian period. Referring to the lowest class of London in 1807, J. P. Malcolm had written:

I shall venture ... to draw the reader's attention to the Alms-houses, Workhouses, Charity Schools, Hospitals and Prisons which surround us; and ask whence they are filled? Who turns his attention to *the second floors, the garrets, the back-rooms, and the cellars* of this Metropolis? [my italics].[14]

Eighteenth century writers had often been perturbed by the 'insolence of the mob' but the mob was in no sense geographically isolated from the more prosperous districts of the town. As Malcolm's remarks show, masters, traders, journeymen and labourers not only inhabited the same areas, but often resided on different floors of the same houses. Distinctions between trades were more important than distinctions between masters and journeymen. As Dorothy George has

---

[12] For a selection of slum-life literature employing this imagery, see Gareth Stedman Jones, *Outcast London*, 2nd edn, London (1984), pt III.
[13] J. R. MacCulloch, *London in 1850–1* (1851), 107.
[14] J. P. Malcolm, *Anecdotes of the Manners and Customs of London*, 2nd edn (1810), vol. II, 413.

written, 'apprenticeship tended to make trades hereditary – trades had their own customs, their own localities, often a distinctive dress and much corporate spirit'.[15] Social distinctions abounded at every level, but there was no great political, cultural or economic divide between the middle class and those beneath them. Despite the great turbulence of the London crowd, its political outlook was generally in accord with that of the City of London's Common Hall which tended to reflect the views of the less substantial merchants and masters.[16] It was only after the Gordon riots that the alliance began to break down. Culturally, there were certainly greater affinities between these groups than were to exist later. All classes shared in the passions for gambling, theatre, tea gardens, pugilism and animal sports.[17] All except the richest merchants lived within a short distance of their work, if not at the place of work itself.[18] The pub was a social and economic centre for all and heavy drinking was as common among employers as among the workmen.[19]

In the period 1790–1840, the distance between the London middle class and those beneath them increased dramatically. Political positions were polarized by the French Revolution. The propertied classes turned increasingly to evangelicalism. The small masters and traders, after an initial flirtation with the London Corresponding Society, found Benthamite ideas of cheap government, franchise extension and political economy more congenial. Their evolution is symbolized by the career of Francis Place. Artisans forged a political position of their own from the writings of Paine and the Jacobinism of the French Revolution. Their ideology was secularist, republican, democratic and fiercely anti-aristocratic. The alliance between middle-class radicalism and artisan democracy came under increasing strain after 1815. The incompatibility between the growth of trade unionism and the radicals' espousal

---

[15] M. Dorothy George, *London Life in the XVIIIth Century* (1930), 157.
[16] See George Rudé, *Hanoverian London 1714–1808* (1971), 183–227; E. P. Thompson, *The Making of the English Working Class* (1963), 69–73.
[17] See Malcolm, *Anecdotes*; Mary Thale (ed.), *The Autobiography of Francis Place* (1972); William B. Boulton, *Amusements of Old London*, 2 vols. (1901); Sybil Rosenfeld, *The Theatre of the London Fairs in the Eighteenth Century* (1960).
[18] George, *London Life*, 95–6.
[19] Brian Harrison, *Drink and the Victorians* (1971), 45–6.

of political economy announced the breach. After the 1832 Reform Bill, the alliance had no common basis. Owenism and the New Poor Law completed the rupture. The direct impact of the Industrial Revolution upon London was slight. The vast majority of firms remained small and factories rare. But the indirect impact was formidable. It can be detected in the decline of the Spitalfields weavers, in the removal of legislative protection of apprenticeship, in the growth of the slop-trades in clothing, furniture and footwear, in the huge expansion of commercial activity, and in the growth of the port of London. Even in the absence of factories, middle-class consciousness developed just as surely. From the end of the 1820s, more and more of the middle class abandoned the city and the industrial quarters for the exclusiveness of the suburbs. The centre became the sphere of the counting house, the workshop, the warehouse and the workers' dwellings, while the periphery became a bourgeois and petit bourgeois elysium – a private world where business was not discussed and where each detached or semi-detached villa with its walled garden and obsession with privacy aspired in miniature to the illusion of a country estate.[20] Shilibeer's omnibus, the Metropolitan Police Act and the 1832 Reform Bill inaugurated a new pattern of class relations in London.

In the forty years after the Reform Bill, this process of segregation and differentiation completed itself. By the 1870s, it had become part of the natural order of things. Rate-payer radicalism of the Benthamite type, which had triumphed with Hobhouse's Act of 1831, degenerated into the meanness of Bumble in Oliver Twist. Only sixteen years after 1832, the middle classes were enrolling as special constables to aid the Duke of Wellington against the Chartists, and by the 1870s they were generally voting Conservative. Evangelicalism and utilitarianism, originally distinct and to some extent opposed philosophies, increasingly coalesced. In 1814, Benthamite reformers had withdrawn their support from the West London Lancastrian Association on the issue of religious teaching in the school curriculum.[21] But Ashley and Chadwick were able to form an alliance on the General Board of Health in the

[20] For an exploration of some of these themes, see Dickens' *Little Dorrit*.
[21] Francis Sheppard, *London 1808–1870, the Infernal Wen* (1971), 217.

1840s, and by the time the Charity Organization Society was founded in 1869, the evangelical and utilitarian traditions were scarcely distinguishable. The social basis of this coalescence was the ever more insistent middle-class striving towards gentility. According to the Bankses, in the years between 1850 and 1870, 'specialist domestic servants were employed in ever increasing numbers. Middle class men and women dined out more frequently and gave more dinner parties at home. They spent their annual holidays at seaside resorts or even abroad. They kept a horse and carriage and employed a coachman and groom.'[22]

Moreover, this style of life, if not its material standards, was increasingly adopted by the growing army of clerks, teachers and new 'professional' men. Not to compete for these trophies, or at least the semblance of them, was to invite ostracism. Even the penniless Marx family found itself compelled to employ two domestic servants, to send their daughters to the 'South Hampstead College for Ladies' at £8 per term and to pay extra for language and drawing lessons. 'And now I have to engage a music fellow', Marx complained to Engels in 1857.[23]

The Marx family was of course exceptional. In general, middle-class incomes were rising. Even so, gentility of this kind was expensive, especially for those whose incomes could not match their aspirations to status. Sacrifices were necessary. The age of marriage was postponed and from the 1870s the size of families began to be restricted. Subtle savings were made in that part of the household budget not on public display. Needlework, ostensibly for charity, often supplemented the family income.[24] In the mid-Victorian period, prudence and thrift – what Harriet Martineau called 'the necessity and blessedness of homely and incessant self-discipline' – were not merely the battle-cries of economists and politicians.[25] They were integral necessities of middle-class domestic economy.

[22] J. A. and Olive Banks, *Feminism and Family Planning in Victorian England* (1965), 71; see also J. A. Banks, *Prosperity and Parenthood* (1954), Ch. 7.
[23] Yvonne Kapp, *Eleanor Marx* (1972), vol. 1, 32.
[24] Booth, *Life and Labour*, Series 2, vol. 5, 36; Series 1, vol. 4, 295–7.
[25] Harriet Martineau, *History of the Thirty Years' Peace* (1850), vol. 2, 705.

How then did these new aspirants to gentility regard the 'unwashed' proletarians crammed together in the smoky regions which they had left behind? In times of prosperity and stability, they probably thought little about them at all, since their major concern was to create a life style as far as possible removed from them. What Walter Benjamin wrote of the Parisian bourgeoisie under Louis Philippe could be applied to their London confrères.[26]

> For the private citizen, for the first time the living-space became distinguished from the place of work. The former constituted itself as the interior. The counting-house was its complement. The private citizen who in the counting-house took reality into account, required of the interior that it should maintain him in his illusions. This necessity was all the more pressing since he had no intention of adding social pre-occupations to his business ones. In the creation of his private environment he suppressed them both.[27]

But in times of political disturbance and economic depression, this complacent self-absorption gave way to fear and anxiety. As the physical distance between rich and poor areas increased, personal acquaintance diminished. Knowledge or rumours about the conditions and attitudes of the working class came not from personal experience, but from Parliamentary enquiries, from the pamphlets of clergymen and philanthropists and from the sensational reports to be found in the press. From these sources, it could be learnt that workers were infidels, politically seditious, immoral and improvident. At these times of insecurity, fears for property were combined with a great emotive yearning to re-establish personal relations between the classes. The enormous popularity of the novels of Dickens in the late 1830s and 1840s, with

---

[26] Evidence of the substantial sums given annually to all forms of London Charity, recorded for instance in the various editions of Samson Low, *The Charities of London* (1850), does not conflict with this argument. Charitable subscription was a mark of gentility. To appear on a published list of subscribers in the company of titled and aristocratic people was to demonstrate genteel status. This neglected aspect of Victorian charity was pointedly satirized by Dickens in the dealings between Boffin and the Duke of Linseed in *Our Mutual Friend*. See Humphrey House, *The Dickens World*, 2nd edn (1942), 80–1. While a high proportion of nonconformists continued to give charity for religious reasons, amongst the rest of the middle class the connection between charity and snobbery became increasingly important.

[27] Walter Benjamin, 'Paris–Capital of the 19th Century', *NLR*, 48, 83.

their nostalgia for Christmas spirit and traditional personal benevolence, was an expression of this desire.[28] But this was only a fantasy solution, a wish fulfilment. In reality, relations of benevolence could only be re-established by proxy. So money was invested in missionary organizations designed to eradicate pernicious customs and dangerous class prejudices from the poor, and to promote acceptance of the moral and political code of their superiors. The policeman and the workhouse were not sufficient. The respectable and the well-to-do had to win the 'hearts and minds' of the masses to the new moral order and to assert their right to act as its priesthood. Propertied London had no need of the new industrial religion of Comte, its ascendancy was to be established through the implantation of self-help and evangelical Christianity.

In the Victorian period, there were three major waves of anxiety among the propertied classes about the behaviour and attitudes of the London working class.[29] The first was a response to the uncertain conditions of the 1840s and early 1850s. There was anxiety about cholera, about Chartism and the Revolutions of 1848, about the inrush of Irish immigrants and the deteriorating condition of artisans threatened by the expansion of the 'dishonourable' and sweated trades. Focal points of concern can be discovered in the growth of the London City Mission reinforced by the findings of the 1851 Religious Census, in the foundation of Lord Ashley's Ragged School Union, in the association of crime and discontent made by Dickens' *Barnaby Rudge*, in the promotion of model dwellings companies and the inspection of common lodging houses, in the hurried attempts to create a public health authority, in the beginnings of Christian Socialism, and finally in Mayhew's investigation of the condition of street people and casual labourers. This period of anxiety about the social condition of London came to an end in the early 1850s. Feelings of insecurity subsided in a new phase of commercial and industrial expansion.

---

[28] See House, *Dickens World*, 46–52.
[29] For a discussion of these themes, see Stedman Jones, *Outcast London*, Pt III; and E. P. Thompson, 'Henry Mayhew and the Morning Chronicle', in E. P. Thompson and Eileen Yeo, *The Unknown Mayhew* (1971), 11–50.

The second peak of religious and philanthropic energy occurred between 1866 and 1872. Anxiety was less intense and certainly less widespread than it had been in the 1840s. Nevertheless, these were the years of the Second Reform Bill and the Paris Commune, of high bread prices coinciding with high unemployment in the East End, of another cholera epidemic and almost equally lethal outbreaks of scarlet fever and smallpox. The country as a whole was stable, but in London the number of paupers rose dramatically and the working class was suspected of republicanism. The spate of reforming concern which these uneasy years produced is reflected in the foundation of the Charity Organization Society, the beginning of Octavia Hill's housing experiments, the promotion of church-run workmen's clubs, Edward Denison's residence in the East End, the foundation of Dr Barnardo's East End Juvenile Mission, James Greenwood's journalistic investigations of the 'wilds' of London and Ruskin's *Fors Clavigera*. But despite the demonstrations, unemployed marches and over-filled stone yards, the problem of order was never acute. By 1873, the last traces of anxiety had passed away.

The third wave of insecurity reached its peak in the years between 1883 and 1888. It was a period of low profits, of high unemployment, of acute overcrowding, of another threatened visitation of cholera and of large-scale Jewish immigration into the East End. Artisans were known to be secularist and to support Henry George's single tax proposals; unemployed and casual workers were suspected of harbouring violent solutions to their misery and appeared to be falling under the sway of socialist oratory. Forebodings were increased by the uncertainties of the Irish situation, by suspicions of police inefficiency and evidence of municipal corruption. The reaction to this situation can be seen in the sensational journalism of Andrew Mearns, G. R. Sims, Arnold White and W. E. Stead, in the novels of Gissing and the first investigations of Charles Booth. Attempts to re-establish harmony ranged from Barnett's Toynbee Hall and Besant's People's Palace to the Salvation Army's Darkest England scheme and a rash of new missions promoted by churches, universities and public schools. But again, the crisis was not long-lived. Fear of disorder and insurrection began to fade as the depression lifted and virtually disappeared after the dock strike of 1889.

In each of these waves, the combination of high unemployment, social unrest abroad, threatened epidemics and doubts about the political loyalties of the masses, created varying degrees of uneasiness among the respectable and the well-to-do. Unemployment encouraged vagrancy. Labourers and broken-down tradesmen tramped into London and filled the common lodging houses in search of work or charitable relief. 'Plagues of beggars' appeared on the streets. The city was full of unemployed artisans and bankrupt small traders. Furniture and tools were pawned. Overcrowding increased as normally prosperous skilled workers and their families were forced to take in lodgers or to move to cheaper and smaller apartments. Epidemics, particularly those like cholera or smallpox which attacked adult wage earners, were known to exacerbate class hostilities. Revolutions abroad could produce disorder at home. Hard winters in years of depression reduced food consumption to dangerous levels and led to disturbing numbers of deaths from starvation. Those with property assumed an intimate link between begging, crime and political disorder. It is not surprising that some of them felt that they were sitting on a powder keg and that each wave of anxiety should leave behind it a new crop of social and religious organizations determined to hasten the work of christianizing and 'civilizing' the city.

Two major stratagems can be detected in this christianizing and 'civilizing' activity. The first was to use legislation to create a physical and institutional environment in which undesirable working-class habits and attitudes would be deterred, while private philanthropy could undertake the active propagation of a new moral code. The material needs of the poor would then be used as a means towards their moral reformation. Thus, in the sphere of housing: street clearance acts, railway promotion, sanitary legislation, common lodging house inspection and Artisans' Dwellings Acts demolished rookeries and slums and dispersed their inhabitants, while model dwellings companies and philanthropic housing trusts provided what propertied London considered to be more appropriate working-class housing. Habits of order and regularity were enforced through the insistence upon regular payment of rent and through detailed regulatory codes governing the use of facilities. The presence of the caretaker was designed to ensure that the rules were observed. Even the architectural design of these buildings, as George Howell noted of the Peabody blocks, was intended to ensure 'regulation without direct control'.[30]

A similar and even more calculated attempt to weight the workers' felicific calculus in favour of middle-class norms of conduct was apparent in the organizational ambitions of the Charity Organization Society (COS). The aim of the Society (never remotely realized) was to act as a clearing house for all requiring charitable assistance in London: all applicants were to have their cases thoroughly investigated; if found 'deserving' (showing signs of thrift and temperance), they were to be directed to the appropriate specialized charity; if found 'undeserving' (drunken, improvident), they were instructed to apply to the workhouse. The COS was a logical complement to the reforms in London Poor Law administration which occurred at the end of the 1860s. The intention of these reforms was to make the workhouse an effective deterrent to the able-bodied pauper and to abolish outdoor relief. Control of charitable outlets allied to strict Poor Law administration would, it was hoped, effectively demonstrate to the poor that there could be no practicable alternative to 'incessant self-discipline'.

These attempts to reform the manners of the working class through the control of its physical and institutional environment were generally accompanied by a firm belief in the civilizing effects of personal relations between the classes. Evangelical in origin, the intensity of this belief grew virtually as a reflex reaction to the growing social segregation of the city. The practice of 'visiting the poor' was pioneered by the Church and increased steadily after the 1851 Religious Census had shown that the christianization of the working class would only be accomplished by active missionary work. In the years that followed, the mission hall became a familiar feature of the slum landscape and evangelical crusades were directed at

---

[30] George Howell, 'The Dwellings of the Poor', *Nineteenth Century* (June 1883), 1004.

every sector of the 'friendless and fallen'. High churchmen, Christian Socialists, nonconformists and Salvationists all competed to implant Christian principles among the poor. But Christianity and 'civilization' were generally synonymous terms. Under the aegis of the local church, household management classes, coal and blanket clubs and penny savings banks were started, teetotal working men's clubs were promoted, ragged school unions were fostered, railway excursions were organized and wholesome athletic sports encouraged. By the end of the 1860s, the idea of inter-class contact was being employed in purely secular missionary enterprises. It was the guiding principle, for instance, of Octavia Hill's use of 'lady rent collectors' to bring in receipts from poor tenements: good examples were set, elevated thoughts implanted, habits of thrift and industry nourished, coarseness and improvidence penalized. Octavia Hill's experiments were carefully costed to show that philanthropy and profitability could go together. Her hope was that all landlords in poor districts would follow her in accepting responsibility for the morality and habits of their tenants. Thus, the moral advantages enjoyed by the inhabitants of model dwellings could be generalized throughout the metropolis.

This belief that missionaries from civilization would dispel the 'shades' and 'shadows' in which the poor dwelt, reached its apotheosis in the settlement houses of the 1880s. According to Samuel Barnett, the founder of Toynbee Hall, the rift between classes had continued to grow despite the previous efforts of philanthropy:

The poor, moved away to make room for railways, left to inhabit back courts and back parts of the town, have not caught the message, unity. Thus it is, that they believe still in conversion rather than in development, and think that progress is to be won by revolution. Thus it is that the great part keep themselves to themselves and 'association', the watchword of the future, is not understood. The good news of a unity greater than rich or poor, greater than creeds, greater than nations, held together by national service is yet to be preached ... humanity will help the poor to see the rich as their brothers and God as their father.[31]

Barnett's preaching found a ready response. Centres of

---

[31] Samuel Barnett, 'The Duties of the Rich to the Poor', in J. M. Knapp (ed.), *The Universities and the Social Problem* (1895), 72.

civilization, 'manor houses,' were established in east and south London. University men, inspired by the idea of 'service' brought their 'culture' to the working class. Through the power of these outposts of civilization, class suspicions were to dissolve in harmony and brotherhood. 'Esau' would put away his bow and join together with 'Jacob' in the appreciation of a national treasure house of art, literature and religion.

The cumulative external effect of this middle-class on-slaught in the Victorian period was considerable. Old haunts of crime, vice and disease were demolished and their inhabit-ants scattered. Writing in 1860 of the once notorious St Giles' district, Renton Nicholson observed:

> The city of cadgers is not what it was. Formerly its boundaries were lawless, like Alsatia ... It was a refuge for the desperado, the thief, the cadger and the prostitute: it now scarcely affords a home for the two latter classes. The introduction of a police station in the immediate vicinity has perhaps caused this revolution in the precinct of the classic ground. The operations of the Mendicity Society have naturally decreased the number of beggars in the Metropolis. These and other multiplied causes have had the effect of reducing the population of St Giles's as well as altering for the better the character of its inhabitants. Working people employed in selling fruit and other things in the streets, and labourers in the markets, are the principle occupiers of the tenements in the 'rookery' at present.[32]

The sites, formerly occupied by these 'Alsatias', were now occupied by acres of model dwellings. By 1891, these blocks housed 189,108 people and by the end of the century the numbers had increased by a further substantial amount.[33]

By the end of Victoria's reign, gin palaces had virtually disappeared. The social and economic functions of the pub had been reduced; drinking hours had been restricted and children had been excluded from the bar. Cock-fighting, bearbaiting and ratting had all but died out. Gambling had been driven off the streets. 'Waits', 'vales' and other tra-ditional forms of 'indiscriminate charity' had been increasing-

---

[32] 'Lord Chief Justice Baron Nicholson', *Autobiography* (1860), 262–3; for the former character of St Giles' see Samuel Bamford, *Passages in the Life of a Radical* (1967 edn), 113–14; Anon., *Dens and Sinks of London Laid Open* (1848), *passim*.

[33] Henry Jephson, *The Sanitary Evolution of London* (1907), 368.

ly resisted by large sections of the middle class.[34] Evangelical disapproval had hastened the disappearance of tea gardens, free-and-easies and judge-and-jury clubs. Public executions at Newgate had ceased in 1868. Southwark, St Bartholomew and the other great London fairs had been abolished. Craft drinking rituals had declined and St Monday had disappeared in most trades. In place of these traditional carnivals and holidays, four regular bank holidays had been instituted in 1871 and a growing number of parks, museums, exhibitions, public libraries and mechanics' institutes promoted a more improving or innocuous use of leisure time.

The churches' ambition to bring the working class into contact with its ideology had also benefited from legislative assistance. From the time of the 1870 Education Act, all children were subjected to religious education and initiated into the rituals of established Christianity through a daily routine of morning prayer. Legislative attempts to change the unsabbatarian habits of adults had not been so successful. Lord Robert Grosvenor's Sunday Trading Bill provoked serious riots in Hyde Park in 1855 and had to be hastily withdrawn. Even in 1880, R. A. Cross, the Conservative Home Secretary, said that if Sunday closing were introduced he would not be responsible for the peace of London.[35] Nevertheless, at an unofficial level, the scale of missionary activity had increased enormously and by the 1890s efforts to establish inter-class contact in working-class areas had in some cases reached saturation point. In Deptford, for example, Booth reported: 'Some time ago (says the vicar) the only workers were church of England, Congregationalist and Roman Catholic; now all sorts are trying ... The poor parts of

---

[34] A street ballad of the 1840s states:
>   Of all the days throughout the year
>   There was never one, I say,
>   That could come up in former times,
>   At all to Boxing Day.
>   But in the windows now you'll see,
>   How shocking, I declare,
>   Notice, recollect, no Christmas Boxes
>   will be given here.

'Boxing Day in 1847', John Ashton, *Modern Street Ballads* (1888), 396. See also James Greenwood, 'Out with the Waits', *In Strange Company* (1873), 328–40.

[35] See Harrison, *Drink and the Victorians*, 244–5.

Deptford are, indeed, a veritable "Tom Tiddler's ground" for missions, and we hear of one woman busy "at the washtub" calling out, "You are the fifth this morning."[36] Salvationists paraded up and down the main streets, while armies of religious volunteers visited the poor in their homes. At the turn of the century, these visible symbols of religious and charitable intervention could be found in every poor borough of London.

How far had this middle-class onslaught changed or influenced working-class attitudes and behaviour? Certainly not in the way it had been intended. By the Edwardian period, it had become inescapably clear that middle-class evangelism had failed to re-create a working class in its own image. The great majority of London workers were neither Christian, provident, chaste nor temperate.

The results of fifty years of Christian missionary activity had been insignificant. The *Daily News* religious census of 1902 concluded that 'the poorer the district the less inclination is there to attend a place of worship'.[37] Charles Booth's encyclopaedic survey of 'religious influences' in London at the end of the 1890s produced similar results. 'The churches', according to Booth, 'have come to be regarded as the resorts of the well-to-do, and of those who are willing to accept the charity and patronage of people better off than themselves.'[38] Where the poor did attend church, it was generally for material reasons. Church attendance was rewarded by church charity. When charity was withdrawn, the congregation disappeared.[39] It was a pleasant irony that the poor should adopt a thoroughly utilitarian attitude in the one realm in which the middle class considered it to be inappropriate. The consequence of this association between church and charity was that religion became a symbol of servile status. Church attendance signified abject poverty and the loss of self-respect. As Booth noted of the Clapham–Nine Elms district, 'the poor are regularly visited, but others are above visitation, and apt

---

[36] Booth, *Life and Labour*, Series 3, vol. 5, 14.
[37] R. Mudie-Smith (ed.), *Religious Life of London* (1903), 26.
[38] Booth, *Life and Labour*, Series 3, vol. 7, 426.
[39] A missionary in Hackney told Booth, 'You can buy a congregation, but it melts away as soon as the payments cease.' Booth, *Life and Labour*, Series 3, vol. 1, 82.

to slam the door, and say, "I am a respectable person." [40] Even among the poor themselves, however, clergymen complained that they were unable to make contact with the men. Dealing with middle-class intruders, like paying the rent and all other activities pertaining to family expenditure and the upkeep of the home, was the province of the wife. Describing the clergy's attempts to make contact with the working class in their homes, Booth reported: 'The visit only results in a conversation on the doorstep, or through the half-closed door, or if the man answers to the knock, he will very likely say "ah you're from the church; you want to see the missus" and will then clear out.' [41] The same impression emerged from the detailed descriptions of the attitudes of the poor, compiled by M. E. Loane, a district nurse. She wrote:

One day while attending to a woman who was seriously ill, I heard a constant rapping at the front door. It would have been against all etiquette for me to offer to go and see what was wanted, but when I observed that the patient was getting nervous and worried by the sound, I went to look for the husband, who had been requested to remain within call. I found him in the backyard, squeezed into the only corner which was not easily visible from the road. 'There is a lady knocking at the door.' No response. 'I think it is Mrs – the vicar's wife.' 'Lerrer knock then,' he replied valiantly, 'I'm not a tome. When the missus is about, she can do's she like.' [42]

If efforts to christianize the working class were largely a failure, efforts to induce temperance appear to have made even less impact. The temperance movement tended to be strong in areas where drunkenness was most prevalent. But drinking habits in London were moderate compared with those in mining districts or centres of heavy industry. Furthermore, as Brian Harrison has pointed out, not only was brewing a major London industry, but a high proportion of London's immigrants were drawn from the south-eastern counties, centres of hop and malt production. [43] It should also be remembered that large numbers of the casual poor depended upon the annual excursion to the Kent hop fields to bridge the slack summer season. Among the mass of the

[40] Booth, *Life and Labour*, Series 3, vol. 5, 190.
[41] Booth, *Life and Labour*, Series 3, vol. 1, 81.
[42] M. E. Loane, *An Englishman's Castle* (1909), 3.
[43] Harrison, *Drink and the Victorians*, 58.

working class, the popularity of music-hall songs extolling the pleasures of drink and lampooning teetotalism was a general indication of antipathy towards the temperance cause. But even among radical artisans, although there were many moderate temperance advocates, temperance never became a prominent feature of the metropolitan radical tradition. A bar was a normal fixture in radical workmen's clubs and provincial socialists were often shocked by the Social Democratic Federation's tolerant attitude towards beer.[44] In the provinces, working-class radicals and middle-class liberals often shared a nonconformist religious background. But in London, there was no common ground between artisan secularism and middle-class nonconformity. Because of this absence of any shared religious outlook, temperance was liable to be associated with sabbatarianism and the 'canting hypocrisy of the nonconformist conscience'. The Liberals' support of the Local Option in the 1895 general election appears to have lost them a considerable number of working-class votes in London.[45]

At the end of the century, Booth reported that drunkenness had decreased but that drinking was more widespread than before. The pub remained a focal point of local working-class life. But its role had changed. It had been shorn of many of its former economic functions and was now more narrowly associated with leisure and relaxation. Women used pubs more frequently, and so apparently did courting couples. Straightforward heavy drinking had become less widespread, as was testified by the virtual disappearance of the gin palace. But there had been no dramatic shift. Frequent and heavy bouts of drinking remained common in traditional London trades and jobs requiring great physical exertion. In the long term, the moderation of drinking habits depended upon the increase of mechanization and the decrease of overcrowding.

---

[44] The possession of a bar in workmen's clubs was in the 1870s in fact the principal symbol of emancipation from aristocratic or ecclesiastical interference. For the struggle around this issue, see John Taylor, 'From Self-Help to Glamour: the Working Man's Club, 1860–1972', *History Workshop Pamphlets*, 7, esp. 1–20; on the friction between the London SDF and provincial socialists on the drink question, see Walter Kendall, *The Revolutionary Movement in Britain 1900–21* (1969), 8, 14.
[45] Pelling, *Social Geography*, 58.

Neither of these tendencies was characteristic of London in the period before 1914.[46]

The results of the pressures exerted by Poor Law officials, charity organizers and self-help advocates to induce thrift among the working class were similarly disappointing. The bulk of the working class did not adopt middle-class habits of saving. What saving there was among the casual workers, the unskilled and the poorer artisans was not for the purpose of accumulating a sum of capital, but for the purchase of articles of display or for the correct observance of ritual occasions. Thus the 'goose club' run by the publican to ensure a good Christmas dinner, or the clothing clubs providing factory girls with fashionably-cut dresses were much more prevalent and characteristic forms of saving than membership of a friendly society which was confined to the better paid and regularly employed.[47] The one form of insurance common among the poor, death insurance, was typical of their general attitude towards thrift. The money was intended not for the subsequent maintenance of dependants, but to pay for the costs of the funeral. If one thought obsessed the minds of those in poverty, it was to escape a pauper's funeral, and to be buried according to due custom. This attitude, which Dickens has immortalized in the character of Betty Higden, was described by one of Booth's informants:

'Funerals,' said the chaplain … 'are still very extravagant, especially in the case of the poorest people, flowers being one of the chief items of expenditure. Plumes on the horses are quite commonly used … Fish and cat's meat dealers and costermongers are the people most addicted to showy funerals. A large proportion of the elaborate tombstones facing the main drive belong to these people. There is a feeling among the poor, that when a man dies if he has saved money, it is his: "he made the money, poor fellow, and he shall have it." '[48]

More generally, evidence about patterns of spending among the London poor suggests that a concern to demonstrate self-respect was infinitely more important than any forms of

---

[46] Booth, *Life and Labour*, final vol., 'Notes on Social Influences', 59–74; and see also Harrison, *Drink and the Victorians*, Ch. 14.

[47] See Charles Manby Smith, *Curiosities of London Life* (1853), 310–19; Booth, *Life and Labour*, Series 1, vol. 1, 106–12; J. Franklyn, *The Cockney* (1953), 183–4.

[48] Booth, *Life and Labour*, Series 3, vol. 1, 249.

saving based upon calculations of utility. When money was available which did not have to be spent on necessities, it was used to purchase articles for display rather than articles of use. An extreme example of this preference was cited with disapproval by the Honourable Maud Stanley who visited the poor around the Five Dials in the 1870s. One cold February, she visited the room of an unemployed painter. The family was on the verge of starvation, the furniture had been pawned, one child had already died and the life of the other was precarious.

I provided her [the wife] with all she wanted for the child, and looked after it constantly until it was out of danger. The man got a promise of work, and I lent him £1 to get his clothes and tools out of pawn, and he gave me his word to repay me in small weekly sums. He got work and changed his house. I went there to Mrs Lin, and to my surprise found the walls of her room hung with little pictures. I asked her how she had got them; and she said that when her husband had brought home his first week's wages on Saturday she had spent 3/6d in buying these pictures, as the room looked so uncomfortable without them. She had not yet bought bed or bedding, and I should have said needed every necessary of life.

I was not over pleased, and said she should have repaid me before buying luxuries.[49]

A similar attitude towards expenditure was described thirty years later by M. E. Loane. Describing the 'pleasures of the poor', she wrote:

Expensive furniture is desired by men, women, and even children, partly as incontrovertible evidence of character and position, partly to satisfy an untrained aestheticism. Comfort has nothing to do with the matter, and use is still less considered. In a home often visited by sickness, and where in earlier days hunger had more than once shown its terrible face, there was a brass fender in the locked parlour. I naturally thought it was a recent purchase, but the second daughter, a girl of 24, told me that it dated from her childhood ... even in the comparatively prosperous days when I made their acquaintance, it would have been easy to pick out 50 things that they needed more urgently than that fender.

Perhaps the real reason why pictures precede other superfluities is because even the most 'keerless' and revolutionary person cannot suggest any method of using them. I almost invariably find that it is the frame and the extent of glass that gives a picture its value; not only is artistic worth entirely unrecognised, but the subject rarely excites the slightest interest.[50]

[49] Anon. (Maud Stanley), *Work about the Five Dials* (1878), 21–2.
[50] M. E. Loane, *Englishman's Castle*, 56.

This concern for display and for keeping up appearances was not confined to the poor, it was predominant throughout the working class. Even the well-paid artisan who could afford to rent a terrace house in Battersea or Woolwich reserved the front room for occasions when he dressed in his best clothes, for Sunday high teas with family relations, to entertain a prospective son-in-law or as a place to lay out the coffin when a death occurred. The room generally remained unused during the week.[51]

For the poor, this effort to keep up appearances, to demonstrate 'respectability' entailed as careful a management of the weekly family budget as any charity organizer could have envisaged. But its priorities were quite different. 'Respectability' did not mean church attendance, teetotalism or the possession of a post office savings account. It meant the possession of a presentable Sunday suit, and the ability to be seen wearing it. At the turn of the century, according to Fred Willis:

Sunday clothes were absolutely essential. Anyone who appeared on Sunday in work-a-day clothes was beyond the pale. The ritual of Sunday clothes was sacrosanct, to the labourer in his respectable black suit, black choker and bowler hat, as much as to the Balham bank clerk in his silk hat and frock coat ... Stiff white shirts and collars, too, were indispensable. On Saturday afternoon and evening children could be seen in every street carrying home the weekly white shirt and collars from the laundry ... [and] he who could not afford the dignity of a white shirt, carefully built up the illusion of one by covering his chest with a 'dicky' and pinning stiff white cuffs to the waistbands of his plebeian Oxford shirt.[52]

To appear without Sunday clothes was to admit inferiority. According to Alexander Paterson writing in 1911:

The mother with a bitter sense of pride, will not allow her family to stray into the main streets should a week of depression have ended in the pawning of Sunday clothes. The father himself, deprived of his best suit and collar, omits to shave, and kicks about his room in socks, having lain in bed till past midday ... The boy of sixteen acquiesces in this subservience to opinion, and remains indoors all day, caged for want of a collar.[53]

---

[51] For the attitude of class 'E' – Booth's typical London artisan – see Booth, *Life and Labour*, Series 2, vol. 5, 329–30; for the atmosphere of the parlour, see Fred Willis, *101, Jubilee Road, London, S.E.* (1948), 102–3.

[52] Willis, *Jubilee Road*, 70; see also M. E. Loane, *The Next Street but One* (1907), 20.

[53] Alexander Paterson, *Across the Bridges* (1911), 38.

But if Sunday was the occasion to demonstrate self-respect and to shut out for a day the pressures of poverty, Monday meant an abrupt return to reality. For Monday meant, not only the return of work, but also the day when the rent had to be paid. According to Paterson again:

> On Monday morning a group of women, with bundles tied in old newspapers, will be seen outside the pawnshop, waiting for the doors to open at 9 am; for this is a common weekly practice, and not the urgent measure of exceptional distress. It is true that on next Saturday night the suit will in all probability be redeemed, but the suit by then will have cost a guinea, instead of a pound, and every time it is pawned in future will add a shilling to the price.[54]

It is clear from these and other accounts that the priorities of expenditure among the poor bore little relation to the ambitions set before them by advocates of thrift and self-help. Joining a friendly society to insure against sickness, medical expenses, unemployment or old age, apart from being enormously expensive for those whose incomes were low or irregular, was too abstract and intangible for families whose whole efforts were concentrated on getting through the week ahead without being beset by disaster. In this respect, the failure of the COS campaign had been total. Even in the East End, where the Society enjoyed the co-operation of local Poor Law officials, Booth remarked: 'Its methods are disliked and its theories attacked ... as regards this particular district, the reformed system of poor law administration and the attempted guidance of charity are, like the efforts of the missions somewhat disappointing'.[55]

Finally, it is clear that although the popular use of leisure time had changed dramatically in the course of the century, the direction of change had not been of a kind to give much encouragement to religious and moral reformers. Certainly, the cruel animal sports of the eighteenth century had declined substantially. In 1869 James Greenwood wrote: 'In the present enlightened age we do not fight cocks and "shy" at hens tied to a stake at the Shrove Tuesday fair; neither do we fight dogs, or pit those sagacious creatures to fight bulls.'[56] By

[54] Ibid., 41.
[55] Booth, *Life and Labour*, Series 3, vol. 2, 52.
[56] James Greenwood, *The Seven Curses of London* (1869), 378.

the end of the century, rat-baiting and bird singing competitions, at the height of their popularity when Mayhew conducted his investigations, had also virtually disappeared.[57] They had given way to the gentler passions for racing pigeons and caged linnets. It is also true that Saturday half holidays established in most trades in the late 1860s and early 1870s had led to an enormous increase in the number of railway excursions to the country and the seaside. But bank holidays, according to clergymen in the 1890s were a great 'curse'.[58] The old association of holidays with betting, drinking and extravagant expenditure remained strong. Derby Day was the major festive event in the calendar of the London poor. Disapproving observers like Maurice Davies and James Greenwood found the roads to Epsom crammed with vans, carts and pedestrians making their way to races where all the 'vices' of the fairground flourished with undiminished vigour.[59] 200,000 people were said to congregate on Hampstead Heath on a fine Easter or a Whitsun, while similarly vast numbers made for Crystal Palace or the Welsh Harp on August bank holidays.[60]

One of the main reasons why fairs and races provoked middle-class disapproval was their association with betting and gambling. Far from decreasing in the second half of the nineteenth century, these pastimes increased enormously. The trend was already apparent at the end of the 1860s. 'There can be no doubt', wrote Greenwood in 1869, 'that the vice of gambling is on the increase amongst the English working classes ... twenty years ago there were but 3 or 4 sporting newspapers published in London; now there are more than a

---

[57] At the time when Mayhew was writing, rat-baiting was a major popular sport. He estimated that there were 70 regular pits attached to pubs in London. See Mayhew, *London Labour*, vol. 2, 56. By the time Greenwood was writing, the sport appears to have become more furtive. See Greenwood, *The Wilds of London* (1874), 271–9. There is no mention of it in the Booth Survey. Dog-fighting and cock-fighting had become illicit sports confined to a minority of sporting aristocrats by the 1850s. See Mayhew, *London Labour*, vol. 2, 57; and 'One of the Old Brigade', in his *London in the Sixties* (1898), 91. Bird singing contests carried on longer. They are mentioned in Booth, *Life and Labour*, Series 3, vol. 1, 252. But the peak of their popularity was undoubtedly thirty or forty years earlier.

[58] Booth, *Life and Labour*, final vol., 51.

[59] Rev. C. M. Davies, *Mystic London* (1875), 141–9; Greenwood, *Wilds*, 318–25.

[60] James Greenwood, *Low Life Deeps* (1876), 176; see also Maurice Davies' description of Fairlop Fair in east London, Davies, *Mystic London*, 123–4.

dozen.'[61] According to Arthur Sherwell, by the beginning of the 1890s, touting was endemic in the craft trades of the West End and sporting papers universal in tailors' workshops.[62] The House of Lords Select Committee on Betting in 1902 concluded that, 'even where due allowance has been made, both for the increase in the population of towns and the rise in wages, betting is undoubtedly more widespread and general than it used to be'.[63] The Booth survey recorded the same impression. 'Betting', the police informed Booth, 'is increasing out of all proportion to other forms of vice', and 'gambling', the clergy told him, 'presses drink hard as the greatest evil of the day'.[64] The situation was aptly summed up in one account of model dwellings where the behaviour of inhabitants was supposed to be subject to greater moral scrutiny than elsewhere: in south London, the boy brought up in model dwellings: 'while yet a schoolboy ... played pitch and toss with secret exuberance on the stairs of his buildings; now that he is older, a group of his mates may entice him to the flat roof of the model buildings some early Sunday morning, and there under the sky, 150 feet above the river, a game of "banker" will be screened from the notice of police and parent'.[65]

The prevalence of these 'unimproving' recreations in the daytime was matched by the enormous popularity of the music-hall at night. Despite the repeated claims made for its educational value by its promoters, the music-hall like the fairs and the races, was subject to constant evangelical disapproval.[66] Music-halls began as extensions to public houses and the sale of drink remained the mainstay of their profits.[67] Added to this there were frequent allegations – often

[61] Greenwood, *Seven Curses*, 377.
[62] Arthur Sherwell, *Life in West London* (1894), 126.
[63] Report of Select Committee of House of Lords on Betting, PP 1902. v, p.v.
[64] Booth, *Life and Labour*, final vol., 57, 58.
[65] Paterson, *Across the Bridges*, 170.
[66] For contemporary defences of music-hall, see the deposition handed in by Frederick Stanley, on behalf of the London Music Hall Proprietors' Association to the Select Committee on Theatrical Licences and Regulations, PP 1866, xvi, appendix 3 (SC 1866); see also John Hollingshead, *Miscellanies, Stories and Essays*, 3 vols. (1874), iii, 254; and the dramatic critic Clement Scott's tribute to Charles Morton, 'the father of the halls', on his eightieth birthday, Harold Scott, *The Early Doors* (1946), 136–7.
[67] Ewing Ritchie, *Days and Nights in London* (1880), 44–5; Harrison, *Drink and the Victorians*, 325.

well-founded – that the halls were used by prostitutes to pick up clients. Yet, despite the efforts of campaigners for temperance, moral purity or a more intelligent use of leisure time, not to mention determined attempts by theatre managers to crush a dangerous rival, the number of music-halls increased dramatically between 1850 and 1900.[68] The first music-hall was built as an extension to the Canterbury Arms, Lambeth, by the publican, Charles Morton, in 1849 and housed 100 people. Its success was immediate and by 1856 it had both been enlarged to hold 700 and then rebuilt to hold 1,500. By 1866, there were twenty-three halls in addition to innumerable pub rooms where music-hall entertainment was held.[69] In the 1870s the number of halls continued to increase at a prodigious rate even though two hundred halls were closed after strict fire precautions had been imposed in 1878.[70] In the 1880s it was estimated that there were five hundred halls in London, and at the beginning of the 1890s it was calculated that the thirty-five largest halls alone were catering for an average audience of 45,000 nightly.[71]

Although music-hall entertainment spread to the provinces, it began and remained a characteristically London creation. According to a Parliamentary Commission in 1892, 'the large collection of theatres and music halls gathered together, the amount of capital used in the enterprise, the great number of persons, directly and indirectly provided with employment, the multitudes of all classes of the people who attend theatres and music halls of London, find no other parallel in any other part of the country'.[72] Apart from the central palaces, which particularly from the 1880s onwards began to attract sporting aristocrats, military officers, students, clerks and tourists, the

[68] For the early development of music-hall in London, see appendix to 1866 Select Committee on Theatrical Licences and Regulations; Scott, *Early Doors*; C. D. Stuart & A. J. Park, *The Variety Stage* (1895).

[69] Select Committee on Theatres and Places of Entertainment, PP 1892. XVIII, appendix 15. (Henceforth SC 1892.)

[70] D. Farson, *Marie Lloyd and Music Hall* (1972). 19.

[71] SC 1892. The estimation of 500 halls is in Colin MacInnes, *Sweet Saturday Night* (1967), 13; the most sensitive evocation of music-hall culture to have appeared so far. It is difficult to make a precise estimate since so many of the smaller music-halls were simply extensions to pubs. For an exhaustive catalogue of all premises known to have been used as music-halls see Diana Howard, *London Theatres and Music Halls 1850–1950* (1970).

[72] SC 1892, iv.

music-hall was predominantly working-class, in the character of its audience, in the origins of its performers and in the content of its songs and sketches. According to Ewing Ritchie who visited the Canterbury Arms in the later 1850s:

> evidently the majority present are respectable mechanics, or small trades-men with their wives and daughters and sweethearts there. Now and then you see a midshipman, or a few fast clerks and warehouse men ... and here as elsewhere, we see a few of the class of unfortunates whose staring eyes would fain extort an admiration which their persons do not justify. Everyone is smoking and everyone has a glass before him; but the class that come here are economical, and chiefly confine themselves to pipes and porter.[73]

The Canterbury, however, was one of the more exclusive music-halls. At the time of Ritchie's account, it cost sixpence admission to the pit and ninepence admission to the gallery. Smaller and cheaper halls attracted a poorer audience. Their character was described by A. J. Munby in 1868:

> about 10 o'clock, I observed just opposite the Shoreditch Station, a brilliantly lighted entrance to a 'Temperance Music Hall'. The admission was only *one penny*; and I went in and found myself in the pit of a small and very dingy theatre, with a narrow stage. The pit was crowded with people of the lowest class; chiefly coster girls and lads, in their working clothes. There was no drinking or smoking as in the grander music halls; both indeed were forbidden. Rough as they looked the audience was quiet and well behaved; and two policemen kept strict order.[74]

The prohibition on drinking and smoking was exceptional, but there were countless small halls of this general character in working-class suburbs between the 1860s and the 1890s. In general the music-hall appealed to all sectors of the working class from the casual labourer to the highly-paid artisan. Its importance as a social and cultural institution in proletarian districts was second only to that of the pub. As one working man told the 1892 Committee: 'The music halls in the East End and South East of London are considered the great entertainment of the working man and his family.'[75] Of its enormous popularity there can be no doubt. Even in 1924,

---

[73] Ewing Ritchie, *The Night Side of London* (1858), 70.
[74] Derek Hudson, *Munby, Man of Two Worlds* (1972), 255.
[75] SC 1892, q. 5171.

thirty years after the music-hall's heyday, 100,000 people turned out to attend the funeral of Marie Lloyd.[76]

From this preliminary discussion of working-class spending habits and leisure-time activity, it is clear that by the beginning of the twentieth century a new working-class culture had emerged in London. Many of its institutions dated back to the middle of the century, but its general shape had first become visible in the 1870s and dominant in the 1890s. By the time Booth conducted his survey of 'religious influences', its general components had already become set in a distinctive mould. This culture was clearly distinguished from the culture of the middle class and had remained largely impervious to middle-class attempts to dictate its character or direction. Its dominant cultural institutions were not the school, the evening class, the library, the friendly society, the church or the chapel, but the pub, the sporting paper, the race-course and the music-hall. Booth's 'religious influences' series was compiled from information provided by clergymen, school board and Poor Law officials, vestrymen, policemen and charity organizers. It could be read as one interminable confession of impotence and defeat. But, significantly, Booth did not draw a pessimistic conclusion from his enquiries. There is an inescapable tone of assurance, even of complacency, running through his final volumes – in marked contrast to the anxiety which coloured his first investigations. This difference in tone could not and was not attributed by him to any substantial decrease in poverty and overcrowding. What principally impressed him was the growing stability and orderliness of London working-class society. Writing of the poorest streets of Whitechapel he remarked, 'as poor as ever, but old rookeries destroyed, black patches cleared away, thieves and prostitutes gone, a marvellous change for the better'.[77] 'The police', he observed, 'have far less trouble in maintaining order.'[78] Describing the elementary schools in the East End, he conceded that the hopes of educationalists had not been fulfilled and that 'the accomplishments of the 4th standard may be all forgotten, so that reading becomes

---

[76] MacInnes, *Sweet Saturday Night*, 24.
[77] Booth, *Life and Labour*, Series 3, vol. 2, 61.
[78] Ibid., 65.

difficult and writing a lost art'. 'But', he went on, 'something still remains. Habits of cleanliness and order have been formed; a higher standard of dress and decency have been attained, and this reacts upon the homes.'[79] Or again in Southwark, he reported that, compared with the situation in 1880, boys were 'much more docile; insubordination, then endemic now almost unknown ... all this, the result of discipline and control at school, reacts beneficially on the home'.[80] Describing the local music-halls, he admitted their vulgarity and unimproving tone, but observed, 'the audiences are prevailingly youthful. They seek amusement and are easily pleased. No encouragement to vice can be attributed to these local music halls.'[81] The general working-class objection to church-going, as Booth described it, stemmed from the class associations of religion. But secularism had sharply declined since the 1880s and the prevailing attitude had changed from hostility to good-natured indifference. In Woolwich it was apparently still 'bad form ... even to nod to a parson in the street'.[82] But this was exceptional. In London as a whole the working class were 'more friendly, more tolerant perhaps of religious pretensions'. The final impression conveyed by the Booth survey was of a working-class culture which was both impermeable to outsiders, and yet predominantly conservative in character: a culture in which the central focus was not 'trade unions and friendly societies, cooperative effort, temperance propaganda and politics (including socialism)', but 'pleasure, amusement, hospitality and sport'.[83]

This impression conveyed by Booth is confirmed by other sources. The secularist, republican and internationalist culture which had been such a characteristic feature of the artisan tradition in the first three-quarters of the century had all but died out by 1900. The Metropolitan Radical Federation, an independent political force well to the left of official liberalism in the 1880s, had degenerated into a canvassing network for Liberal MPs in the early 1890s and had steadily lost members.

[79] Ibid., 54.
[80] Booth, *Life and Labour*, Series 3, vol. 4, 202.
[81] Booth, *Life and Labour*, Series 3, vol. 4, 'Social Influences', 53.
[82] Booth, *Life and Labour*, Series 3, vol. 5, 121.
[83] Booth, *Life and Labour*, Series 3, vol. 7, 425.

The *Star* which had been launched in a wave of radical enthusiasm in 1888, and had reached an unprecedented daily circulation of 279,000 in 1889, had lost both circulation and political influence by 1895. The attempt by *Reynold's News* to revive a radical campaign between 1900 and 1902 proved a total failure.[84] The secularist movement which had possessed thirty branches in London in the mid-1880s had almost disappeared by the late 1890s. Working-class internationalism, still a significant force in the 1860s and early 1870s, had similarly declined by 1900.[85] Even in the 1880s, radical artisans had frequently and exhaustively debated the Eastern Question, Irish coercion and British rule in India. But in 1900, far from standing out against the Mafeking celebrations, the radical working men's clubs joined in the general euphoria. 'The relief of Mafeking has caused great enthusiasm in the club during the last few days', wrote a correspondent from the Paddington Radical Club, 'when I ventured to point out to one member that the cost of the present war would have put old age pensions on a sound basis, the answer I received was "to Hades with Old Age Pensions"'.[86]

These workmen's clubs had been the focal point of artisans' radicalism in the 1870s and 1880s. But a declining interest in politics was noted by radical clubsmen from the early 1890s. Its place was usurped by an increasing demand for entertainment. Entertainments, in the form of amateur dramatics, dances and sing-songs had always formed an intrinsic part of the weekly routine of these clubs – even in the mid-1880s when lectures, political debates and demonstrations had occupied the predominant place in club activity. But in the 1890s, as the pioneering research of John Taylor reveals, the political and educational side of club life faded. Entertainment became the dominant attraction and the balance of power within the clubs shifted from the political council to the entertainments committee. According to the Club Journal, it was already

[84] P. Thompson, *Socialists, Liberals and Labour, the Struggle for London 1885–1914* (1967), 179.
[85] For discussions of London working-class international interests in the 1860s and early 1870s, see Royden Harrison, *Before the Socialists* (1965); H. Collins and C. Abramsky, *Karl Marx and the British Labour Movement* (1965); Stan Shipley, 'Club Life and Socialism in Mid-Victorian London', *History Workshop Pamphlets*, 5.
[86] Price, *Imperial War*, 75.

known in 1891 that political 'lecturers have a poor chance of getting an audience, no matter how clever or gifted they may be, while the comic singer and the sketch artiste, however lacking in real ability, can always draw a hall full'.[87] Furthermore, it was always entertainment of the lightest kind. Formerly Shakespeare plays and ballad singing had been popular items of a social evening. Now music-hall entertainment was all that was demanded. According to a report of a social in one south London club: 'A gentleman so far forgot himself as to sing two Ballads at the South Bermondsey Club the other evening, and was hissed by the younger people present, who left the hall in disgust. This is the result of giving the younger people "Hi-ti" and "Get Yer 'Air Cut", and pandering to a vitiated taste.'[88]

It is sometimes implied that the decline of radicalism was simply the result of its displacement by socialism. But this cannot be the whole explanation. For socialism, when distinguished from a vague predisposition towards collectivism or the defence of trade union rights, remained a peripheral force in London between the 1890s and 1914. Neither the SDF nor its successor, the BSP (British Socialist Party), ever possessed more than 3,000 members in a population of 6½ million (1900) – which compares unfavourably with the 30,000 members reputed to have belonged to the London Republican Clubs in 1871.[89] The strength it did possess was mainly concentrated in the new outlying working-class areas like West Hammersmith and Poplar. Areas where trade union or labour candidates could win elections – Deptford, Battersea and Woolwich – were similarly situated on the outskirts.[90] The inner working-class area, the old home of radical working-class activity, remained largely unresponsive to socialist influence.

---

[87] Cited in Taylor, 'From Self-Help to Glamour', 59; for a discussion of this theme see 57–70.

[88] Ibid., 62.

[89] For membership of London socialist groups, see P. Thompson, *Socialists, Liberals and Labour*, 307; for the numbers engaged in republicanism, see R. Harrison, *Before the Socialists*, 233. But this estimate was probably an exaggeration.

[90] For accounts of working-class politics in West Ham, see Leon Fink, 'Socialism in One Borough: West Ham Politics and Political Culture 1898–1900' (1972 unpublished); for Hammersmith, see E. P. Thompson, *William Morris, Romantic to Revolutionary* (1955); for Woolwich, see P. Thompson, *Socialists, Liberals and Labour*, 250–63; for Battersea, see Price, *Imperial War*, 158–70.

It is also sometimes implied that the socialist movement carried over the most positive aspects of the old artisan tradition. It is true that the first socialist groups began as a direct extension of artisan radicalism. But by the Edwardian period, the decay of these distinctively metropolitan traditions was as evident within the socialist movement as outside it. In 1887, the year of Victoria's Golden Jubilee, radical and socialist clubs had protested vigorously against public money being spent to celebrate '50 years of royal flunkeyism'.[91] But in 1902, at the time of Edward VII's coronation, the SDF sent a loyal address, specifically denying any intention to replace the monarchy by a republic.[92] Secularist attitudes also appear to have declined within the socialist groups. By the Edwardian period, two SDF branches were meeting in churches, another branch had established a labour church and the prevalent tone of the branches had become suffused with a vague but intense religiosity more akin to the middle-class ethical movement than to the tradition of Paine, Carlile and Bradlaugh.[93] Finally, the anti-jingoist, anti-imperialist character of artisan radicalism was also to a considerable extent modified within the SDF. This has generally been attributed to the peculiarities of Hyndman and his associates. But the fact that Hyndman could generally determine SDF policy on international issues without effective challenge is an indication that the bulk of the London membership either accepted his positions or considered such issues to be of subordinate importance. When at last in 1910 Hyndmanite views on imperialism were decisively challenged, the revolt in London was led by Russian and Jewish political refugees.

The decay of indigenous metropolitan political traditions and the marginal appeal of socialism in the late Victorian and Edwardian period were accompanied by the stagnation of London trade unionism.[94] In the years between 1800 and 1820, London had been the greatest stronghold of trade unionism in the country. Even in the 1850s and 1860s, the new

[91] Taylor, 'From Self-Help to Glamour', 49.
[92] Cited in Kendall, *The Revolutionary Movement*, 19.
[93] See P. Thompson, *Socialists, Liberals and Labour*, 209–10.
[94] For the numerical strength of London trade unionism, see Booth, *Life and Labour*, Series 2, vol. 5, 136–82; S. and B. Webb, *History of Trade Unionism* (1920 edn), 423–7; P. Thompson, *Socialists, Liberals and Labour*, 39–67.

model, the Nine Hours' movement and the trades council were largely London creations. But in the third quarter of the century, London trade unionism declined rapidly both in strength and imagination, and by the 1880s only possessed two unions (the engineers and the compositors) with more than 6,000 members. The great upsurge of new unionism of 1889–91 temporarily reversed this situation. The membership of the new unskilled unions soared and the membership of all unions substantially increased. The London Trades' Council was revitalized after years of inactivity and for a moment it looked as if London could once again become a bastion of trade union strength. But the recovery was not sustained. The return of depression in 1892, the employers' counter-offensive particularly against unskilled trade unionism, disagreement between unions and a series of badly-planned strikes once again crippled London trade unions. The London Trades' Council relapsed once more into passivity and did not even make any arrangements to assist the 1897 engineering strike. The unskilled unions were severely hit. The Dockers' Union, for instance, which had possessed 20,000 members in 1890, had been reduced to 1,000 in 1900; it only survived the bleak years up to 1910 through the strength of its provincial branches. The Gasworkers' Union held on to its London membership more successfully and in 1900 still possessed 15,000 members; but, by 1909, it too had been reduced to 4,000 members. Compared with other industrial regions, London had once more become strikingly weak. In 1897 trade unionists composed 3.5 per cent of the population of London compared with 8 per cent in Lancashire and 11 per cent in the north-east. Furthermore, despite the upheavals of new unionism, the bulk of London unions remained parochial and exclusive. Of the 250 London unions listed in 1897, 75 were purely metropolitan, and only 35 had memberships of more than 1,000. In the cabinet-making trade alone, there were twenty-three competing unions. As Ernest Aves concluded at that time: 'metropolitan conditions militate against trade unionism, just as they do against other democratic institutions that depend largely for their vitality on the maintenance of intimate personal relationship between their members'.[95]

[95] Cited in Booth, *Life and Labour*, Series 2, vol. 5, 175.

In a period in which working-class politics was in retreat and trade unionism remained stagnant, it is not suprising to find that large numbers of the working class and the poor, when they expressed any political preferences, were motivated by sectional rather than class interests. Thus watch-makers and sugar refiners supported the Conservatives because they thought tariff reform would arrest the decline of their trades. Lightermen supported them because they promised to defend their traditional corporate privileges; munitions workers and engineers in the Arsenal, because they believed that an aggressive foreign policy would mean fuller employment and higher wages; brewery workers, because a Liberal government would mean the threat of temperance legislation; costers and cabmen, because they disliked the restrictions imposed on them by the Progressive majority on the London County Council (LCC); dockers and unskilled workers in the East End, because they thought that restrictions on foreign immigration would ease pressure on housing and employment.

Psephologists also tell us that workers in small and medium-sized enterprises were more likely to support the Conservatives.[96] In the inner London region, the vast majority of enterprises were small; firms employing more than 500 men were exceptional. Thus in the craft workshops of the West End, which involved personal dealings with the rich, conservatism could be the result of 'Admiration for the high-ups, but a contempt for the half-way-ups.'[97] Amongst the unskilled and semi-skilled, where the labour market was almost always over-filled, the retention of regular employment in small firms often depended on retaining the patronage of the employer or the foreman. To step out of line was to invite dismissal. Independent working-class politics was unlikely to result. In the new outlying areas, where the larger factories and gas works were mostly situated and enterprises tended to be more impersonal, the chances of recruiting trade unionists or socialists were better. But everywhere in the London region, except in years of good trade, sheer poverty and constant anxiety about employment were the overriding

---

[96] See Pelling, *Social Geography*, 422. Workers in very small enterprises (1–20) inclined towards radicalism.
[97] See Willis, *Jubilee Road*, 105–6.

concerns of the unskilled and the semi-skilled.[98] Except for home rule or Catholic education in the case of the Irish, larger political issues were abstract and remote. The result in the riverside districts of South London was described by Paterson:

> Politics stir them very little, even at the time of election. Very many have no vote, because they are always moving; the majority of the more settled do not attend the party meetings, but profess great indifference. They have but the vaguest notion of the issues before the country, or the meaning of party catchwords. Old scandals sink deep and live for ever; anything that affects the reputation of the candidate is likely to prove a more potent influence than the gravest flaw in his cause.[99]

But it would be wrong to assume that this sort of political apathy among the unskilled and the poor was simply in the nature of things, or to imagine their outlook can adequately be deduced from voting figures in elections. The evidence suggests that when economic circumstances promised any chance of success, as happened in 1854, 1872, 1889 or 1911, they did strike and join unions. There is also evidence that considerable numbers of the poor had identified with the Chartist cause in the belief that Chartism would relieve their poverty and end their oppression. At the very least they imagined it would mean the end of the daily oppression of the police and the Poor Law. Since most of them could not write, and few were interested in recording their opinions, it is not easy to reconstruct their attitudes. But their general feelings about Chartism were probably accurately expressed by one street ballad of the 1840s:

> And when that the Charter, Old England has got,
> We'll have stunning good beer at three half pence a pot:
> A loaf for a penny, a pig for a crown
> And gunpowder tea at 5 farthings a pound:
> Instead of red herrings, we'll live on fat geese,
> And lots of young women at two pence a piece.[100]

It is true that Mayhew considered the unskilled as 'unpolitical as footmen', but it should be remembered that

---

[98] Reasons for the saturation of the London labour market are discussed in Stedman Jones, *Outcast London*, Part I.

[99] Paterson, *Across the Bridges*, 215.

[100] Cited in Ashton, *Modern Street Ballads*, 336.

Mayhew began his investigations when Chartism had already been defeated.[101] It is not so certain that he would have come to the same conclusion had he conducted his investigations in 1842 or in the period leading up to 1848.

So far I have argued that from the 1850s a working-class culture gradually established itself which proved virtually impervious to evangelical or utilitarian attempts to determine its character or direction. But it has also been shown that in the latter part of the century, this impermeability no longer reflected any widespread class combativity. For the most prominent developments in working-class life in late Victorian and Edwardian London were the decay of artisan radicalism, the marginal impact of socialism, the largely passive acceptance of imperialism and the throne, and the growing usurpation of political and educational interests by a way of life centred round the pub, the race-course and the music-hall. In sum, its impermeability to the classes above it was no longer threatening or subversive, but conservative and defensive. Two questions remain to be asked: firstly, what factors had combined to produce a culture of this kind? And, secondly, what were the central assumptions and attitudes embedded within this culture?

Undoubtedly, the primary cause was the undermining of the distinctiveness and cohesion of the old artisan culture in London. In the period between 1790 and 1850 it was this artisan class which had provided political leadership to the unskilled and the poor. But in the second half of the century, it became increasingly defensive and concerned to protect itself from below as much as from above. In 1889, far from welcoming the opportunity to organize the unskilled, its most prominent spokesmen and its Trades' Council offered no constructive assistance and reacted more often with alarm than with enthusiasm to the upsurge of new unionism.

In the course of the nineteenth century, this artisan culture based upon traditional London trades was undermined by a variety of disintegrating tendencies. A few trades managed to maintain their traditions intact. The strongly unionized wet-

---

[101] Mayhew, *London Labour*, vol. 3, 233; some evidence of the participation of the unskilled in Chartist agitation is provided in Iorwerth Prothero, 'Chartism in London', *Past and Present*, 44 (August, 1969), 90.

coopers and silk-hatters, for instance, maintained control over apprenticeship and the work process and continued to express a strong sense of craft solidarity reinforced by traditional rituals of communal drinking and conviviality.[102] But these trades were small and exceptional. The larger trades either declined in the face of provincial competition or else were broken up through the subdivision of the work process into separate semi-skilled tasks. Silk-weaving, ship-building, watch-making and leather manufacture were examples of the first tendency; the clothing, footwear and furniture trades examples of the second. It was artisans in the latter trades who had formed the backbone of London Chartism.[103] But even at that time, Mayhew had estimated that only one-tenth of these trades were made up of 'honourable men' (that is, members of trade societies, properly apprenticed, working for accepted rates and controlling the speed, quality and location of work). In the second half of the century, these honourable men were increasingly threatened on the one hand by home work and its tendency towards 'sweating', and on the other by the gradual invasion of the bespoke sector by high-class ready-made goods produced in provincial factories. Visiting the West End clothing and shoe-making workshops in the 1880s, Beatrice Potter and David Schloss still found that the men were republicans or socialists and that traditional customs and rituals of conviviality continued in full force.[104] But these craftsmen now constituted a minute proportion of the trade. They were not threatened by East End slop-workers, because they served a luxury market, but they could not maintain their traditional position in the face of competition from the ready-made sector. In the 1890s, their position rapidly declined. A strike of shoe-making unions in 1890 successfully outlawed home work, but this only accelerated the removal of the trade to Northampton. The work of bespoke tailors and cabinet-makers also became markedly irregular. Skilled artisans could still earn good wages in the ready-made sectors of these

---

[102] On these trades see Willis, *Jubilee Road*, 88–100 (on the hatters); Bob Gilding, 'The Journeymen Coopers of East London, Workers' Control in an Old London Trade', *History Workshop Pamphlets*, 4.

[103] See Prothero, 'Chartism in London', 103–5.

[104] Booth, *Life and Labour*, Series 1, vol. 4, 141.

trades. But the conditions which had sustained a strong political culture no longer existed. The skilled workshop in which the trade society controlled the work process, and in which artisans had taken turns in reading aloud from Paine or Owen, had been replaced either by home work or else by the warehouse where the skilled operative was surrounded by semi-skilled 'greeners' and unskilled slop-hands.

The traditional culture of all London artisans had been work-centred. In the first half of the nineteenth century, most London trades worked a twelve-hour day, six days a week, with a daily break of two hours for meals.[105] Workers generally lived in the immediate vicinity of their work. Political discussion, drinking and conviviality took place either at the workplace itself or at a local pub, which generally served as a house of call and a centre of union organization. Trade feasts, carnivals and outings were normal. Intermarriage, a hereditary tendency in apprenticeship and a distinctive language and dress all reinforced trade solidarity; even broad political movements like Chartism were to some extent organized on a trade basis.[106] If this was the 'republic of artisans', it was a very masculine republic. Homes were cramped and uncomfortable; where they were not the place of work, they were little more than places to sleep and eat in. Even if some artisans discussed politics with their wives, women were excluded *de facto* from the focal institutions of this culture.

In the second half of the century, this work-centred culture began to yield to a culture oriented towards the family and the home. By the mid-1870s, weekly hours of work had been substantially reduced in most skilled trades. A 54–56½-hour week, or a nine-hour day and a Saturday half holiday became general. The growth of sporting interests, seaside excursions, working men's clubs and music-halls from about this time is therefore not accidental. In London, however, this increase in leisure time should be seen in connection with another tendency – the growing geographical separation between home and workplace. As early as 1836, the Owenites had

---

[105] On working hours see M. A. Bienefeld, *Working Hours in British Industry, An Economic History* (1972).

[106] For a discussion of this artisan culture, see Prothero, 'Chartism in London'.

complained that organization was difficult 'owing to the distance of the members from each other in this large metropolis'.[107] But the difficulties they faced were insignificant compared with those which lay ahead. From the 1870s, the migration of the skilled working class to the suburbs became a mass phenomenon. While the residential population of the City declined from 75,000 in 1871 to 38,000 in 1891, its daytime population increased from 170,000 in 1866 to 301,000 in 1891.[108] The old skilled artisan centre of Holborn and Finsbury was reduced from 93,423 to 66,781 in the same period. By the time of the Booth survey, the majority of workers commanding skilled wage rates commuted to work on a tram, a workman's train or on foot.[109]

This combination of increased leisure time and suburban migration would alone have eroded the strength of the work-centred culture. But it was combined with a number of other factors which further reinforced this process. The fall of prices in the Great Depression period produced a rise in real wages spread over the whole employed population. This increased spending power again strengthened the importance of home and family. In the eighteenth and early nineteenth century, all wives were expected to work in some capacity.[110] By the 1890s, however, Booth found that the wives of workers in skilled trades did not normally work.[111] Increased earnings were not generally spent in trade drinking customs, but were handed over to the wife who became the decision-maker in all aspects of household expenditure. In many households the husband was only entrusted with pocket money to be spent on fares, beer, tobacco and a trade union or club subscription.[112] The effect of this division of labour could be seen in the growing institutionalization of the Sunday suit and the

[107] Ibid., 88.
[108] Anon., *Ten Years' Growth of the City of London* (1891), 14.
[109] See Booth, *Life and Labour*, Series 2 (industry series), *passim*, for commuting habits of skilled workers in various trades, and see Series 2, vol. 5, Ch. III, for summary. In the last quarter of the nineteenth century, working-class use of commuter transport increased sharply, but even in the 1890s a high proportion of workers travelled long distances to work on foot. See T. C. Barker and Michael Robbins, *A History of London Transport* (1963), vol. I, XXVI–XXX.
[110] George, *London Life*, 168.
[111] Booth, *Life and Labour*, Series 1, vol. I, 50–1.
[112] Paterson, *Across the Bridges*, 32; Loane, *Englishman's Castle*, 183.

elaborately furnished front parlour.[113] By the Edwardian period, according to Fred Willis who was apprenticed as a silk-hatter, 'the boy wanted to get into a position that would enable him to keep a wife and family, as it was considered a thoroughly unsatisfactory state of affairs if the wife had to work to help maintain the home. The home was regarded as the sanctuary of married life, and practically all the leisure of the working classes was spent there.'[114]

This stricter division of roles between man and wife was to an increasing extent generalized throughout the working class by the 1870 Education Act. Once children, particularly girls, were forced into school, it became more difficult for the wife to go out to work and leave household cleaning and the care of the infants to the older children.[115] Among all sectors of the working class, the association of mother with home became increasingly axiomatic. Even the poorest women in the riverside districts, once encumbered with children, generally took in home work, garment making, matchbox making, envelope making, etc. Furthermore, as the home increasingly became the wife's sole domain, her control over it appears to have become increasingly absolute. In Southwark and Bermondsey in the 1900s, for instance, it was stated:

The care of the children is delegated to the mother. It is she who chooses the school, and interviews the teacher, the inspector or the magistrate.

   The care and management of the house is so much in the mother's hands that it is really more her home than his. The man rarely brings in a friend to sit by the fire and chat. Such social delights are tasted elsewhere. The neighbours who do come in are, as a rule, the wife's friends. It is she who entertains and makes the laws of hospitality. In her hands will rest the management of the furniture, the decision of what shall be pawned or redeemed. If a move is to be made, she will choose the new home and superintend the removal on a small cart or coster barrow. The husband only demands that, as far as possible, his conservatism in small things shall be respected. He would object with some force to the removal of some old photograph that for 15 years has been perched on a chest of drawers. A new wall paper would dismay him, and if he could not find his spare pipe in its

[113] See Booth, *Life and Labour*, Series 3, vol. 5, 330; Loane, *The Next Street but One* (1907), 20.
[114] Fred Willis, *Peace and Dripping Toast* (1950), 54.
[115] The care of the house and of babies fell particularly on girl children. See James Greenwood, *Low Life Deeps* (1876), 140.

usual place there would be grave dissatisfaction. If a stranger calls he will leave it to his wife to represent the family interests. Though still maintaining his headship of the family, and asserting it on occasions with ruthless force the wife on ordinary days reigns as ruler of the home.[116]

Since wives had generally had little contact with the traditional centres of political discussion, the workshop, the house of call, the coffee shop, and since in the second half of the century wives increasingly retreated from productive employment itself except in the form of home work, home and family life tended to become a depoliticized haven. With the shortening of the working week and the separation of living quarters from workplace, home and the family occupied a larger place in the working man's life. Yet, despite its growing ideological significance the home remained a crowded and unrelaxing environment. After the evening meal, therefore, men and to some extent women continued to pass a high proportion of their evenings in the pub. If the man commuted to work, however, the regular pub visited would no longer be the trade pub near the workplace, but the 'local'. At the 'local' he would mingle with men of different trades and occupations. Conversation was less likely to concern trade matters, more likely to reflect common interests, politics to a certain extent, but more often, sport and entertainment. In the past, Ewing Ritchie complained in 1880:

the bar parlour or whatever it might be called, of the public house, was the place in which men gathered to talk politics, and to study how they could better themselves. When Bamford, the Lancashire Radical, came to town in 1817, the working men were principally to be found discussing politics in all the London public houses ... such things are out of fashion nowadays ... In London there are but few discussion forums now, and the leading one is so fearfully ventilated and so heavily charged with the fumes of stale tobacco and beer, that it is only a few who care to attend.[117]

Of course, the picture was not quite as bleak as Ritchie painted it. The radical working men's clubs of the 1870s and 1880s constituted perhaps the most impressive attempt to adapt the old artisan culture to these new conditions. But in the clubs too, as has already been noted, politics were finally displaced by entertainment.

---

[116] Paterson, *Across the Bridges*, 210–12; see also, Loane, *Englishman's Castle*, 178–206; Julian Franklyn, *The Cockney* (1953), 179–87.

[117] Ritchie, *Days and Nights*, 41–2.

Ritchie hoped that this situation would be remedied by the London School Board. But in fact the elementary education provided by the 1870 Act appears to have acted as yet another solvent of artisan traditions of self-education. The London *Mechanic's Magazine* had stated in 1816: 'men had better be without education than be educated by their rulers. For then education is but the mere breaking in of the steer to the yoke; the mere discipline of a hunting dog, which, by dint of severity, is made to forgo the strongest impulse of nature, and instead of devouring his prey, to hasten with it to the feet of his master.'[118] Board School education between 1870 and 1914 appears to have confirmed this judgement. Apart from the instillation of the three Rs, constant attendance (rewarded by medals) and habits of cleanliness and order (enforced by unremitting drill) appear to have been the qualities generally aimed at in the average lesson:

The teacher will in all probability be standing at the blackboard, the boys ranged in exact rows, each head covering the one in front, hands clasped behind the neck in unanimous response to the command 'neck-rest' given at the beginning of the lesson. The class is being taught as one whole, the teacher thinking necessarily of no particular boy. Individual tuition is all but impossible when the average class is but a few short of sixty.[119]

In addition to this basic recipe, teachers vainly attempted to interest their cohorts in the Christian religion and the middle- and upper-class view of Britain's history and its place in the world. According to one ex-pupil:

'History', as taught by the board school, left us with a vague impression that up to the time of Queen Elizabeth this country had been occupied exclusively by kings and queens, good, bad and indifferent and from Queen Elizabeth onwards were the Dark Ages, since we never heard of anything happening in that period. The American War of Independence, indeed the existence of the United States of America, was hushed up ... Geography was confined to the British Empire and countries were assessed not by their peoples but by the magnitude and wealth of their products. The only reference to people that I remember was 'the Indian can live on a handful of rice a day', which made us feel a particularly opulent race when we were enjoying our Sunday dinners.[120]

---

[118] Quoted in Brian Simon, *Studies in the History of Education 1780–1870* (1960), 230.
[119] Paterson, *Across the Bridges*, 76.
[120] Willis, *Jubilee Road*, 76–7.

Discipline was maintained by the habitual resort to the cane. This caused particular offence to working-class parents who might hit a child when annoyed, but did not generally employ a formalized system of corporal punishment. It is now generally recognized that one important working-class objection to the early factory system was the removal of children from parental control and the exercise of discipline by an impersonal supervisor. But it is not so often realized that one of the main working-class objections to the Board School was of a similar kind. It took some time before working-class parents accepted their inability to stop this treatment. One headmaster comparing the situation in one poor board school in 1882 and 1900, noted:

Parents in relation to teachers: Much more friendly; hostility, insolence, violence or threats, common in 1882, now hardly ever occur.[121]

In general, it is not surprising that the new education system aroused no gratitude or enthusiasm among the working class and that remarks about the indifference of the English working class to education begin to become commonplace from the late 1880s onwards.[122] It is certainly significant that when radicals in the working men's clubs began to look for reasons why members were taking less interest in the political and educational side of club life, they assigned a place to the effects of elementary education.

The combination of declining industries, the breakdown of skilled crafts into a mass of semi-skilled processes, the prevalence of home work, the decline of a work-centred culture, the growth of commuting and the deadening effects of elementary education made a politically demobilizing impact in London. Some of these tendencies were of course present elsewhere in Britain. But they did not generally produce such demoralizing results. What intensified the purely negative aspect of these developments in London was the continuation of small-scale production combined with chronic unemployment. The problem of unemployment, as Paul de Rousiers

---

[121] Booth, *Life and Labour*, Series 3, vol. 4, 202; on the hostility of working-class parents to the discipline of their children at school, see M. E. Loane, *From Their Point of View* (1908), 150.

[122] See Royal Commission on the Elementary Education Acts, Final Reports, PP 1888, xxxv, 131.

wrote in the 1890s, was largely a problem of London.[123] In the years before 1914, London was stranded between a small workshop system which refused to die and a system of factory production which had scarcely begun to develop. Its workforce was divided between a highly skilled but technically conservative elite and a vast mass of semi-skilled and un-skilled workers subject to varying degrees of under-employ-ment. In the 1920s and 1930s, London was to be transformed by the development of light industry on its peripheries. But few would have prophesied this transformation before 1914. In the late Victorian and Edwardian period, rents and prices rose, wages remained stagnant and unemployment was a permanent feature of the landscape. Yet London continued to grow at a phenomenal rate. The new suburbs were flooded with rural immigrants from the depressed and conservative home counties.[124] With the exception of a few outlying areas like Woolwich or Stratford, London working-class districts were shifting and unstable. The eviction of the poor from the central area continued and everywhere 'shooting the moon' (moving furniture from an apartment after dark before the landlord collected the rent) was a familiar feature of London working-class life – one need only think of perhaps the best known of all music-hall songs, 'My Old Man said follow the Van'. The family as a working-class institution may have grown in importance, but in London there was nothing very settled about the home. Co-op and professional football, two of the most prominent features of the new working-class culture of the north, were still of minor importance in London. Like trade unionism and friendly societies, their strength was greatest in more stable and homogeneous industrial areas. If we wish to find a peculiarly metropolitan form of the new working-class culture, it is to the music-hall that we must look.

Once the evidence is sifted critically, the music-hall can give us a crucial insight into the attitudes of working-class London.

---

[123] P. de Rousiers, *The Labour Question in Britain* (1896), 280, 357.
[124] It may be significant that it is in the mid-1870s that Sam Weller-type cockney pronunciation with its substitution of *v* for *w*, is said to have died out. See Franklyn, *The Cockney*, 22.

But this can only be done if working-class music-hall is disentangled from its West End variant with which it is generally confused.

Music-hall was both a reflection and a reinforcement of the major trends in London working-class life from the 1870s to the 1900s. 'Music halls and other entertainments', wrote T. H. Escott in 1891, 'are as popular among the working men of London as they are the reverse with the better stamp of working men out of it.'[125] Music-hall was a participatory form of leisure activity, but not a demanding one. The audience joined in the chorus, but if they didn't like the song or the sentiments expressed, they 'gave it the bird', and it was unlikely to be heard again. Top stars could earn up to £100 a week by rushing from one hall to another in the course of each evening.[126] But the profession was also crowded with less successful aspirants. The vast majority of performers came from poor backgrounds and began by doing turns in pubs or trying themselves out in a newcomer's spot in one of the smaller halls. Since most singers were generally too poor to pay a song writer, they composed the lyrics themselves, usually adapting them to an already known tune. Until it was transformed by the coming of the more pretentious palaces of variety in the Edwardian period, the atmosphere of the halls was more like that of the pub than the theatre. Indeed, many of the smaller halls were simply extensions to pub premises. Performances were continuous from six to eleven p.m., but the audience could move freely to and from the bar which was responsible for half the profits of the proprietor. The great boast of music-hall and of Charles Morton, its self-appointed 'father', was that it was a 'family entertainment'. Unlike the old 'free and easies' and pub sing-songs which had been popular in the 1840s, the music-hall admitted women, and avoided overtly obscene songs. In fact, the bulk of the audiences were composed of young unmarried workers, male and female; but all witnesses agreed that there was always a fair sprinkling of families as well.[127]

[125] T. H. S. Escott, *England, Its People, Polity and Pursuits* (1891), 161.
[126] See Booth, *Life and Labour*, Series 2, vol. 4, 137–40.
[127] See Scott, *Early Doors*, 139–40; Ritchie, *Days and Nights*, 47; Booth, *Life and Labour*, Series 2, vol. 5, 334.

In working-class districts, where the multiplicity of occupations, the separation of home from workplace and the overcrowding and impermanence of apartments made any stable community life very difficult, the local hall with its blaze of light and sham opulence, its laughter and its chorus singing, fulfilled, if only in an anonymous way, a craving for solidarity in facing the daily problems of poverty and family life. Music-hall stood for the small pleasures of working-class life – a glass of 'glorious English beer', a hearty meal of 'boiled beef and carrots', a day by the seaside, Derby Day and the excitements and tribulations of betting, a bank holiday spent on Hampstead Heath or in Epping Forest, the pleasures of courtship and the joys of friendship.[128] Its attitude was 'a little bit of what you fancy does you good'. Music-hall was perhaps the most unequivocal response of the London working class to middle-class evangelism. As Marie Lloyd told her critics in 1897:

You take the pit on a Saturday night or a Bank Holiday. You don't suppose they want Sunday School stuff do you? They want lively stuff with music they can learn quickly. Why, if I was to try and sing highly moral songs they would fire ginger beer bottles and beer mugs at me. They don't pay their sixpences and shillings at a Music Hall to hear the Salvation Army.[129]

Or, as the *Era* put it in 1872: 'The artisan tired with his day's labour, wants something to laugh at. He neither wants to be preached to, nor is he anxious to listen to the lugubrious effusions of Dr Watts or the poets of the United Kingdom Alliance.'[130]

Music-hall appealed to the London working class because it was both escapist *and yet* strongly rooted in the realities of working-class life. This was particularly true of its treatment of the relations between the sexes. While its attitude towards courtship could be rhapsodic, there were few illusions about marriage. Writing about marriage among the London poor in the 1870s, Greenwood remarked of the couples he saw entering and leaving the church, 'they are as a rule, cool and business like, as though, having paid a deposit on the purchase of a donkey or a handsome barrow, they were just

[128] See MacInnes, *Sweet Saturday Night*, 106–23.
[129] Quoted in Farson, *Marie Lloyd*, 57.
[130] A. E. Wilson, *East End Entertainment* (1954), 215.

going in with their witnesses to settle the bargain'.[131] Paterson
observed a similar attitude in 1911:

A funeral demands special clothes and carriage, very considerable expense,
and to attend such an event, second cousins will take a day off work, and
think it but dutifully spent. Yet a marriage is, by comparison, almost
unnoticed ... It occurs most frequently on a saturday or sunday, as it is
hardly worthwhile to lose a day's work ... few attend it outside a small circle
of lady friends.[132]

Among the poor, marriage was normally the result of
pregnancy, but among all sectors of the working class,
marriage meant children and the constant drudgery of work
on a declining standard of living until they were old enough to
bring money into the home. Marriage as a 'comic disaster' is
an endless refrain of music-hall songs. The titles of the best
known male songs are self-explanatory: Tom Costello's 'At
Trinity Church I met my doom', Charles Coburn's 'Oh what
an Alteration', Gus Elen's 'It's a great big shame'. The lead in
translating courtship into marriage was normally taken by the
woman. For working-class women, marriage was an economic
necessity and unlikely to happen after the age of twenty-five.
Booth stated that among the poor, marriage banns were
almost invariably put up by the woman.[133] The anxiety of
girls to get married was the theme of many female songs like
Lily Morris' 'Why am I always the bridesmaid, never the
blushing bride?' or Vesta Victoria's 'Waiting at the Church'.
According to Dan Leno, in his sketch of the lodger entitled
'Young Men taken in and done for':

I'll tell you how the misfortune happened. One morning Lucy Jagg's mother
came upstairs to my room, knocked at the door and said, 'Mr Skilley are you
up?' I said, 'No, what for?' Mrs. Jaggs said, 'Come along get up, you're
going to be married.' I said, 'No, I don't know anything about it.' She said,
'Yes you do, you spoke about it last night, when you'd had a little drink.'
Well, I thought, if I did say so, I suppose I did, so I came downstairs half
asleep (in fact I think every man's half asleep when he's going to be
married).[134]

But despite their determination to achieve wedlock, the

[131] Greenwood, *Low Life Deeps*, 140.
[132] Paterson, *Across the Bridges*, 130.
[133] Booth, *Life and Labour*, final vol., 45.
[134] *McGlennon's Star Song Book* (1888), 10, 4.

attitude of women to marriage was no more romantic than that of men. The pros and cons were summed up by Marie Loftus in 'Girls, we would never stand it':

> When first they come courting,
>   how nice they behave,
> For a smile or a kiss,
>   how humbly they crave
> But when once a girl's wed,
>   she's a drudge and a slave.

Nevertheless, she concludes:

> I think we would all prefer
>   marriage with strife
> Than be on the shelf
>   and be nobody's wife.[135]

The same comic realism dominated the depiction of relations between husband and wife. Husbands make themselves out to be dominated by the tyranny of their wives. They escape to the pub, go off to the races and lose money on horses or are cheated out of it by 'welshers', they get drunk and return home to face the consequences. Males are generally represented as incompetent at spending money and are endlessly getting 'done'. But if a wife is incompetent at managing the household, the results are much more serious. In the end the wife who 'jaws' is preferable to the wife who drinks. The problem of the lodger, the landlord and the pawnbroker's shop are also constantly discussed. Finally, the threat of destitution in old age, once children no longer contribute to the family income and the man is too old to work, is not evaded. The whole point of Albert Chevalier's famous song, 'My Old Dutch' is that it is sung in front of a backdrop representing the workhouse with its separate entrances for men and women.

In music-hall, work is an evil to be avoided when possible. But the only real escape suggested in the songs is the surprise inheritance or the lucky windfall. It is the same sort of fantasy escape from poverty that could be detected in the passionate interest with which poor Londoners followed the case of

---

[135] Ibid., 4, 3.

Arthur Orton, the Tichborne claimant, between the 1870s and the 1890s. Nevertheless, when such an escape is made in the songs, the result is consternation; the former friend begins to 'to put on airs', as Gus Elen sang, 'E don't know where 'e are'. Class is a life sentence, as final as any caste system. The pretensions of those who feigned escape aroused particular scorn, as did those who suggested that education would change this state of affairs. According to a *Daily Telegraph* report of Mrs Lane's Britannia Theatre in Hoxton in 1883:

> Here is a large audience mainly composed of the industrious classes, determined to enjoy itself to the utmost ... Mrs Lane's friends feel the disgrace which attaches to a fulfilling of the requirements of the School Board so that when one of the characters upon the stage pertinently asks, 'if every kid's brought up to be a clerk, what about labour? Who's to do the work?' there rises a mighty outburst of applause.[136]

There was no political solution to the class system. It was simply a fact of life. It was certainly not considered to be

---

[136] Wilson, *East End*, 183. The rapid growth of clerical labour during this period was another demoralizing feature of London working-class life. Skilled artisans in nineteenth century London unquestionably regarded themselves as an elite, the natural spokesmen for the whole of their class. Both Mayhew and Escott regarded a distinct and sometimes exaggerated sense of his own importance to be one of the defining traits of the London artisan. In the second half of the nineteenth century, however, this artisan pride was increasingly threatened by the increase of white-collar workers. This latter group was overwhelmingly recruited from the skilled working class, tended to earn comparable wages, and generally inhabited the same districts. Far from recognizing these affinities however, clerks ostentatiously rejected them. They drew *salaries*, not *wages*; their occupations were genteel; their clothes and their hands were clean; their mode of life was modelled upon that of the professional middle class. They were loyalist in politics and came to form the ballast of what Lord Salisbury referred to as 'villa toryism'. Like 'Mr Pooter', they were prepared to go to any lengths to stake their claim to gentility. Therefore, far from accepting the traditional artisan division between those who possessed a trade and those who did not, they erected a new caste-like distinction between those who worked with their 'hands' and those who worked with their 'brains'. The growth of this clerical stratum as a wedge between the working class and the middle class accentuated the cultural gulf between two distinct ways of life. The anxious and often absurd pretensions of clerks reinforced working-class cultural identity, if only by force of repulsion.

The friction between clerks and artisans was exacerbated by the educational programme of the London School Board which was disproportionately geared towards the production of an adequate supply of clerical labour. It thus accentuated working-class estrangement from public education. See, on this, Booth, *Life and Labour*, Series 1, vol. 3, 231–4. I am grateful to Professor Eric Hobsbawm for pointing out some of the ramifications of the growth of clerical labour in London.

just, for as Billy Bennett sang, 'it's the rich what gets the pleasure, It's the poor what gets the blame.' But socialism was just a lot of hot air. As little Tich put it, in his sketch of the gas-meter collector, 'My brother's in the gas trade too, you know. In fact he travels on gas. He's a socialist orator.' Music-hall never gave class a political definition. Trade unionism was accepted as an intrinsic part of working-class life and the music-hall songs of 1889 supported the 'Docker's tanner'.[137] But music-hall didn't generally sing about the relationship between workers and employers, and the capitalist is completely absent as a music-hall stereotype. The general music-hall attitude was that if a worker could get a fair day's wage for a fair day's work, that was a good thing, but if the worker could get a fair day's wage without doing a fair day's work, that was even better. The attitude towards the rich was similarly indulgent. The general depiction of the upper class was, as MacInnes has remarked, not hostile but comic.[138] Upper-class figures like Champagne Charlie, Burlington Bertie, the 'toff' and the galloping major were incompetent and absurd, but there was no reference to the source of their income.

Music-hall has often been associated with a mood of bombastic jingoism, associated with MacDermott's 1878 song, 'We don't want to fight but by jingo if we do' or 'Soldiers of the Queen' sung at the time of the Boer War.[139] The audiences of Piccadilly and Leicester Square sang these songs with undoubted gusto, and, judging by the innumerable song sheets on these themes, could never get enough of them. But the predominant mood of the working-class halls was anti-heroic. Workers were prepared to admire and sing about the bravery of the common soldier or the open-handed generosity of the sailor, but they did not forget the realities of military life. Men joined the army usually to escape unemployment, and, if they survived their years of service, it was to unemployment that they would return. According to one song

---

[137] See 'The Dock Labourers' Strike' and the 'Dock Labourer' in *New and Popular Songs* (1889).

[138] MacInnes, *Sweet Saturday Night*, 108.

[139] According to one report, Disraeli used to send his secretary, Monty Corry, to the music-hall to listen in on MacDermott's song to assess the extent of support for his foreign policy. See J. B. Booth (ed.), *Seventy Years of Song* (1943), 38.

of the 1890s which recounts a conversation between Podger
and his lodger, a soldier on leave:

> Said he, now Podger, Why don't you enlist,
>   you'll get cheap beer
> The glories too, of war in view
>   Come be a soldier bold
> Said I, not me. No not me,
>   I'm not having any don't you see
> Might lose my legs, come home on pegs.
>   Then when I'm O-L-D
> Not wanted more.
>   Workhouse door
> Not, not, not, not me.[140]

In a song which was enormously popular in the 1890s,
Charles Godfrey's 'On Guard', an old Crimean veteran asks
for a night's shelter in the workhouse casual ward. 'Be off you
tramp', exclaims the harsh janitor. 'You are not wanted here.'
'No', thunders the tattered veteran. 'I am *not* wanted *here*, but
at Balaclava, I *was* wanted *there*.' This scene which was a
working-class favourite, was apparently curtailed in the West
End because officers from the household brigade complained
that it was bad for recruiting.[141]

Working-class music-hall was conservative in the sense that
it accepted class divisions and the distribution of wealth as
part of the natural order of things. By the 1890s, the class
resentment expressed in Godfrey's sketch was as near as it
came to political criticism. But the music-hall industry was
not merely a passive barometer of working-class opinion. And
here lies the difficulty of using it simply as an index of
working-class attitudes. For in the period between 1870 and
1900 it became actively and self-consciously Tory. There were
two major reasons for this development.

The first reason was the growth of a second audience for
music-hall entertainment, alongside that of the working class.
This new audience consisted of sporting aristocrats, from the
Prince of Wales downwards, guards officers from St James',
military and civil officials on leave from imperial outposts,
clerks and white-collar workers, university, law and medical

---

[140] *MacGlennon's Star Song Book* (1896–7), 105.
[141] Scott, *Early Doors*, 215.

students, and the growing number of tourists from the white Dominions. This audience can be dated back to the 1860s, but it first reached boom proportions in the 1880s, as witnessed by the opening of the new Pavilion in 1884, rapidly followed by the Empire, the Trocadero, the Tivoli and the Palace.[142] The Empire was the most famous centre of this new audience. It provided a natural focus for jingoism, upper-class rowdyism and high-class prostitution. The most popular event in its annual calendar was boat race night, a drunken saturnalia in which all breakable objects had to be removed from the reach of its tipsy 'swells'.[143] There was little in common between these imperial playgrounds and the working-class halls, except for the important fact that these new palaces drew upon the working-class halls for many of their performers. Furthermore, as the entertainment business became more organized and monopolistic, and combines began to take over the proletarian halls, the turns offered in Hackney or Picca-dilly to some extent converged.[144]

In the 1860s many of the songs sung in the working-class halls were still anti-aristocratic and populist in tone. They were still at a halfway stage between the old street ballad and the mature music-hall song.[145] Even Frederick Stanley, defending music-hall interests before a Parliamentary enquiry in 1866, conceded as the one valid objection to the music-hall 'the immense difficulty of improving the comic element'. 'I believe,' he stated, 'it is impossible to get a comic song written worthy of the present age.'[146] But the atmosphere changed in the 1870s with the appearance of stars like Leybourne, Vance and MacDermott. The anti-aristocratic element in the songs disappeared, the intellectual level fell, and a jingoist tone became prominent. The effects of the new audience were clearly evident by the late 1880s when Vesta Tilley stated:

---

[142] See Stuart and Park, *The Variety Stages*, 191 ff.

[143] Farson, *Marie Lloyd*, 60.

[144] Real convergence was more possible in variety than in music-hall. Even Marie Lloyd found herself booed in the East End music-hall when she attempted to sing some of her more risqué West End numbers. See Farson, *Marie Lloyd*, 75.

[145] See for instance the songs of J. A. Hardwick in *Comic and Sentimental Music Hall Song Book* (n.d. [1862]).

[146] SC 1866, appendix 3, 307.

Nowadays, nothing goes down better than a good patriotic song, for politics are played out as they are far too common. Talking of that suggests the oddity of the music hall audience in their political bent. Every such allusion must be Conservative.[147]

This first reason for music-hall Toryism, the growth of an aristocratic and jingoist clientele, had little to do with any marked shift in working-class opinion. But the second reason affected slum and West End music-halls alike. This was the increasing association between Toryism and the drink trade. In the first half of the nineteenth century, as Brian Harrison has shown, the pub was not the exclusive property of any particular political interest and in fact London brewing magnates tended to be Whig or Liberal rather than Conservative. But the rise of the teetotal movement and its growing tendency to operate as a pressure group on the flank of the Liberal party began to push publicans and music-hall proprietors towards Toryism. This tendency became increasingly apparent after the 1871 Licensing Act of the Liberal government.[148] In the 1880s, Liberals, teetotallers and radical temperance advocates attacked both the central pleasure palaces and the working-class halls with equal vigour, for both were associated, although in unequal proportions, with drinking, gambling, prostitution, crude chauvinism, and the absence of educational content. In the early 1880s, the temperance crusader, F. N. Charrington, launched his attack on Lusby's Music-Hall on the Mile End Road and the Salvation Army made an unsuccessful attempt to close down the Eagle in the City Road.[149] But reformers did not confine their assaults to the working-class halls. In 1894, Mrs Ormiston Chant of the Social Purity League, challenged the licence of the Empire in the name of 'the calm steady voice of righteous public opinion, the non-conformist conscience'.[150] Supported by the Progressive party and the Labour bench on the LCC, Mrs Chant was successful in getting a screen erected between

[147] *McGlennon's Star Song Book* (1896–7), 8, 2.
[148] Harrison, *Drink and the Victorians*, 319–48.
[149] On Charrington, see Guy Thorne, *The Great Acceptance, the Life Story of F. N. Charrington* (1912), Ch. v; on the attempt to close down the Eagle, see H. Begbie, *Life of William Booth* (1920), vol. 2, 10–13.
[150] Mrs Ormiston Chant, *Why We Attacked the Empire* (1895), 5.

the auditorium and the bars, thus fencing off the audience from the provision of drink and the solicitation of prostitutes. But the young 'swells' and 'toffs' of the period who regarded the Empire as their spiritual home, violently resisted this restriction of their prerogatives. On the Saturday following the erection of the screen, 200–300 aristocratic 'rowdies' smashed it down again with their walking-sticks and paraded in triumph around Leicester Square, waving its fragments at the passers-by. The ringleader of this group then made a speech to the assembled crowd: 'You have seen us tear down these barricades tonight; see that you pull down those who are responsible for them at the coming election.'[151] The speaker was the young Sandhurst cadet, Winston Churchill.

Music-hall proprietors, 'swells', cabmen and bizarrely, George Shipton, the Secretary of the London Trades' Council (he also ran a pub just off Leicester Square), enrolled in defence of the Empire's rights. A 'Sporting League' was formed. According to one of its spokesmen:

They were now approaching the County Council Elections, and it would be the duty of every true lover of sport to see that no 'wrong'uns' got on the council again ... These faddists came upon them in all shapes and kinds, either as members of the Humanitarian League, or the anti-Gambling League, or Anti-Vaccination. They were all acting on the same principle, trying to interfere with the enjoyment and pleasures of the people.[152]

This incident was no doubt the origin of the myth, assiduously cultivated by the upper class after the war, of an affinity of outlook between the 'top and bottom drawer' against the 'kill-joys' in between.[153] It is true, however, that for different reasons both the proletarian halls and the West End pleasure-strip were devitalized in the succeeding twenty years. The West End became more decorous after the Wilde scandal, while the working-class halls were bought up by the Moss–Stoll syndicate whose policy was to replace the 'coarseness and vulgarity' of the halls by the gentility and decorum of the Palace of Variety. Music-hall entertainment was given its final kiss of death with the achievement of a Royal Command Performance in 1912. Music-hall artistes removed from their

---

[151] Winston Churchill, *My Early Life* (1930), 71.
[152] Chant, *Why We Attacked the Empire*, 30.
[153] See Shaw Desmond, *London Nights*, 84–92; Willis, *Jubilee Road*, 30–6.

acts any allusions that could be considered offensive or coarse and vainly tried to win the approval of King George V, 'a lover of true Bohemianism' according to Conan Doyle's unctuous description of the proceedings.[154]

If these had been the only tendencies at work in music-hall since the 1870s, it would be difficult to explain its prominent position in London working-class culture. But it was the mid-1880s which also witnessed the emergence of the greatest and best-loved music-hall performers – Dan Leno, Marie Lloyd, Gus Elen, Little Tich, Kate Karney and others. These artistes, who all sprang from poor London backgrounds, articulated with much greater accuracy than their predecessors the mood and attitudes of the London masses. Although they were popular both in the West End and in the East End, they sang or spoke not about the Empire or the Conservative party, but about the occupations, food, drink, holidays, romances, marriages and misfortunes of the back streets. It is from their songs that the specificity of London working-class culture can best be assessed.

Unlike the ballad, the songs of these performers expressed neither deep tragedy nor real anger. They could express wholehearted enjoyment of simple pleasures or unbounded sentimentality in relation to objects of affection. But when confronted with the daily oppressions of the life of the poor, their reactions were fatalistic. In the middle of the century, Mayhew had written:

Where the means of sustenance and comfort are fixed, the human being becomes conscious of what he has to depend upon.

If, however his means be uncertain – abundant at one time, and deficient at another – a spirit of speculation or gambling with the future will be induced, and the individual gets to believe in 'luck' and 'fate' as the arbiters of his happiness rather than to look upon himself as 'the architect of his fortunes' – trusting to 'chance' rather than his own powers and foresight to relieve him at the hour of necessity.[155]

This was precisely the attitude to life projected by the London music-hall. The two greatest products of that culture, Dan Leno and Charlie Chaplin, play little men, perpetually 'put upon'; they have no great ideals or ambitions; the characters

[154] See Farson, *Marie Lloyd*, 88–97.
[155] Mayhew, *London Labour*, vol. 2, 325.

they play are undoubtedly very poor, but not obviously or unmistakably proletarian; they are certainly products of city life, but their place within it is indeterminate; their exploits are funny, but also pathetic; they are forever being chased by men or women, physically larger than themselves, angry foremen, outraged husbands, domineering landladies or burly wives; but it is usually chance circumstances, unfortunate misunderstandings, not of their own making, which have landed them in these situations, and it is luck more than their own efforts which finally comes to the rescue.

The art of Leno and Chaplin brings us back again to the situation of the poor and the working class in late Victorian and Edwardian London; to that vast limbo of semi-employed labourers, casualized semi-skilled artisans, 'sweated' home workers, despised foreigners, tramps and beggars.

In this paper, I have attempted to put into relationship two themes which traditionally have been kept apart: on the one hand, the history of the labour movement, on the other, the investigation of working-class culture. It is only a preliminary analysis, based upon the study of one city, and any conclusions that might be drawn from it can only be provisional. Nevertheless, the mere conjunction of these two themes points towards the necessity of questioning some of the traditional assumptions of English labour history.

Music-hall highlighted the peculiarities of the working-class situation in London. But it also reflected the general development of the English working class after 1870. Fatalism, political scepticism, the evasion of tragedy or anger and a stance of comic stoicism were pre-eminently cockney attitudes because the decline of artisan traditions, the tardiness of factory development, the prevalence of casual work, and the shifting amorphous character of the new proletarian suburbs were particularly marked features of London life. But it would be a mistake to overemphasize the purely local significance of these themes. In industrial areas more homogeneous than London, trade unionism tended to occupy a much more commanding place in working-class culture. In such communities, co-ops, friendly societies, choral clubs and football teams were also more likely to flourish. But these were differences of degree, not of kind. There are good historical reasons why after 1870 London pioneered music-hall, while coal, cotton and ship-building areas in the north generated the most solid advances in trade unionism.[156]

Trapped in the twilight world of small workshop production, London was not well-placed to sustain the defensive corporate forms of solidarity upon which working-class politics was increasingly to be based. The strength of its own political tradition had not been founded on the factory. It therefore registered the new situation in predominantly cultural forms. But music-hall did spread to the provinces and trade unions were slowly able to secure important pockets of strength in certain areas of London. There was great diversity of local experience, but no unbridgeable gulf. What is finally most striking is the basic consistency of outlook reflected in the new working-class culture which spread over England after 1870.

If the 'making of the English working class' took place in the 1790–1830 period, something akin to a remaking of the working class took place in the years between 1870 and 1900. For much of the cluster of 'traditional' working-class attitudes analysed by contemporary sociologists and literary critics dates, not from the first third, but from the last third of the nineteenth century. This remaking process did not obliterate the legacy of that first formative phase of working-class history, so well described by Edward Thompson. But it did transform its meaning. In the realm of working-class ideology, a second formative layer of historical experience was superimposed upon the first, thereby colouring the first in the light of its own changed horizons of possibility. The struggles of the first half of the century were not forgotten, but they were recalled selectively and reinterpreted. The solidarity and organizational strength achieved in social struggles were channelled into trade union activity and eventually into a political party based upon that activity and its goals. The distinctiveness of a working-class way of life was enormously accentuated. Its separateness and impermeability were now reflected in a dense and inward-looking culture, whose effect

---

[156] See Webb and Webb, *History of Trade Unionism*, 299–325.

was both to emphasize the distance of the working class from the classes above it and to articulate its position within an apparently permanent social hierarchy.

The growth of trade unionism on the one hand and the new working-class culture on the other were not contradictory but interrelated phenomena. Both signified a major shift in the predominant forms of working-class activity. What above all differentiated the Chartist period from the post-1870 period was the general belief that the economic and political order brought into being by the Industrial Revolution was a temporary aberration, soon to be brought to an end. This belief sustained the activities of moderate Chartists like Lovett and Vincent no less than Harney and O'Connor. It was this half-articulated conviction that had made Chartism into a mass force.

Once the defeat of Chartism was finally accepted, this conviction disappeared. Working people ceased to believe that they could shape society in their own image. Capitalism had become an immovable horizon. Demands produced by the movements of the pre-1850 period – republicanism, secularism, popular self-education, co-operation, land reform, internationalism etc. – now shorn of the conviction which had given them point, eventually expired from sheer inanition, or else, in a diluted form, were appropriated by the left flank of Gladstonian liberalism. The main impetus of working-class activity now lay elsewhere. It was concentrated into trade unions, co-ops, friendly societies, all indicating a *de facto* recognition of the existing social order as the inevitable framework of action. The same could be said of music-hall. It was a culture of consolation.

The rise of new unionism, the foundation of the Labour Party, even the emergence of socialist groups marked not a breach but a culmination of this defensive culture. One of the most striking features of the social movements between 1790 and 1850 had been the clarity and concreteness of their conception of the state. There had been no hypostasization of the state into a neutral or impersonal agency. It had been seen as a flesh and blood machine of coercion, exploitation and corruption. The monarchy, the legislature, the Church, the bureaucracy, the army and the police had all been occupied by 'bloodsuckers', 'hypocrites', 'placemen', etc. The aim of popular politics had been to change the form of state. The triumph of the people would replace it by a popular democracy of a Leveller or Jacobin sort – an egalitarian society of independent artisans and smallholders – a society built upon petty commodity exchange on the basis of labour time expended (the Chartist land plan and the Owenite labour bazaar formed part of a single problematic). The Charter, a purely political programme, was to be its means of realization.

Late Victorian and Edwardian labour leaders had no such concrete conception of politics or the state. The emphasis had shifted from power to welfare. Socialism, as Tom Mann defined it, meant the abolition of poverty. The founding moment of the Labour Party was not revolution abroad or political upheaval at home, but a defensive solution to the employer's counter-offensive of the 1890s. The ending of Britain's industrial monopoly did re-create an independent labour politics, as Engels had prophesied, but not in the way he had intended. The LRC (Labour Representation Committee) was the generalization of the structural role of the trade union into the form of a political party. It was not accountable directly to its constituency, but indirectly via the trade unions upon which its real power was based. Its mode of organization presumed mass passivity punctuated by occasional mobilization for the ballot box. As a form of political association, it was not so much a challenge to the new working-class culture that had grown up since 1870 as an extension of it. If it sang *Jerusalem* it was not as a battle-cry but as a hymn. It accepted *de facto*, not only capitalism, but monarchy, Empire, aristocracy and established religion as well. With the foundation of the Labour Party, the now enclosed and defensive world of working-class culture had in effect achieved its apotheosis.

5

WHY IS THE LABOUR PARTY IN A MESS?

The present crisis of the Labour Party has deeper roots than the Conservative victory of 1979, the rise of the Bennite left and the emergence of the SDP (Social Democratic Party). These are only the final acts in a drama of a more secular kind and, if we are to understand it, we must step back from the present apologias being offered on the right and left of the Party and attempt to situate the crisis in a longer term historical perspective.

Of course, history of a kind is not absent from the present debate. But the history on offer is generally of the 'golden age' variety and, curiously, both right and left are at one in the dating of that 'golden age' – the Labour governments of 1945–51. Political memories are short. In the late 1950s and early 1960s, the predominant tone of discussion of 1945 was critical. For the right, it had identified the Party too closely with obsolete 'shibboleths' like nationalization and the 'cloth cap' image; for the left, it had represented a failure to capture the 'commanding heights' of the economy and a capitulation to market forces, the civil service and the cold war – in either scenario, it had generated 'thirteen wasted years' of Tory rule. But, in the light of the failures and frustrations of the Wilson and Callaghan years, the post-war Labour government has come to be seen in increasingly benign terms. It has come to be associated with a magical moment to which all sections of the party have yearned to return. 1945 has been summoned up as much by Social Democrats as by Tony Benn. 1951 is the time from which everything started to go 'wrong' for Jeremy Seabrook and it is the point at which Eric Hobsbawm's 'forward march of Labour halted'. The talismanic character of that epoch has been as evident in the recent television drama of Trevor Griffiths, as it has been in appeals to ageing working-class voters at election times: a recent Islington Social Democratic election address claimed that 'a vote for Eden is a vote for trusted Labour Leaders like Clem Attlee, Hugh Gaitskell and George Brown'.

The present appeal of 1945 is not primarily based upon an assessment of its policies, but rather upon a nostalgia for the social and political alliance upon which it was based. If the 1970s and 1980s have witnessed the fragmentation of Labour's alliance – between PLP (Parliamentary Labour Party) and constituency activists, between constituency activists and Labour voters, between TUC (Trades Union Congress) and Labour governments and between trade union activists and ordinary workers – then 1945 represents the time when all these different elements appeared to pull in the same direction. The post-war Labour government was relatively free from fundamental clashes between government and the TUC or between PLP and Conference. It was a time when individual constituency membership reached its peak, as did the Labour Party's percentage of the popular vote. It was the high tide of the 'labour movement' in all the peculiarly British connotations of that phrase, in which a 'working-class party' committed to 'socialism' gained, and for a time held the support of, the clear majority of the nation.

While there is general agreement that changes in British society since the 1950s have in some sense been responsible for the gradual disintegration of the 1945 consensus, the discussion of what kinds of changes have been responsible, and how, has tended to be crude and one-sided. Generally, both the Marxist left and the Social Democratic right have focussed overwhelmingly upon changes in the distribution of wealth, income and power and shifts in the social structure – as if such changes have found or should have found quasi-automatic correlates in the state of British politics in general and Labour politics in particular. Such an approach first surfaced in the writings of Crosland and the Social Democratic revisionists of the 1950s. Crosland's revision was not so much of Marxism as of traditional Fabianism.[1] Rather than tracing a Fabian

---

[1] C. A. R. Crosland, *The Future of Socialism* (1956).

evolution from competitive capitalism to collectivism, Crosland substituted an evolution from capitalism to a mixed economy based upon equality of opportunity and the social security afforded by the welfare state. Such an argument was reinforced in the early 1960s in the writings of Goldthorpe and Lockwood in which it was suggested that Labour's traditional corporate working class base was cracking up under the impact of affluence.[2] On the other hand, in the gloomier atmosphere of the 1970s, the assumption of a welfare state and full employment creating real classlessness and equality of opportunity became increasingly hard to sustain. Already the researches of Richard Titmuss in the 1950s had shown that it was the middle, rather than working class, who had derived disproportionate benefit from the welfare state.[3] Peter Townsend's poverty survey and the studies of Frank Field have documented the increasingly regressive trend in fiscal policy since the 1950s and have dramatized the inability or unwillingness of successive governments to reform the social security system in such a way as to remove or even significantly ameliorate the actually existing forms of poverty which have continued or even increased in the last decade.[4] There has been no 'fundamental shift in the balance of power and wealth in favour of working people and their families' since the 1940s, nor have the more modest aims of increasing equality of opportunity through institutional reform been as significant as their proponents hoped. According to the recent study of social mobility by John Goldthorpe, chances of social mobility between social groups in proportional terms have not increased, even though in numerical terms a greater proportion appeared to move because of the increase in service and non-manual occupations in the long post-war era of relatively full employment and economic growth.[5]

The point of mentioning such studies is not to argue that the right was wrong and the left was right or vice versa, but rather to suggest that there is no obvious way in which the

[2] J. Goldthorpe and D. Lockwood, 'Affluence and the British Class Structure', *Sociological Review* (1963); *The Affluent Worker in the Class Structure* (1969).

[3] R. Titmuss, *Essays on 'The Welfare State'* (1958); id., *Income Distribution and Social Change* (1962).

[4] F. Field, *Low Pay* (1973); P. Townsend, *Poverty in the United Kingdom* (1979).

[5] J. Goldthorpe, *Social Mobility and Class Structure in Modern Britain* (1980).

course of British politics since 1951 could be deduced from them. Changes in the social realm necessarily form a large part of the raw material out of which different political languages and practices may be forged or reforged. But such changes are not bearers of essential political meaning in themselves. They are only endowed with particular political meanings so far as they are effectively articulated through specific forms of political discourse and practice. There are no simple rules of translation from the social to the political. Relatively minor phenomena may be endowed with enormous significance, while major secular changes may be invested with no particular significance at all. Thus the 'objective' realities of class discerned by social surveys and sociological analysis do not have any unambiguous bearing upon the fate of class-oriented political parties. The nineteenth century shift in popular politics from Chartism to Gladstonian liberalism did not occur because the country had become in some Marxist or sociological sense less class-defined. The final breakaway and popular success of the Social Democrats has not occurred in a bland period of social peace such as the 1950s, but amidst the din of riot sirens and the dismantling of the very social services which theorists of this tendency had originally taken to be a presupposition of the viability of their politics. Similarly, actual poverty (however defined) and the discovery of poverty are two different things. Poverty has always been there to be discovered, but only in certain political and ideological contexts did its discovery become an explosive issue. Hence the impact made by Booth and Beveridge, compared with the general indifference towards the findings of Townsend. The same criticism could be applied to Eric Hobsbawm's interesting essay, 'The Forward March of Labour Halted?'.[6] Hobsbawm, among other reasons, has ascribed Labour's crisis to a growing sectionalism in the trade union movement and the growth of public sector employment. According to his argument, this has meant that trade union struggles have increasingly taken the form of strikes against the public as consumers, rather than against private employers, and have thus divided the labour

---

[6] E. J. Hobsbawm *et al.*, *The Forward March of Labour Halted?* (1981).

movement against itself. Although, as a description of 'the winter of discontent', this portrayal undoubtedly captures something of what did happen, it is by no means clear that this is primarily to be seen as a simple reflex of the post-war growth of the state sector. Other sections of the labour movement and the general public were far worse hit by the miners' strikes of the early 1970s and yet, politically, the results were the reverse of 1979.

All this suggests that we need different ways of asking why the Labour Party is in a mess. The whole idea of a 'forward march of Labour' is something of an optical illusion or, more specifically, part of the social democratic mythology of Labour in the 1940s: an understandable one at the time, encapsulated very well in Francis Williams' *Magnificent Journey*. It is no less ephemeral than Harold Wilson's less sympathetic canard of the 60s – for a time earnestly debated by media academics – that Labour had become 'the natural party of government'. If we are to understand the history of the Labour Party, we must understand it in terms of a number of discontinuous conjunctures which enabled it to achieve particular and specific forms of success at rather widely separated points of time, rather than as a continuous evolutionary movement which at a certain point mysteriously went into reverse.

Historically, it appears that Labour's electoral viability as a majority party has depended upon a social alliance between the organized section of the working class and the professional middle class broadly defined. Since approximately one-third of the working class has throughout the twentieth century either voted Conservative or not voted at all, Labour has only been able to form majority governments when it could achieve alliance with sections of the population not by nature predisposed to look with any particular favour to a party so closely tied to the trade union movement. Labour has never divided the nation in any simple vertical sense. Despite the efforts and occasional successes of Labour leaders like Herbert Morrison, the Labour Party has never been able to achieve a stable alliance between organized working class and lower middle class, except when it has also attracted significant support from social groups above them. The constituencies to which the Labour Party has wished to appeal are not very different from that of the pre-1914 progressive alliance espoused by the Liberal Party. Labour's definition of 'working people' has generally reiterated the emphases of pre-war progressivism. According to Ramsay MacDonald:

> The true separation in society is the moral and economic line of division between the producer and the non-producer, between those who possess without serving and those who serve, whereas the separation between the professional classes and labour has made the line of division a purely psychological one which is not without its reason in the different modes of life of the two classes, but which nevertheless is mischievous and ought to be obliterated.[7]

This is not to suggest, however, that the terms of the combination or its centre of gravity have remained the same. The cases of John Burns and Arthur Henderson in the period before 1918 suggest that the liberal progressive alliance could never have embodied the undeferential proletarian note sounded by Ernest Bevin in the 1940s, and the barely disguised contempt for the intellectual capacities of the working class expressed by Edwardian progressives was replaced by Gaitskell's 'humility' as the correct outward stance to be adopted by the Oxbridge-educated Labour leaders in their dealings with the TUC. Moreover, the Labour Party has managed to appeal to sections of the working class not reached by the Liberals, while conversely never securing the same success among rural workers, free trade businessmen and a rump of Whig magnates.

Looked at in these terms, it is clear that Labour between the Wars never came near to forming the necessary alliance to achieve a majority. Despite the existence of the mainly middle class ILP (Independent Labour Party), and the adhesion of otherwise politically homeless pacifists and feminists after 1918, Labour was not able to attract significant electoral support outside areas where industrial trade unionism was strong (mining, heavy industry, textiles). While Labour ousted the Liberals as the major opposition party, it did so more by driving former Liberals towards the Conservative Party than by attracting them into its own ranks. Mac-Donald's Party may have been moderate and constitutional,

---

[7] Cited in R. Lyman, *The First Labour Government 1924* (1958); and see also on this period, R. McKibbin, *The Evolution of the Labour Party 1910–1924* (1974).

but it was neither by character nor inclination effectively reformist. It only became so under trade union influence in the 1930s after the débâcle of 1931 with *Labour's Immediate Programme* of 1937. Even so, however, there was no sign of Labour's 'forward march' in the 1930s. It was the conjuncture of the War that gave it its unique opportunity to reconstitute the old progressive alliance under its own name.

If the Second World War did generate a new alliance between the organized working class and professional middle-class progressivism, this was not least because, in policy terms, the progressives were in the saddle. As Paul Addison has written of reconstruction in *The Road to 1945*, 'in every area of policy-making the main principles of advance had been defined before 1939 by non-party experts'.

What is important to stress here is not so much the character of the policies of 1945 – which arc well known – as the unspoken social premises upon which the alliance was based. Dunkirk radicalized the thinking of the old service class, but only to reinforce their sense of the working class as the object of compassion or reform. Their outlook was summed up in extreme form by Beatrice Webb writing of Beveridge in 1940:

Beveridge realises that if the war is to be won, and still more if the industrial state of Britain is to be saved from decay, planned production and consumption has to be undertaken. But as of old, Beveridge is obstinately convinced that he and his class have to do the job, and the Trade Unionists have to be ignored and the wage earner ordered to work ... he agrees that there must be a revolution in the economic structure of society; but it must be guided by persons with training and knowledge.[8]

This sort of diktat was the one thing the trade unions would not accept after the experience of 1914–18 and Bevin on their behalf protected the formal structure of free collective bargaining throughout the Second World War. But the assumption of social reform and post-war reconstruction for the welfare of, rather than by the agency, power and intelligence of, the working class remained deeply ingrained. Even the Solomon of the left socialism of the day, Harold Laski, reproduced the assumption when he wrote unguardedly of

[8] Cited in P. Addison, *The Road to 1945* (1977), and see also J. Harris, *William Beveridge, a Biography* (1977).

'the pride every citizen of this country is bound to have in the amazing heroism and endurance of the common people'. Moreover, the organized working class kept its side of the bargain. Once its essential interests were secured by the preservation of free collective bargaining during the War, the reversal of the 1927 Trades Disputes Act, and the commitment to social security and full employment, it made little concerted attempt to challenge the policy of the post-war government. Keynes' reasons for his distrust of the inter-war Labour Party – 'I don't believe that the intellectual elements of the Labour Party will ever exercise adequate control' – were not vindicated.[9] Fiscal policy, American loans, the cold war, the public corporation approach to nationalization, the preservation of the existing constitution, and Britain's imperial role – all testified to a continuity of assumptions from the days of pre-1914 progressive liberal imperialism. Globally and nationally, the post-war Labour government was the last and most glorious flowering of late Victorian liberal philanthropy.

Perhaps this provides some clue to Labour's difficulties in reconstituting its social alliance from the 1950s onwards. For one thing was certain, once Britain's global role contracted and its caste-like social structure began to loosen up, that alliance could never successfully be put together again on the same terms. As was stressed at the beginning of this chapter, emphasis upon the minimal or even regressive character of the redistribution of wealth and income since 1945 misses the social changes of the period which have been more important in shaping the pattern of politics. More important than any changes in relative shares were the long years of relatively full employment and rising real wages, the gradual evaporation of Britain's independent position, and the secular decline of class consciousness both among middle and working classes.

Class consciousness in twentieth century Britain has been a conservative rather than a revolutionary phenomenon. The consciousness of the working class in the period from 1900 to 1950 – summed up more by music-hall, cinema, sport, pubs, working-men's clubs and distinctions of accent, residence and dress than by chapel, trade unionism or labour politics – was

[9] For this strand of liberal progressivist thinking, see, in particular, P. Clarke, *Liberals and Social Democrats* (1981).

the consciousness of the separateness of a caste rather than of the hegemonic potentialities of a particular position in production.[10] Among the organized working class – apart from a revolutionary minority which formed and led the Communist Party – it was the consciousness of an estate with definite interests to defend and advance within the existing polity. Among the professional middle classes, it was the ethic of service, of intelligence and expertise in pursuit of humanitarian ends, of a civilizing mission both at home and abroad. Removed from the daily worries of domestic toil by the continuing, if diminishing, availability of servants, the progressive middle classes possessed the consciousness, both locally and nationally, of being notables, untiring in the pursuit of good causes but expecting in return a deference due to their position as experts, teachers, scientists, doctors, civil servants or preachers. The potential terms of alliance between such people and organized labour between the Wars was most vividly exemplified in the teaching professions, in the relationship between tutor and class in University Extension and the WEA (Workers' Educational Association). Apart from canvassing and some educational work, the least frictional point of rapport between local professionals and working-class Labour stalwarts was to be found in the organization of treats and multifarious acts of benevolence for the benefit of the slumland poor. Toynbee Hall has as much claim to be counted among the ancestors of the Labour Party as methodism, Taff Vale or William Morris.[11] The career of Clement Attlee exemplifies the point.

After 1951, the type of class consciousness encapsulated in the 1945 victory began to dissolve both among the working and professional classes. Most commentaries on this process have concentrated upon changes in working-class living standards and life style, but certainly of equal importance for the fate of the Labour Party was the way in which these changes impinged upon the professional wing of the alliance.

[10] For an analysis of the genesis of this type of working class culture, see Ch. 4 in this volume.

[11] For a depiction of the mid-Victorian pre-history of this middle-class evangelism, see G. Stedman Jones, *Outcast London*, 2nd edn, London (1984); and for the way in which it defined the ethos of adult education, see Sheila Rowbotham, 'Travellers in a Strange Country', *History Workshop Journal*, 12 (1981).

To the extent that the professional classes had given their allegiance to a trade union based party in the first half of the century, it was premissed upon a representation of trade unionism as the vehicle of the poor and the underprivileged. In many ways the attitudes of this stratum were a continuation in a more or less secularized form of Christian evangelical impulses deriving from the late nineteenth century. Seen in this light, the changes of the 1950s and 1960s were undermining. Not only was Christianity itself a fading force among the educated middle classes, but trade unions and the indigenous working class were no longer associated with the poor and underprivileged. While real differentials might not have narrowed, there was undoubtedly a narrowing in perceived styles of consumption. Much of the self-esteem of the old professional middle class stemmed from their sense of difference from the working class and of helping the labour movement from an unassailed privileged position. The perception therefore of a working class owning cars, televisions and washing machines and even being able to follow them on package holidays to the Mediterranean was corrosive of a sense of evangelical mission; just as the generalization of an ethic of undifferentiated consumerism projected by advertising and oiled by hire purchase – climaxing in the 1960s in a chic but socially amorphous youth culture signified by jeans and pop-music – was an incitement to a sense of injured or lost notable status. Mortgage relief and country cottages could not repair this felt loss of position, and the expansion of higher education and the advance of comprehensive schools made it all too vulnerable to *Black Paper* talk of 'declining standards'.

But by the end of the 1960s it was anyway no longer possible to speak of the professional classes as a unitary group. The enormous post-war expansion of the state and service sector had produced increasing differentiation among the professional classes themselves. The traditional professions were joined by social workers, polytechnic lecturers and whole new grades of state and municipal employees. Many of these new positions were occupied by women. Divisions, partly of generational outlook, opened up both between and within professions. Old demarcations of status and etiquette came under attack. New forms of radicalism appeared among students, social workers, lecturers, school teachers and, to a lesser extent, among doctors and lawyers. Lines of distinction between professional associations and trade unions that had formerly been clear began to blur. CND (Campaign for Nuclear Disarmament), the Vietnam Solidarity Campaign, ecological concerns, life style and community politics, New Leftism and diffuse forms of Marxism, the students' movement and, most fundamentally, the women's movement divided this class against itself. The hierarchical distinctions of the 1940s, still vigorous in the Indian summer of the 1950s have not regained their self-assurance in the aftermath of the euphoric anti-authoritarian thrust of 1966–72. Meritocratic ambition and vanguardist illusion commingled uneasily with democratic and egalitarian sentiment in this groundswell of opinion and agitation. Dependence on the public sector inoculated large sections of this constituency against Toryism, but concerns about the costs, inefficiencies and injustices of the public sector destroyed most of the residual idealism about the welfare state. The difficulties of providing any clear political profile to the preoccupations of this sector as a whole is reflected in the editorial difficulties of the *New Statesman* since the departure of Kingsley Martin, in the conflicts exposed by the *Time Out* dispute, and in the schizophrenia of the *Guardian* exemplified by the uneasy conjunction of Posy Simmons and Peter Jenkins. It would be comforting to interpret the conflict as a simple battle between left and right, to align the hardcore SDP to the affronted dignity of the traditional professional sector, to associate Bennism with the assertive stridency of the new. But such a dichotomy would be false. Simple sociological correlates will not work. It would be fairer to say that in so far as either Bennism or the SDP represent coherent positions, each plays in different ways upon elements of evangelism, elitism, egalitarianism and populism, both new and old, from across the whole spectrum of professional groups.

Among the organized working class, long years of a buoyant labour market – particularly in the south and the midlands – led to a gradual erosion in the authority of the trade union leadership to speak on its behalf. Plant bargaining tended to displace national agreements, shopsteward committees became the most vital embodiment of trade union effectiveness and unofficial strikes became increasingly numerous, often challenging both traditional managerial prerogatives and the authority of trade union officials. If cohesive consciousness among the professional stratum has fragmented, the fragmentation has been even more acute among the organized working class. In the 1940s, Ernest Bevin, both as trade union leader and as member of a Labour cabinet, could talk unselfconsciously about the organized working class as 'our people'.[12] But from the 1950s onwards, the automatic equation between trade unionism, Labour voting and a cluster of labour movement loyalties became increasingly hard to make. Trade unionism has always been associated first and foremost with free collective bargaining, but never, until recently, only that. From the days in which trade union organization risked the threat of sacking and blacklisting and in which channels of working-class self-expression were severely limited, trade unionism had been invested with all kinds of moral and political labour-movement aspirations. However, now that the Tories of the 1950s had come to accept social security and full employment, and the vast majority of British employers had come to accept trade union channels of negotiation, the link between trade unionism and political loyalty became less compelling. While the left applauded the rise of shopstewards and unofficial strikes as signs of shopfloor emancipation from the 'bossism' of right-wing trade union leaders, they remained largely oblivious of the increasingly tenuous connection between wage militancy and working-class politics. Trade union leaders themselves accepted with more or less good grace the decentralization of trade union power as a means of adapting the structure of unionism to the novel possibilities of the labour market. Moreover, trade unionism became increasingly generalized as the appropriate form of bargaining for every type of employee group, if they were to maintain their relative position in a ladder of wages and salaries. In an increasingly inflationary situation, those who held back, and those too weak to organize, lost out. In the process, the distinctively proletarian connotations of trade

---

[12] On Bevin, see A. Bullock, *The Life and Times of Ernest Bevin*, 2 vols. (1960, 1967).

unionism, and its cultural penumbra, receded and public representation of the trade unions shifted from that of a potential class threat to that of a powerful sectional set of vested interests.

Trade unionists found it increasingly difficult to talk with any conviction on behalf of the politics of their members – a problem, it emerged in the 1970s, not just of general secretaries, but of shopstewards as well. Only in defence of the lowest common denominator of trade union politics – the defence of free collective bargaining on behalf of those already organized – could trade unions count on mass support, whether against *In Place of Strife* or Heath's *Industrial Relations Act.* But this was an issue which divided state administration and the leadership of all three political parties from trade unionists, rather than a divide between workers and capitalists, Labour and Conservative. On an issue raising trade union questions of a more fundamental labour movement and class type – the struggle to gain recognition at Grunwick's – trade union support was uneven and the trade union movement went down to an ominous defeat. Already, in the Common Market Referendum, it was clear that the majority trade union position was not accepted by large sectors of the membership. It was only a matter of time before Tories – and most notably Thatcher – began to appeal with some success to trade union members over the heads of their representatives, and employers attempted directly to address the shopfloor in defiance of agreed negotiating procedures and shopsteward mediation. Finally, the archaism of official trade union fictions about the views of their members were cruelly and irrevocably exposed in the half-hearted consultation procedure employed by the TGWU (Transport and General Workers' Union) in the deputy leadership battle. Whatever validity the trade union block vote had once possessed, it had now disappeared with the public admission of the cumulative detachment of trade union membership from class consciousness and Labour loyalty – an equation which the pre-war Labour Party could regard with some justification as axiomatic.

It is not right, however, to view this disintegration in purely negative terms any more than some might bemoan the passing of an old professional ethic. What the changes of the 1950s and 1960s suggested was that the working class as a whole had become far more permeable to practices and ideas from outside its own political and cultural inheritance; and among younger thinking workers, this meant they could often become more readily engaged in politics in other than their purely trade unionist or labour movement personae. The fairly rigid demarcations between the political and industrial sides of the Labour Party were already beginning to break down in the early 1950s, when the Bevanites began to appeal to a rank and file left within the trade union section against the policies of right-wing trade union leadership; and the lines crossed more seriously when Gaitskell attempted to revise clause four and the trade unions took their revenge with a brief espousal of unilateralism. But more significant were the types of popular politics and cultural movements which grew up wholly outside the constitutional and bureaucratic procedures of the pre-existing labour movement. CND, Anti-Apartheid, Vietnam Solidarity, diffuse forms of libertarianism and pop-culture and, finally, the women's movement were not confined in their impact to the youth of the professional classes; they attracted significant elements of proletarian support as well. Radical students were not altogether wrong in believing that their activities might have an exemplary effect on other sectors of society. The actions on the Upper Clyde and the wave of factory occupations in the early 1970s possessed no precedent in trade union rule books. The growth of single-issue campaigns was yet another indication of the non-coincidence of class ascription and political engagement. Of course, this situation has given new opportunities to the right as well as to the left. But there is nothing predetermined in the form through which such changes have found and will find political expression. The present phenomenon of punk music, with its spectrum of political positions from extreme left to extreme right, exemplifies the politically protean character of the young working-class movement of the present.

Finally, it is quite wrong to treat developments within either the professional or working classes over the past three decades in abstraction from the politics of the Labour Party itself. Neither politics in general nor the Labour Party in particular can be regarded as a passive victim of social change. Social alliances do not simply happen, they are brought into being and re-created by the construction and periodic reconstruction of a common political discourse. The alliance constructed between the professional classes and the organized working class of the 1940s, as I have argued, was of a type which could not be rebuilt on the same terms. It was the revisionist right of the 1950s who first discerned this situation, but only understood it in narrowly economistic terms. Although they called rightly for a greater emphasis upon democracy and equality, their conception of these demands was narrowly hemmed in by their acceptance of the managerial ethos of the welfare state and the public corporation and their allegiance to the cold war priorities of American foreign policy. The left could point to the cultural poverty of this vision and its State Department deference, but provided little in the way of a positive domestic counter-strategy. In the 1960s and 1970s, its intellectual and political energies were focussed increasingly upon the progress of anti-imperialist movements abroad, while 'labourism' was left to fester at home. In the meantime, however, one last effort had been made by the Labour leadership to renegotiate the terms of the social alliance upon which Labour's viability as a majority party was based. Wilson, with his Panglossian talk of an arrest to industrial decline and a new society which would emerge from the 'white heat of technology' and the sweeping of dead wood from the board-rooms, did momentarily capture the imagination of the contending constituencies upon which the Labour Party was based, and in 1964 managed to poll 44 per cent of the popular vote. Unfortunately, however, it was only talk. The contradictions of this strategy, with its utter acceptance of existing economic power relations, both national and international, which it imagined could be transformed by paper-planning and rhetoric rather than controls, and not least its increasingly blatant political and moral vacuity, rendered the whole fragile concoction vulnerable to the first slight buffeting. Thereafter, there was a political vacuum in the leadership of the Labour Party, and the different social constituencies upon which it was based were left to go their separate ways, bereft now even of the residual political integrity that the party had retained until Wilson. In the PLP the increasingly predominant professional strata, whose guiding philosophy was now technocratic rather than moral (even in the revisionist sense of Crosland), attacked the trade union side in the name of a productivism devoid of any larger political purpose. This move was stymied at the end of the 1960s by old-style operators of Labour's political machine in the name of a pragmatism equally devoid of any longer term programme. From this impasse, the Labour Party has never recovered. In 1974, it was the trade union statesmanship of Jack Jones rather than any new initiative from the political leadership which provided what strategy there was. The breakdown of this 'social contract' from the time of the IMF (International Monetary Fund) loan and its predictable outcome in 'a winter of discontent' severed what remained of the residual attachments among large sections of middle and working classes alike, and the scene was set for Thatcher, Bennism and the SDP.

In what way a socialist politics could reconstruct an alliance between the working and professional classes, and whether the Labour Party could again be the medium of such an alliance, are questions to which it would be foolish to attempt a confident answer in the present situation. But one formal conclusion at least suggests itself in the light of the preceding analysis. This is that the Labour Party will never be able to make a credible appeal to either of its former constituencies unless it attempts to ally them in a new way by taking account of the profound changes wrought by the welfare state, the mixed economy and national decline, both upon the forms of consciousness and the relative material situation of each.

At the beginning of the twentieth century, when trade unions first formed a political party, whatever 'social security' was available to the working class outside the Poor Law, narrowly depended upon the strength of their collective organizations. Even after the social reforms inaugurated by the Liberal Government of 1906, trade union institutional bargaining power and its capacity for political mobilization and the channelling of political allegiance remained crucial. If money wages did not simply fall in line with prices in the inter-war years, and if the unemployed, however miserable their dole payments, were not simply condemned to the workhouse, this was primarily because trade unions in conditions of manhood suffrage represented an irremovable obstacle to the revanchist schemes of Conservative politicians, bankers and employers. It was therefore not surprising that consciousness among workers grew naturally out of, and was strongly defined and limited by, trade union membership. The union was a lifeline, both locally and nationally, against employers and the state; and out of the necessary solidarity which trade unions entailed grew many of the larger loyalties and values which held the labour movement together.

The advent of the welfare state, the acceptance of the normality of trade union bargaining, and concomitant changes in the pattern of employment gradually and unevenly transformed this situation. A gulf opened up between trade unionism and the crusade against poverty, for poverty was now either of a wageless type which had to be fought at the level of the state or of a low wage type effectively beyond the purview of the ordinary bargaining process. Or, to put it less politely, poverty, which remained extensive, was mainly the lot of coloured immigrants and 'single parent families', i.e. women, and was thus not an overriding priority for a Party whose appeal was pitched to white male organized workers. But even among indigenous workers of this type, the wage packet now formed only part of the social wage and the male wage only a diminishing part of the organized worker's family income. Consciousness no longer derived overwhelmingly from union involvement. If anything, the reverse was becoming true. Political consciousness, generally derived from other sources, could take the form of union militancy. It was not so much that trade union experience bred militancy, but rather that new forms of social and political discontent, not shaped primarily in the workplace, found a form of expression – and often a cramped form – through trade unions. In this sense, the precipitants of political activism among workers were not so different from those present among broad sectors of the professional classes, no longer so conscious of their gentility and no longer so averse to expressing their occupational grievances through trade unions.

In the face of these changes, the preservation of the pre-existing constitutional structure of the Labour Party – with its primary representation of working-class interests by indirect trade union means – has maintained an ever more inappropriate demarcation between its two principal constituencies and has stifled the emergence of forms of politics which could draw in new ones. If the Labour Party is ever to reverse its present involution, it will have to rethink the social alliances upon which it could be based in terms of what they now potentially share in common. At the moment, the emergence of new and potentially unifying strategies is thwarted by an enduring major premiss of Labour Party thinking: the perception of one part of its constituency as a homogeneous proletarian estate whose sectional political interest is encompassed by trade unions, and of the other part as a heteroclite aggregate of idealists, notables or entrists to be humoured, promoted or circumvented. This ingrained assumption has survived intact through all the recent constitutional reforms and informs both right and left, whether justified in the language of tired pragmatism, liberal progressivism or mechanical Marxism. It is this premiss, still embodied in the structure and constitution of the Labour Party, which inhibits a believable appeal to today's real poor or oppressed (immigrants, women, the unemployed), is productive of unreal and unworkable solutions to Britain's economic plight, and deflects to the sidelines what should be a central socialist debate about the distribution of non-material goods (knowledge, democratic control, environment, quality of life) of interest to all its potential constituencies. Unfortunately, it is not possible to discuss these substantive issues here. All that can be suggested as a formal precondition to such a discussion is that in the present grim situation of the country, Labour will not be able to construct a socialist politics that addresses this situation as long as its inherited thinking and practices continue to be deformed by the largely unquestioned acceptance of an anachronistic and now disastrous social distinction between mental and manual labour.

INDEX